I dedicate my research to the sleeping, dreaming and awakening feminine consciousness of the universe and all its benefactors—from the tiniest piece of rock to the grandest mountain ranges, from the ant to the elephant, from the earth to the skies, from the children to the ancient ancestral mother—this, that and everything.

Rising Daughter
Silent Mother
Fading Grandmothers

A Study of Female Sexuality within a
North Malabar Nayar Family Structure

An organic inquiry by
REKHA GOVINDAN KURUP

Published by
CreateSpace Independent Publishing Platform

Rising Daughter, Silent Mother & Fading Grandmothers
A Study of Female Sexuality within a North Malabar Nayar Family Structure

Copyright ©2014 Rekha Govindan Kurup
First Edition. All Rights Reserved. No part of this publication may be reproduced, stored in a retrieval system, or transmitted by any means – electronic, mechanical, photographic (photocopying), recording, or otherwise – without prior permission in writing from the author.

Book Design, Layout, Art Work & Research Photos By Rekha Govindan Kurup.
Copyright © 2014 Rekha Govindan Kurup. All Rights Reserved.

Research Study Edited By Colleen Bol
M.A Thesis Chairperson: Dr. Dianne E. Jenett
M.A Thesis Committee Member: Vicki Noble, Author
Photos of Maternal/Paternal Grandparents Edited By Rajiv Anand
About Author Photograph by Robin Ruth (http://www.robinruth.com)

Front Cover Photo 1 *(Top Left): Rekha's Maternal Grandparents.*
Front Cover Photo 2 *(Center Left): Rekha and her Mother, Balamani*
Front Cover Photo 3 *(Bottom Left): Rekha's Paternal Grandparents.*
Back Cover Photo *(Bottom): Yashoda Amma and her Daughter, Anita*

ISBN-13: 978-1492810414
ISBN-10: 149281041X
Printed in the United States of America

CONTENTS

Dedication	iii
Foreword by Dr. Dianne Jenett	vi
Preface	viii
Blessing	ix
Invocation	x
PART I: SETTING THE STAGE	1
1 Introduction	2
2 The Research Methodology	10
PART II: THE RISING DAUGHTER	26
3 Social, Cultural, and Religious Upbringing	27
4 Relationship with Body and Sexuality	37
5 Relevance and Emergence of this Study	48
PART III: LITERATURE REVIEW	58
6 Matriarchal Societies of Peace	59
7 Women's Spirituality	81
8 Nayars of Kerala	88
PART IV: NAYAR FEMALE-CENTERED RITUALS	103
9 *Thirandukulli*: The Obligatory Menarche Ritual	104
10 Story of Kamadevan: Kerala's Sexual God	115
11 The *Thiruvathira* Festival	118
12 The North Malabar *Pooram* Festival	123
PART V: THE INTERVIEWS	126
13 Letting go and Surrender	127
14 Balamani Amma : *The Silent Mother*	132
15 Madhavi Amma : *The Fading Grandmother*	165
16 Meenakshi Amma : *The Fading Grandmother*	198
17 Yashoda Amma : *The Fading Grandmother*	225
PART VI: HARVESTING THE FRUITS	247
18 *Onnara* : Feminine Wear of Yesteryears	248
19 Embodied Sexuality and Spirituality	249
20 My Matrilineal Awakening	251
21 Integrating Transformative Change	256
22 Answering Her Call	258
Acknowledgements	264
References	266
Glossary	272

FOREWORD BY DR. DIANNE JENETT

During the last two decades there have been a number of US feminist scholars in the fields of religious studies, anthropology and women's spirituality who came to India to study women and their spiritual practices, particularly those centered on the Goddess. No matter how sensitive and thoughtful their work, most of these women came as outsiders to the cultures they were studying. Thankfully, this is changing and there are a growing number of India women, such as Rekha Kurup, who are examining their own spiritual culture and history using a feminist and post-colonial lens.

During similar time frame, a field of matriarchal studies developed, beginning in Europe and spreading around the globe as women researched historical and extant matrilineal and matrifocal cultures and this work which documents a fast fading history of the lived experience in Nayar Taravad three quarters of a century ago is an important contribution to this field.

In the literary tradition of articulate and passionate Malayali women who have gone before her, Rekha Kurup's work bravely and honestly illustrates the psycho-spiritual development of a contemporary Indian woman during her exploration of her family history and her subsequent reclamation of her matrilineal heritage. This work, originally her Master's Thesis in Women's Spirituality, explores three generations of Malayali women all of whom have lived in the midst of extreme social change from her grandmothers who lived in a world where the traditional female centered matrilineages were being dissolved and replaced by patriarchal nuclear families, to her mother who raised her family in the pan-Indian military culture outside Kerala, and finally to Rekha, who trained as an engineer and became a NRI living in Silicon Valley before returning to her roots. Her work is a gift to women and men who want to examine and resist the patriarchal norms which discount and devalue the female and which are the sources of violence which is rising in a globalized, sexualized, capitalistic economy.

For me, personally, Rekha has been a great gift from the Goddess and I know her work will move, educate, and inspire others.

Dianne E. Jenett, Ph.D. is one of four co-authors of the groundbreaking qualitative research methodology, Organic Inquiry, first published as 'Organic Inquiry: If Research Were Sacred' in Transpersonal Research Methods for the Social Sciences (Sage). She holds a Ph.D. in Integral Studies with a concentration in Women's Spirituality and an M.A. in Transpersonal Psychology. She founded Serpentina, a collaboration in support of 'woman-centered research for everybody.' She also, served as the Co-Director of the Women's Spirituality M.A. program at the Institute of Transpersonal Psychology (now known as Sofia University), as well as Adjunct and Research Faculty at California Institute of Integral Studies and Sonoma State University. Her passionate love for Kerala, India takes her there almost every year where she researches and participates in community rituals to Bhadrakali. Her research interests are women's rituals and community rituals to the Goddess in South India, women's psycho-spiritual development, and qualitative research methods. Her research has been published in the U.S., Europe and India. Dianne Jenett was also the chairperson for Rekha Govindan Kurup's masters thesis work (this study).

PREFACE

For My Sisters:
(who will choose to read this thesis)

Hope it makes you angry. Hope it makes you cry.
Hope it makes you breathe deep & embrace what you deny.

Hope it makes you happy. Hope it makes you sad.
Hope it makes you question every belief that you ever had.

Hope it wakes you up,
from the deep slumber of our fall.
Hope it forces you to rise up and stand tall.

Hope it challenges your "shoulds"
and messes up your "should nots."
Hope it shows you new ways to question and fear not.

Hope it empowers you to open up,
embrace your body & sexuality.
Hope it opens new doorways to your spirituality.

For My Brothers:
(who will choose to read this thesis)

Hope it bridges:
the widening gap between masculine & feminine.
Hope it encourages:
you to step without shame into your feminine.
Be patient.
Be true.
Be brave.
Be kind.
As you read, please have an open mind.

Life is Mysterious, Mystical & Magnanimous!

Color Me *Yoni Mandala*

Instead of asking *why?* at the mysterious and sometimes seemingly outrageous unveiling of our own life, may we have the awareness, courage and willingness to slide into the *wow!* of the happening, take positive action and stand tall in our knowing!

Blessed Be!

INVOCATION

**Mother Saraswati,
Goddess of Wisdom**
*"Saraswati Namasthubhyam,
Varade Kamaroopini,
Vidyarambham Karishyami,
Sidheer Bhawathume Sada"*

**Mother Lakshmi,
Goddess of Prosperity**
*"Namasthesthu Mahamaye,
Shree Peethe Surapoojithe
Shankh-Chakra Gadaa-Hasthe,
Maha Lakshmi Namosthuthe"*

**Mother Durga,
Goddess of Valor & Courage**
*"Sarva Mangala Maangalye,
Shive Sarvartha Saadhike.
Sharanye Thrayambake Gauri,
Narayani Namosthuthe"*

*Loka Samastha Sukhino Bhavanthu!
Loka Samastha Sukhino Bhavanthu!
Loka Samastha Sukhino Bhavanthu!*

*Shanti,
Shanti,
Shantihi!*

PART I

SETTING THE STAGE

"I see myself as the Rising Daughter of my matrilineage called upon to stand tall—holding the unsaid Silent whispers of my Mother on one hand and the fruit-bearing wisdom of my Fading Grandmothers on the other hand."

CHAPTER 1.

INTRODUCTION

This research study explores my journey as a modern-day city-bred daughter to redefine, reclaim and re-inform my female sexuality by reconnecting with the matrilineal lived experience of two earlier generations of indigenous women—my mother and three grandmothers from my near and extended Nayar family living in the North Malabar Kannur district of Kerala. As a daughter, this study gave me the freedom to engage in questions I would otherwise never have explored with my mother and grandmothers. As a researcher, it gave me the opportunity to intellectually explore the written works of various anthropologists, historians and philosophers on the Nayar community. Using the qualitative research methodology of organic inquiry, I engaged in conversations with my mother and three grandmothers on female sexuality and the various factors that influenced the forming of their relationship to their bodies as each of these women blossomed from a young girl into an adult woman.

This study is deeply influenced by my own perception that is daughter-centered, mother-centered, woman-centered, and Nayar-centered. I see myself as the *Rising Daughter* of my matrilineage called upon to stand tall—holding the unsaid *Silent* whispers of my *Mother* on one hand and the fruit-bearing wisdom of my *Fading Grandmothers* on the other hand. I see this study as my first step into reclaiming my indigenous Nayar roots. Personally, I hope this study inspires daughters from my immediate and extended maternal and paternal families to explore and reclaim their connections with indigenous Nayar female-centered rituals, and stand up tall in their bodies and sexuality. On a broader scale, I sincerely hope that this study inspires daughters like me everywhere to re-define, re-engage, and re-claim not just their own stories but also, those of their mothers and grandmothers. I have consciously narrated my story as I felt, saw and experienced it. I have also shared resources in the form of books, practices and rituals.

Throughout my life, my relationship with my body and sexuality has been in state of constant flux. I often found myself navigating the ups and downs of this relationship by myself. In fact, the western and so-called civilized cultural influences in my life through education, media, and literature led me to believe that my indigenous earth-based rituals are primitive, uncivilized and backward and this further alienated me from my indigenous culture that celebrated menstrual blood, feminine body, and her erotic sexuality (de Tourreil, 1995, 2009; Gough, 1952, 1955, 1961, 1965; Grahn, 1999; Jayakar, 1990; Jenett, 1999; Moore, 1988; Neff, 1995). This journey made me question everything—gender perceptions, cultural and social conditioning around gender, the "do"s and "don't"s of a feminine identity, the age-old dogmas defining womanhood, the shame, disgust and silence surrounding body and sexuality, and most importantly the direct and indirect influences of mother-centered and father-centered civilizations in defining a woman's relationship with her body and sexuality. I transformed my attitude from having complete disregard for my body and sexuality to revering and honoring them. This research study is my conscious effort to share with women and men around the world the journey of reclaiming my matrilineal indigenous knowledge around female body and sexuality.

It is important that I define *female sexuality* in my own words. To me female sexuality represents the very essence of being a woman in body—wild, open, sensual, innocent, shy, erotic, intuitive, earthy, mysterious, magical, naked, creative, raw, simple, grounded, free and complicated—all at the same time. I have chosen not to use the word *erotic* in place of *female sexuality* because *erotic* has many negative connotations attached to it especially in India such as vulgar, cheap, indecent, and also pornographic. Moreover, I felt that I did not need a separate word to define my essence. Just like when I say rose, everyone understands the essence of a rose in spite of the different categories of roses available, I feel that female sexuality needs to reflect the infinite essence and vocabulary of the feminine without negative or positive associations, *erotic* being only a part of that vocabulary.

From my own experience, I feel that female sexuality is deeply connected to a woman's menstrual blood, her breasts, genitals, and her ability to create and sustain life. It is ingrained in her body and invoked by the sensation of touch. Female sexuality gives a woman the innate ability to connect, feel, and emotionally relate to other life effortlessly in her various relationships as daughter, sister, lover, friend, mother, grandmother, and wife. It defines her. Scholar and healer, Vicki Noble (1991) describes, in *Shakti Woman*, "how a woman relates sexually in her life is deeply connected to her sense of self-esteem and her ability to receive and transmit powers and energies of transformation" (p. 179). I grew up hearing that to engage sexually would result in the loss of vitality or life force energy. In recent years, through the work of women scholars (Eisler, 1995; Lorde, 1985; Noble, 1991) and talking to other women, I have realized that in the feminine body sexuality and spirituality are not separate but deeply intertwined, and that a woman is capable of multiple orgasms without the loss of any vitality:

> We have the insatiable capacity to be stimulated to one orgasm after another, with the entire process building on itself in intensity, no peak in sight, and without any apparent loss of vitality. There is no "little death," no sacrifice of arousal, no spending of one's energy. (Noble, 1991, p. 186)

On reading this it struck me that by keeping women disconnected from our sexual and spiritual knowing, male-dominated societies have exercised *power over* us for thousands of years. Contrary to this, ancient indigenous earth-based traditions have celebrated the auspiciousness of the feminine sexual energy through rituals, practices and ceremonies for millennia. This study is my step toward reclaiming that knowing through my own indigenous tradition.

Limitations of This Study

One of the biggest limitations of this study was that Malayalam is not my first language. Although I speak, write, and read Malayalam, my vocabulary and conversational skills are not that of a native speaker. However, Malayalam is the first language for my mother and the grandmothers. They are not English speakers. Given the sensitivity of the topic, I knew I had to find the right choice of words to transfer the meaning of relationship with body and sexuality in a way that was empowering. It did not take me long to figure out that there were no exact words or phrases in Malayalam that could convey the meaning in a positive way. My mother worked with me on the translation from English to Malayalam. I spent considerable time explaining to my mother about the meaning of female sexuality as I intended it in the study. Then my mother and I narrowed down words and sentences that closely conveyed the meaning of relationship with body and sexuality. We also formulated specific examples and stories using real-world people and situations to explain the topic of study to the grandmothers. In this process, I learned many nuances of the Malayalam language. For instance, both shy and shame are expressed in the word *nannum*. Depending on the context, it could mean shame or shy—the former reflecting a negative context and the latter a positive one. So I had to pay close attention to the meanings transferred in the conversation, and also in the transcribing process. My biggest concern was the possible loss of meaning in the translation of the interviews from Malayalam to English. However, my mother's guidance helped me overcome this concern.

Another limitation was the personal and private nature of the study. I realized early on that invariably women and men, mostly friends and acquaintances of mine, equated my topic, the study of female sexuality, to having sex, sexual experiences, orgasm and things like that. Without even waiting to hear further, some people checked out upon hearing my topic as if they could not even bear the thought of it. Some would look at me with such sternness as if to say, "Do you have no shame?" It brought some discomfort and restlessness in the beginning. At the same time, it also helped me to (a) be more sensitive, (b) drop any expectations about the outcome, and (c) keep the questions more open-ended with the grandmothers.

Delimitations

Based on the time and budgetary constraints, the vastness of the field of research and the various controversies surrounding the ancient history of India and Kerala, I have consciously drawn two definite boundaries for this study:

1. I have confined my study to a small number of co researchers from within my family belonging specifically to the North Malabar region of Kerala. I wanted to keep this study simple, easier to complete and hence, I chose the scope of my research within parameters known and familiar to me in terms of people, the environment, and the region. My study is

localized to a small geographic region of Northern Kerala, and thus culturally the experiences of these women are closely bound to be similar.

2. I will not be engaging in an in-depth discussion on the how and why factors that contributed to the changing face of female sexuality in India and Kerala. The history of Indian civilization, the caste system, the Aryan versus Dravidian viewpoint, and the various other social forces that have influenced the patriarchal shift on the Indian subcontinent like Sanskritization, Christianization and more are highly sensitive, controversial and debatable. I feel this could be a research topic in itself beyond the scope of this study. However, I will use scholarly sources to support the presence of these influences on female sexuality based on my own upbringing.

An Overview of Chapters

This book is divided into six parts; each part describes a different aspect of my study.

The *first* part (this one) of this book lays the foundation for my research. It consists of 2 main chapters. While the first chapter is an introduction; the second chapter describes in detail the qualitative research methodology of organic inquiry. I feel that understanding the various aspects of my research methodology are key to understanding why I chose to share what I did as part of my story.

The *second* part of this book narrates my story as the *Rising Daughter*. It consists of three main chapters. Chapters 3 and 4 narrate my life story while chapter 5 illustrates the significance and relevance of this research study.

Chapter 3: Social, Cultural, and Religious Upbringing
Chapter 4: Relationship with Body and Sexuality
Chapter 5: Relevance and Emergence of this Study

The *third* part of this book describes the literature I reviewed for this study. I realized that to understand the shift in Nayar matriliny across the ages, the relevance of its practices supporting female sexuality and the various cultural, political, and religious influences plagueing the culture of present-day Kerala, I needed a broader perspective spanning across time (from Paleolithic to present civilizations) and space (matriarchal societies across the world). Also, I believe that positive and negative gender construction is directly connected to the perception, observation, and expression of the female body and sexuality within any culture. For this reason, I chose to focus and present the literature around matriarchal, patriarchal, and religious influences on body and female sexuality around the world before presenting literature about Nayar matriliny. I hope that the literature reviwed will provide the foundation to understand the shifts in Nayar matriarchy caused in large part by colonization and westernization. Whereever possible, I have infused scholarly writings with my own personal reflection and experiences.

Chapter 6: Matriarchal Societies of Peace
Chapter 7: Women's Spirituality
Chapter 8: Nayars of Kerala

Part *four* of this book presents detailed ethnographic accounts of the Nayar female-centered rituals and festivals. I chose rituals that were shared by the grandmothers in their interviews. It consists of four chapters:

Chapter 9: Thirandukulli: The Obligatory Menarche Ritual

Chapter 10: Story of Kamadevan – Kerala's Sexual God
Chapter 11: The Thiruvathira Festival
Chapter 12: The North Malabar Pooram Festival

Part *five* of this book consists of the translated interview transcripts of my mother and three grandmothers. I have also shared my personal experience and reflections through the process of interviewing and transcription. This constitutes chapter 13 through 17.

Chapter 13: Letting go and Surrender
Chapter 14: Balamani: The Silent Mother
Chapter 15: Madhavi Amma: The Fading Grandmother
Chapter 16: Meenakshi Amma: The Fading Grandmother
Chapter 17: Yashoda Amma: The Fading Grandmother

Part *six* of this book compiles the results of this study. It constitutes of five small chapters.

Chapter 18: Onnara : Feminine Wear of Yesteryears
Chapter 19: Embodied Sexuality and Spirituality
Chapter 20: My Matrilineal Awakening
Chapter 21: Integrating Transformative Change
Chapter 22: Answering Her Call

Chapters 18 through 22 synthesizes the shifts in the perception, observation and expression of female sexuality within the culture across three generations of women—three grandmothers, my mother, and myself. Chapter 22 is conclusive beginning of my transformative journey.

CHAPTER 2.

THE RESEARCH METHODOLOGY

I used the transpersonal qualitative research methodology of organic inquiry (1999, 2011) to examine the lived feminine experience of my mother and three grandmothers from the North Malabar Nayar family structure, and explore the various factors that influenced their relationships with their bodies and sexuality as they blossomed from young girls into adult women. I contrasted their experiences with mine. I chose organic inquiry as my main research methodology because it is based on storytelling and transformative change, which may be expected to occur during the research process.

> The fundamental technique of organic research is telling and listening to stories. The topic of an organic research study grows out of the researcher's own story, and the methods used in the research are expected to creatively evolve in response to influences from within the researcher's psyche and from external events that affect the work in progress. At its core is an emphasis on the transformative power of inviting, listening to, and presenting individual participants stories about significant experiences, using the participants voices and words as much as possible. Because the study of a study is recorded and told in the researcher's voice, organic research presupposes a moderately high level of psycho-spiritual development by an organic researcher. Ultimately, organic research seeks to nourish personal transformation in the researcher, co-researchers (research participants), and readers alike. (Anderson & Braud, 1998, p. 31)

In addition to listening and narrating the stories of my mother and grandmothers, I recorded my transformation evolving from the responses of my co-researchers who are close family members. So I chose a methodology that honored the relational, spiritual and transformative aspects of my journey.

If Research Were Sacred

> What if we honored our own experiences, made them part of our research story, wrote about the deepest, most vulnerable parts of ourselves? What if we could support each other to find our authentic voices and those of our co-researchers? What if we incorporated the stories of how we were led, given information, and supported by dreams and synchronicities? (Clements, Ettling, Jenett, & Shields, 1999, p. 17)

During my Master's program, I did a small study (Kurup, 2011) on a woman's connection to her *Yoni*, a Sanskrit word for feminine sexuality and genitalia, for my organic inquiry research class. It required me to engage in conversation with two women acquaintances and during the research, I experienced moments of intense fear, doubt, and confusion. These emotions acted as a catalyst and pushed me further into the topic of feminine sexuality. By accepting the various challenges and experiences emerging during this explorative journey as organic and sacred, I was able to step beyond my comfort zone, thus expanding my embodied awareness and deepening my relationship with my body and sexuality. In that moment, I realized that organic inquiry provided a safe and sacred container to embody, embrace and engage in the personal nature of my research topic without compromising on the deeply transformational aspects for the researcher, co-researchers and the individual readers:

> Organic inquiry offers a systematic process for including trans-egoic influence within a context of disciplined inquiry. An ultimate goal is to offer transformative change for its individual readers, encouraged by the study's report of similar changes in the researcher and the participants. Readers, in effect, are invited to engage with the study using mind as well as heart, allowing it to relate to and impact their own experience of the topic. (Clements, 2004, p. 30)

My research was situated in telling and listening to stories of deeply personal nature (female sexuality) narrated by my mother and grandmothers. These grandmothers have either known my mother and/or me since childhood. I had never indulged in a conversation of such personal nature with these women because conversations of such private nature (around sexuality) are not encouraged in the social culture. So I needed a methodology that honored the private nature of our discussions and gave my co-researchers the freedom to share (or not) their stories, allowing for their stories to emerge in the narration in their own words as much as possible. I also wanted the freedom to narrate, and also document, my own story and transformative journey during the course of this study, which organic inquiry provided. This method values the stories of human experience, honors the voice of the co-researchers, and gives the researcher the freedom to engage with the readers intimately from the heart.

To me, the whole process of research—from preparing for the interview, to creating the space for the interview, to the process of interviewing, to the subsequent acts of transcribing, to narrating the story, and holding space for myself and for my co-researchers—was closely embedded in the organic unveiling of life. Organic inquiry supported me in honoring this journey of research as sacred, "Every aspect of the research including the method, the collaboration with the co-researcher, the content and the implication of the inquiry—everything is considered sacred allowing for organic growth" (Clements et al., 1999, p. 86).

Throughout this journey I used the guidance of dreams, past memories, prayers, and embodied spiritual practices to deepen the psycho-spiritual experiences around my topic. Unnamable energy forces more powerful than myself guided me through this journey. With the methodology of organic inquiry, I was able to incorporate these experiences as part of the research (Clements et al., 1999, p. 88). I also, engaged in numerous ways of gathering and reporting data using methods such as journaling, mandala drawing, making collages, conversations, meditation, movement, tarot cards, and poetry. These non-rational and non-verbal ways of self-exploration deeply contributed toward my understanding of the topic (Clements et al., 1999, p. 86).

The open-ended nature of conversation supported by organic inquiry allowed me to facilitate the discussion with my mother and grandmother using six simple semi-structured questions:

1. How did your relationship with your body and sexuality transform as you blossomed from a young girl into an adult woman?
2. Do you remember participating in any *female-centered* rituals? Can you describe what they were like? How did you feel?
3. Did you bathe with your maternal kin in a pond or *kullam*? What was it like? What conversations did you have? Were women shy around their nakedness or comfortable in their bodies?
4. How did the girls or women respond to the flirtatious advances of boys and men? Was talking to boys and men outside the *taravad* allowed?
5. Would women talk openly about their sexual fantasies or their flirtatious encounters with men?
6. Have you noticed a change in the images of female sexuality over the years?

These questions supported my mother and grandmothers to speak freely about their experiences without prejudice and hesitation. It felt more like engaging in an intimate conversation between family members versus gathering information based on questions and answers. My co-researchers had fun answering these questions and at the same, felt empowered about remembering their past—however, the past might have been. They felt safe in sharing not just the so-called positive experiences but also, in sharing what they thought of as negative.

The last and the most important reason I chose organic inquiry was because it honored "influences from both within the researcher's psyche as well as from the outer progress of the study" (Clements et al., 1999, p. 87). For my research, I knew I had to travel to Kerala, India to conduct the interviews. I also, knew that I had no control over people, events, and situations in Kerala and that they could organically shift for better or worse. Just as I predicted, numerous unforeseen changes occurred at the last minute, such as when two of my co-researchers could not make it to the interviews due to unpredictable circumstances. In spite of my detailed planning, on many occasions I had to surrender to the intelligence and guidance of a higher knowing. In those moments, I was grateful to have organic inquiry as my methodology of research. In short, organic inquiry made the entire research a sacred journey of personal transformation for those involved in the research directly as well as indirectly.

Ethical Considerations and Challenges

One of the biggest challenges was how to reveal the identity of my co-researchers as well as their relationship to me, while maintaining ethical considerations. Since my co-researchers were close family members, it was important for their identities to be revealed because it deeply contributed to the personal as well as transformational aspect of my study. However, it meant that complete privacy, confidentiality, and anonymity could not be guaranteed for the participants, and there was the possibility that they could be identified in the final published study through their relationships to me.

Prior to every interview, I met with each grandmother to discuss in detail the concerns about privacy and confidentiality using the consent form. I also proposed to them the idea of having a pseudonym if they chose to do so. However, they did not care for a pseudonym; they wanted their names published. I assured them that I will seek their permission at all times—before recording any conversation during the interview, and before including any information shared by them that I feel is too personal and/or private. I also, told them that I would not make assumptions on what information can or cannot be included.

None of the three grandmothers were concerned about the issues of privacy, confidentiality, and anonymity, insisting instead to be identified with their real names and their relationships to me. Seeing no value in using a pseudonym, each grandmother said the same thing: "I can only tell you what I know. It does not matter to me if it got published or appeared in a newspaper. It would still be the truth." I was deeply inspired by their strength and conviction in their own words and life experiences. They gave me their consent to work in anyway I desired with the information they were sharing. I was humbled by their trust in me and I thanked them for that. I gave the grandmothers the opportunity to review the transcribed interviews, but they did not want to be involved in any of the reviews. They told me to take care of it. So my mother agreed to review all the transcribed interviews before I incorporated them into my thesis. Whenever I had some doubts, especially around family relationships and rituals, I first crosschecked with my mother and then, if needed, my mother called up the respective grandmother or her daughter for further clarification. I valued the opinion of my mother and grandmothers. It was of utmost importance to me to make sure that they felt comfortable before, during and after the interview. Furthermore, I saw this research as an opportunity to deepen my relationships with them, which required greater accountability on my part in understanding their stories without compromising my relationship to them.

There was another dimension to the research based on the relationship between the researcher and the subjects of the research that I was struggling with in writing the thesis. In my case these subjects were not just people, they were *my* people—an integral part of my life. Relationships are viewed in India very differently from the West. For example, every elderly person is a grandmother to me. I treat them exactly the way I treat my grandmother from the moment I meet them. Similarly any person older than me is either a sister or brother or uncle or aunt; that is how I address them. In that sense, not just for this research but also for any research that I do in future, what is my responsibility toward that relationship? It is a deeper question for me. I have realized that even the use of the word *co-researcher* in writing shifts the dynamics of my relationship, taking it to a level of equality. However, relationships in India are not based on the premise of equality, since they involve the factors of age, knowledge, and so much more. In fact, they are infinitely complicated. So my first and foremost need is not only protecting the information, but also, honoring my relationships with my mother and grandmother, and giving them their true voices. The stakes of loss are high for me.

Although I never expressed these concerns to my chair, she recommended *Research is Ceremony: Indigenous Research Methods*, by Shawn Wilson, a new book in the field of indigenous research. Shawn Wilson is an Opaskwayak Cree Native now living in Australia. This book described a research paradigm shared by the indigenous scholars in Canada and Australia based on the indigenous knowing that relationships do not just shape the indigenous reality, but they *are* the reality. Wilson (2008) wrote that within an indigenous research methodology the most important and meaningful role is to be "accountable to your relations" (p. 77). It made total sense to me. The researcher's interpretation of the knowledge has to be respectful and should help deepen the relationship between the researcher and the subject of the research (Wilson, 2008, p. 77). He recommended three R's for maintaining a healthy relationship: respect, reciprocity, and responsibility (Wilson, 2008, p.77). I realized that my role as a researcher was not just based on receiving something from the co-researchers, but *giving back* in full in a way that it demonstrated respect, integrity, and love for the relationships. This book helped me greatly in my writings, and I hope my actions reflect the depth of my admiration and respect for these women.

My Co-researchers

The first co-researcher I interviewed for this study was my mother. Her role as a silent witness to the changes between the two generations—my grandmother's and mine—was key to understanding the shifts that happened in the maternal family. She is my first Guru, my inspiration and my strength. She radiates patience, strength, compassion and generosity; she is the glue that keeps the extended family together. She patiently mediates conflicts between siblings, maintains intimate connections with her step-siblings, and stays in touch with the community in North Malabar at large. Most importantly, she understood the need for this study and supported my undertaking it whole heartedly. On numerous occasions during the period of interviews, I have forced her to step out of her comfort zone and she has bravely done so. I am proud of her. In this study, she was not only my co-researcher but she was also my translator and constant companion at every interview. As soon as I arrived in Bangalore, we spent a couple of days translating the consent form from English to Malayalam, engaging in various conversations around the topic of female sexuality. I was able to share intimate personal stories with her that influenced my engagement with this topic, which helped clear many of her doubts and understanding around *female sexuality* and the need for this study. These conversations deepened our friendship in addition to strengthening the mother-daughter bond. She kept a journal to record her experiences as well as any memories that surfaced from the past during the entire journey. She also gave me permission to use her journal for my research.

In addition to my mother, I interviewed three grandmothers (or *ammammas*) between 80 to 90 years of age. They are all from my home city of Kannur. I am only giving their names in this section. You may refer to the part five of this book for a detailed description of their family background as well as their relationships to me.

The first grandmother I interviewed was Madhavi Amma. She is the oldest living grandmother 92 years of age and connected to my mother's *taravad*. She is mischievous, enthusiastic and witty. Her eyes twinkled with excitement when she spoke of her childhood. Her humorous sarcasm made the challenging moments of life sound funny. Thanks to this interview, I got connected to her.

The second grandmother, Meenakshi Amma, was from my paternal side—my paternal great grandfather's sister's granddaughter. She is one of the strongest women I know. She has not left the perimeters of her ancestral property in many years, and yet, she exudes qualities of deep knowing, strength and wisdom, and her face reflects deep contentment and peace. In fact, all the women in her family are enterprising, open and free. She is the glue that keeps the entire matriliny together. In the last four decades I have not seen this grandmother age, a clear indication of the harmonious family structure among other factors.

The third grandmother, Yashoda Amma, is my father's younger brother's wife's mother. She is nearly 80, and currently lives with her daughter at my father's ancestral home in Taliparamba.

My sister was also part of this research, acting as a constant source of psychological and emotional support for me. She played the role of the videographer for the first interview.

During the interviews my co-researchers shared their experiences of participating in three female-centered rituals that were performed exclusively by women, focused on celebrating and guiding female sexuality. Although I did not get to observe or participate in any of these rituals or festivals during my visit, I feel that sharing them is gift for the younger generation since they are hardly observed or celebrated in the dominant culture of North Malabar.

I have organized my research journey in this book in a way that it unveils the organic emergence of the five key stages of Organic inquiry namely, **sacred, personal, chthonic, relational and transformative.** These various stages guided and supported my research work. I will begin with the first two stages in this chapter. The last three stages of organic inquiry will be discussed in the interview section of this book.

Sacred: Preparing the Ground

> Before any seeds are planted, the earth must be spaded and broken up, old roots and stones thrown to the side, and fertilizer added. Similarly, participation in the organic approach either as a researcher or as a reader calls for spading up one's old habits and expectations and achieving an ongoing attitude which respects and allows for the sacred to emerge on all levels, from the everyday level to the transpersonal. (Clements et al., 1999, p. 14)

In order to engage with my research topic sincerely and to be committed to the transformational journey that presented itself every day, it was most important that I seriously invested in preparing myself physically, mentally, emotionally and spiritually. That was *Preparing the Ground*—creating a sacred container for research.

I was pursuing the Master's program while holding a full time job as program director for a youth nonprofit. I worked with high school youth on a daily basis in a public school setting teaching yoga, breath work and life skills steeped in transpersonal wisdom. It did not take too long for my research world and my work world to cross paths, intermingle, and blend. Sometimes the awareness of one world conflicted with the other, and other times they complemented each other. Instead of resisting and avoiding, I used those opportunities to confront my inner fears, understand my judgments, refine my perceptions, and drop my positions around gender, sexuality, and body. This helped me bridge the gap between my work, life, and research study.

I invested nearly 1 to 2 hours every day in my spiritual practice of yoga, breathing, and meditation. No situation, remark or visual image that caused physical, mental, or emotional discomfort around gender, sexuality, and body went unnoticed by me. I engaged in self-reflection through writing, speaking aloud, moving, drawing, collaging, and dancing. I used every opportunity of art and embodied work in school to deepen my engagement with the topic of female sexuality.

I also participated in events that challenged my understanding of sexuality. One such opportunity was participating in a performance of the Vagina Monologues at the Institute of Transpersonal Psychology (now Sofia University) 2 years in a row. I embraced the performance as a sacred setting in which to overcome my hesitation, shame and discomfort around sexuality, and it worked. In the initial days in spite of my severe discomfort and shock, I sat through the entire narration and practice sessions of the Vagina Monologue with an open mind and complete awareness around my discomfort, shame, and even numbness in my body. Slowly the discomfort dropped and a sense of playfulness dawned in my body as I listened to the monologues. By the second year, I actually volunteered when the assigned reader could not make it to the practice session to read some of the monologues, which were the cause of my discomfort. For the first time I was able to understand and enjoy the humor in some of the readings. There was no longer any discomfort based on my vagina being something *unknown, unattractive* or *yucky*. In fact, I feel the brutalities and pain in the readings with more intensity. The Vagina Monologues have changed me sexually as a woman.

I believe that life is overseen, guided and orchestrated by an unseen intelligence. This intelligence flows through me into everything, and from everything back into me, shaping my intuition and intention. I do not see anything as a coincidence. Surrendering to this intelligence consciously was one of the practices I did. I set up a Goddess altar with Her images from around the world. I lit a candle at that altar every time I prepared to work on my thesis. I also did prayer, chanting and singing in front of the altar. I used the wisdom of the MotherPeace Tarot deck (Noble, 1983; Noble

& Vogel, 1988) to seek guidance from this intelligence. I laid the cards on the Goddess altar, and drew one card, sometimes once a week and other times, less or more frequently. I took the cards with me as I traveled in Kerala for the interviews. The appropriateness of guidance from the cards has left me speechless eliminating unnecessary doubts in the mind, as they reaffirmed my knowing and intuition.

I also, reached out to the guidance of my ancestors by creating an ancestral shrine or altar in my house on the night of the *Day of the Dead*. On that shrine I placed pictures of my grandparents and offered prayers frequently. The first time I prayed, I had a powerfully transformational dream around my marriage. In the dream, I was with my husband in a public place. Our relationship was easy going. When he asked me to accompany him home, I gently refused and said that I already have company at home. Then I came home to that company and in that presence I felt true intimacy. It was then I saw the face of the person I was with; it was my own self. I was in my own company. I woke up from the dream feeling a deep sense of love and connectedness with my body and sexuality. The title of this research also, came through that dream. I used a combination of the Goddess and Ancestor altar at every interview site. A lit *nellavillakku* (traditional lamp of Kerala), few red hibiscus flowers and my cowry shells used in ancestor practice adorned every altar. Additionally, I encouraged my co-researchers to place some image or object from their matrilineal past on the altar, helping to create a sacred space of intimacy and remembrance.

I engaged regularly in the sacred practice of drawing a Yoni Mandala (cover photo), a unique technique that happened through me and to me during my organic inquiry class at ITP. The first step in the Yoni Mandala drawing was to draw a line in the center of the page. Around that line I drew a *mandorla*—an ancient symbol of two circles coming together, overlapping one another to form an almond shape in the middle, the line going through the center. This represented the Yoni. The Yoni Mandala was drawn from this *mandorla* expanding outwards through intricate designs freely flowing on paper. This practice helped me transition easily into the space of research amidst the chaos and busyness of life and work. My professor, author Vicki Noble, introduced me to an early coloring book, *The Cunt Coloring Book*, by Tee Corrine, first published in 1975, consisting of illustrations of real yonis of women. This book (Corrine, 1975) celebrated feminine sexuality in a sacred and beautiful sort of way.

In addition to these practices, I used the world I drew around myself through people, situations and events as a reflection of my intention, intuition and guidance.

Personal: Planting the Seed

> Once the ground has been prepared, the gardener plants the seed deep in the darkness of the earth. This seed represents the initial concept for an organic study, which comes out of the researcher's own profound personal experience. The researcher's story of her or his subjective experience of the topic becomes the core of the investigation. (Clements et al., 1999, p. 26)

The central core for organic inquiry is the researchers' own profound personal experience. That story acts as the seed for birthing the relational aspects of the study—the stories of the co-researchers. Together these stories trace a path of transformation, not just for the reader but also for the researcher and co-researchers. How much of my life do I reveal? What do I hold back? How do I share the intimate personal aspects of my story that involved the life of another person? And the deadliest of all questions: who cares about my life and what I went through? I wrestled with many of these questions in my mind.

I read the personal narratives of other researchers who used organic inquiry as their key methodology: Framm (2010), Jamal (2007), Jenett (1999), and Shields (1995). One thing that stood out in the narratives was the portrayal of life by the researcher as a conscious witness. Though it was written in first person, it felt like it was presented in the third person. This mode of writing had a profound effect on me as the reader. I felt the need to sincerely portray my personal story around my body and sexuality as felt, seen, and experienced by me, without projecting judgment onto others. This required me to be more aware of my feelings, bodily sensations, and intense emotional moments while writing.

During the writing of my thesis, my husband and I were going back and forth about our separation. Finger pointing, accusations and blame were unavoidable. In the moments that followed I sincerely questioned the victim in me—where did I go wrong, what did I lack in knowing in the relationship, and what was I unable to see? These questions really helped me step out of the victim mode, and see my life experience in a truthful way. Prior to interviewing the grandmothers, I staged an interview with myself. My sister facilitated the process by asking me the six semi-structured questions. I recorded the whole interview. I wanted to experience the questions and the response for myself. My sister was only a presence witnessing the unfolding of the answers. She never uttered a word apart from asking the questions. Before answering every question, I closed my eyes, remembered my ancestors and the Goddess, and spoke without interruption or thinking, without editing the thoughts that flowed through me. When I completed the transcription of the entire interview, I saw visually how minimal my responses were for questions two through six in comparison to my response to the first question. So many unexpected memories surfaced during this mock interview. The entire interview lasted 90 minutes. At the end, I felt like a huge waterfall had washed over me creating an expanded feeling. My sister who was silent throughout the interview shared that every word I spoke affected her deeply. She felt that something in her had shifted as well. The self-interview process gave me a firsthand experience of hearing the questions and answering them. It also, prepared me for my interviews with the grandmothers.

Now I invite you to read my story of the *Rising Daughter*.

PART II

THE RISING DAUGHTER

"I was beginning to realize that my feminine body and sexuality served no purpose outside marriage, belonging to a man, or becoming a mother. Although fully clothed, slimly clothed, naked, and erotic images of the Goddess adorned temple walls and palaces, these images did not have any relevance to the living bodies of women in my culture."

CHAPTER 3.

SOCIAL, CULTURAL & RELIGIOUS UPBRINGING

My relationship with my body and sexuality has been deeply influenced by my relationship with the Indian subcontinent, the Nayar culture of Kerala, and the cultures dominant in each. I will describe this relationship first before diving into my personal journey around body and sexuality. I will share my experience as it happened, highlighting the timeline of the experience for the understanding of the reader.

My family. I was born in a small town called Cherukunnu in the North Malabar district of Kannur in Kerala. When it was time for my birth, my mother went and stayed in her natal home with my grandmother (her mother) to give birth to me. This was and still is the custom for most families in South India, although now that is changing. My parents are simple, hard working, sincere people. My father joined the army as a soldier immediately after completing eleventh grade, an average education for his generation. My mother also quit school after 10th grade to take care of her siblings. She was a homemaker all her life, also the norm for her generation. My sister was born nearly 5 years after me. My father's transferable job took us through the different states of India from the North to the South. Most of my student life I lived within the Army campus so I had friends from every religious, social, and cultural background of India.

I am very close to my family; we share and openly discuss everything —from simple to complex, from private to public—and there are hardly any secrets in the family. As a teenager and even as an adult, I chose to spend time with my family. My family relaxes, nurtures, and supports me. I laugh the most in their company. My father is the most dynamic, joyful, and enthusiastic father I know of. He is the one who encouraged me to dream for the stars, and made me believe that I am no less than any boy. My mother is the enlightened one in the family, embodying grace, compassion and wisdom; she laid the foundation for my unshakable faith in the divine. My sister is my reflection and my best friend. We shared many life experiences directly and indirectly around the same time in our lives—influencing each other in our world views and perspectives—and protecting and supporting each other.

My close-knit family is different. Early on in life, I learned that my parents were different from other parents, being more on the casual side—and never strict. They gave my sister and me complete freedom to think, act, and be the persons we wanted to be. My father was big on education, encouraging my sister and me to get professional degrees and jobs before we even considered marriage. It was on his insistence that I got a degree in engineering and graduated second in my class and my university. I never experienced the pressure of getting married that was experienced by most of my girlfriends. Often, when I visited my friends' homes, I observed that the interactions between the families were more restrained and formal, and their relationships were compartmentalized: the children, the mother, and the father. In our house, we were one unit.

I am an Indian Malayali. Growing up I identified myself first and foremost as an Indian, and then a Malayali, a native of Kerala. In fact, even as a child I spoke Hindi (India's national language) more fluently than Malayalam. Now would be a good time to introduce you to India—my beloved country and my first love. India is a land of an amazingly vast religious, ethnic, cultural, and social diversity with 28 formal states and seven union territories. Each state has its own language, cuisine, attire, appearance, and so much more. Even within each state there is a huge variation in the ethnic and cultural makeup across different regions. Hinduism is the dominant religion and culture of India, and Hindi is the national language. It is almost impossible to define and confine Hinduism into a particular form and construct. The word Hindu was coined by outsiders to identify the people living on the other side of the Sindhu river, and Hinduism became identified with their way of life (Flood, 1996, p. 8). Hinduism has many disguises, forms, expressions, appearances, religious texts, and more (Flood, 1996, pp. 5-22). In fact, it is thoroughly confusing even to an Indian to attempt to define what constitutes Hinduism. The spirit of India is reflected in the spirit of its people, and in the values of friendliness, compassion, and non-violence embodied by the people of India irrespective of the religion they belong to.

My connection to Kerala. My knowledge of Kerala is mostly embedded in the memories of my childhood all the way until high school. Every summer we took short vacations there and for 3 years, seventh through ninth grade, we stayed at my grandparent's house, while my father was stationed in the remote villages of North East India. The frequency of my visits to Kerala dropped significantly after completion of high school when I entered a professional degree course, followed by my getting a job, marrying, and eventually coming to the United States. However, I have always felt a deep connection to the land and its people, like it was part of my spirit from another time and place. There was something strangely mysterious, ancient, and magical about the folk songs, myths, rites, and rituals of Kerala. I recognize them today as earth-based and indigenous, but I did not know that then. Each time I left Kerala as a child, I longed to return. I got to know the land through the numerous stories shared by my parents and grandparents, watching *Malayalam* movies, reading *Malayalam* literature and popular magazines, and interacting with the people of Kerala during my vacations.

My Malayali Hinduism was different. As a child and then a teenager, I observed that the Hinduism of every Indian was very different in terms of the rituals, festivals, food, folk culture, dances, music, clothing, and belief systems. In my experience, the North Indian Hindu was completely different from the South Indian Hindu. In the South, my state Kerala was unique in every possible way. Although religiously I was a Hindu, my Malayali Hinduism was in stark contrast with the rest of my friends there. Our favorite divinities of *Bhagawathi* (the goddess), *Guruvayoor Appan* (a form of Lord Krishna), and *Ayyappan* (son born of the union of Shiva and Mohini, Vishnu's female form) were unknown to most of my non-Malayali friends. In addition, popular Hindu festivals of India, such as *deepavali, holi,* and *navarathri* were either completely absent or celebrated in an entirely different way in Malayali homes, and popular festivals of Kerala, like *vishu, thiruvathira, pooram* and *onam,* were absent from the rest of India. When asked about this, my mother's usual response was, "In Kerala we are different." Among the many things about Kerala differing from the rest of India, a few in particular are of interest to this study.

The auspicious daughters of Kerala. The most important difference is that a daughter was, and still is, considered auspicious. She is honored and celebrated, associated with prosperity and, most importantly, she is considered to be the Goddess Bhagawathi herself. I was the first female grandchild on my father's side of the family. I received special attention because of that from my paternal grandparents—getting excused for mischief, getting an extra piece of desert from Grandmother, and the constant acknowledgement of my birth in the family. I felt powerful, beautiful, and smart just because I was a girl, and this positive acknowledgement of my femininity was reflected in the eyes of my parents, my uncles, aunts, grandparents, granduncles, grandaunts, and everyone else in my extended maternal and paternal families. My father took pride in having two daughters, a very different situation from most traditional Hindu families where sons are favored, the continuation of the family heritage and lineage is associated with boys and men, and girls bring shame and are felt to be a burden. My sister and I never felt less in any way because we were girls. Everyone assumed that we would study, get jobs, and reach great heights in our professions. There was no conflict with marriage and work. In fact, it was common to see working women in Kerala.

The bond of the maternal family. The other important feature of Kerala is the men and women's attachment to their maternal families—their mothers, the maternal grandparents, maternal uncles and aunts, maternal home, maternal food, maternal village, and the maternal festivals. The maternal family was and still is spoken of in pride and remembered fondly. I myself felt a strong connection to my mother's side of the family, beyond words, expression or feeling. It was rooted in my body and knowing. In spite of the fact that I was cherished as a granddaughter on my father's side, I longed to be in my mother's home during vacations. I felt intimately close to my maternal land; it spoke to me. Although this might be true for most Hindus across India, what stands out in Kerala is that a woman continues to maintain this connection even after her marriage.

Traditionally she is always a daughter. She is free to go back to her mother's home, stay there, and seek support anytime—nobody questions her rights to return to her mother. In most Hindu families outside Kerala, the daughter becomes a member of her husband's family upon marriage. In many cases, she is even required to change her first name to go with this new identity. Her relationship with her maternal family changes completely. She is discouraged from visiting, talking, or speaking to them frequently, in direct contrast with what I see in Kerala, and especially within my own family. A majority of my summer vacations were spent in my mother's home. My father would stay at most for a day and then go back to his family. We would visit and stay with him for a few days at my paternal grandparent's house. This was true for others in my family as well. My aunts (wives of my maternal uncles) mostly stayed at their maternal homes during vacations and were guests in our family. They were never expected to stay with my grandmother or take care of her; they lived with my uncles in nuclear homes. However, this did not affect my maternal uncles from having close relationships with their mother. They financially supported my grandmother's affairs, and visited her on their own when she was alive. My father never objected or stopped my mother's relationship with her maternal side, and vice versa. In fact, when my father had to spend 3 years away from his family, my maternal grandmother's home in Kerala was the natural choice for us to stay. The maternal family is considered the most natural bond and deeply respected especially in the case of women. These bonds are closely tied to the matrilineal history of Kerala, which I was completely unaware of at that time in my life and which I will describe in detail in Chapter 7.

Sexuality of Kerala women. The last and most relevant aspect of Kerala, even today, is the visible sexuality of her women—the grandmothers, the mothers, the sisters, the daughters, and the women workers in the paddy fields, in the marketplace, in the temples, in buses and on the streets. As I recall from my years in Kerala, feminine sexuality expressed itself through the earthiness of women's bodies. In the way their hands moved, their hips moved, and their whole bodies moved—even the clothing of the women suggested a deep sense of sexual freedom and groundedness from within and without. In those days, they mostly wore off-white *mundu-veshti* (also called set-mundu), another unique asset of

Kerala—a figure-fitting blouse outlining the woman's breasts, a long piece of cloth called *mundu* tightly wrapped around her waist with her bare midriff showing, and then the thin muslin cloth called *veshti* worn over her shoulders. It was a common sight to see bare breasted grandmothers going about their daily activities without shame or being self-conscious. The more I saw the women of Kerala, the more they appeared in direct contrast to the *saree* or *salwar-kameez*-wearing modest contemporary Hindu women (including myself) outside of Kerala. The women in Kerala were different—dynamic, educated, vocally loud, mostly cheerful, working, and moving without shame or fear amidst men, their interactions open, casual, and free. I saw this freedom of interaction even in my father and mother, who had their own set of close friends from school and from the community which included both men and women with whom they spoke freely. I did not see that kind of freedom in the interaction of married women outside of Kerala, especially with men other than their husbands or brothers.

During my 3-year stay as an adolescent in Kerala, I saw that the younger generation of school or college girls in Kerala embodied sexuality in a different way from the older generation of women. I do not have an English word to describe this behavior and, hence, I will use the Malayalam word *sringarikukka* derived from the Sanskrit root word *sringaram* (meaning the dance of love) to describe their behavior—young girls in buses throwing innocent sideway glances at young boys through kohl-covered eyes with half smiles on their lips, all the while giggling with their girlfriends, and sometimes the boys reciprocated humming love songs and passing love letters to girls. Culturally nobody made a big deal about this behavior. However, my own sense of morality acquired in those days through media and education made me look down upon this behavior.

My cultural shadow. Before I step into my story around my body and sexuality, I would like to briefly mention why I chose to exempt myself from being identified as a Hindu or Nayar. One of the scars of Hinduism in India is the caste system, which is an extremely complex, controversial, and sensitive topic for most Indians, and outside the scope of this study. Growing up I experienced this system as something that hierarchically divided and separated people based on birth and their ancestral trade or skill, combined with severe practices of purity and impurity within and between the different categories of castes (Flood, 1996, pp. 58-61).

My parents never spoke of caste at home, and so as a child I had very little knowledge of it. I remember being asked what caste I was by a non-Malayali friend and I did not know the answer. I only knew I was a *Kurup*. I came home and asked my parents about it, whereupon I was told that every Hindu was born into a caste associated with an ancestral profession or skill: *Brahmins* were the guardians of spiritual knowledge, *Kshatriyas* the protectors of the land, *Vaishyas* the business class, and *Sudras* the working class who supported the daily lives of people. I learned that there were people classified as "untouchables," ranked lowest in the hierarchy. It was explained to me that the *Kurups* of Kerala were generally considered as belonging to the *Kshatriya* class, because they were the warriors or martial experts. Over the course of time, through movies and literature, I learned that in Kerala the caste systems were extremely complex, rigid, and complicated. In addition to the four castes and the untouchables, people were also classified as un-approachable and even un-seeable—so much so that breaking these rules was punishable by death.

Several reform movements over the last 60 years have shifted the shadows surrounding castes considerably in Kerala compared to the rest of India. My generation's knowledge and experience around the caste systems was mostly learned from observing the adults: parents, uncles, grandparents, neighbors and more. However, my father and many men of his generation had most of the castes across Kerala and India memorized. Though my father meant no harm, he like many men of his generation could effortlessly identify a person's caste or profession from his or her last name and could list the prejudices that went with that caste. For instance, if I said the name of my teacher or friend, the first thing my father mentioned was the caste: He is a warrior like us or a barber or a shoemaker or a blacksmith or a washer man. It bothered me immensely. Although I embraced the spiritual values, I moved away from rituals, rites, symbols, and ceremonies that in my opinion segregated people. Sadly, this decision also kept me away from the rich tradition of my own indigenous Nayar culture.

I lived in two worlds. Growing up I mostly lived in two worlds, my home space with my parents and sister, which was the safest and most comfortable of the two, and the world of my friends, teachers, and people in general. Many times I felt that my parents did not understand the world well enough, and that they were not cool enough. They did not speak fluent English, were not modern or western in anyway, and did not read English novels or magazines or watch Hollywood movies. When I entered adolescence, I was caught up in the world of influences through my immediate friends, my school and, most importantly, western literature and media. It was a world I kept from my parents, especially my mother, thinking that she would not be able to relate. I began to confide in my sister when she was in high school. I was an aspiring feminist—fearless, angry, powerful, and ready to fight with anyone for women's rights. I wanted to be seen as a modern woman—educated, independent, and free. However, there was also the traditional me that was committed, giving, duty bound, respectful of societal norms, and secretly wishing for a wise intelligent honest man to take care of me. These two identities were often in conflict, which clouded my intellect and mind, and influenced the way I showed up in the world as a woman. I had no access to the natural wisdom and knowing that came from my body and sexuality, since that relationship had been deeply compromised through various happenings in my life as I journeyed from a young girl into an adult woman.

CHAPTER 4.

RELATIONSHIP WITH BODY AND SEXUALITY

My childhood. As a child, I was very comfortable in my body. That connection was pure, innocent, free, and playful—boys and/or girls together without shame or perverseness, enjoyed intimate cuddling, touching, hugging, lying next to each other, on top of each other, holding hands, giggling and laughing, kissing. My voice was clear; it came from my gut. My laughter was loud and clear; it echoed joy. My body moved without inhibition—hopping, swinging, singing, and humming. My genitals evoked wonder, my hands often going there without feeling shame. My world was alive; the butterflies, dragonflies, ants, cows, birds, trees, and clouds spoke to me. My sexuality presented moments of complete awareness, as if every cell in my body were alive. My body was sacred, sweet, and beautiful. I was natural and free.

My adolescence. My connection with my body and sexuality shifted with adolescence and the onset of breasts, menstruation, and hormonal body changes when I was in eighth grade living in Kerala at my maternal grandmother's home with my grandmother, my mother, sister, mother's younger sister and her children, and my youngest uncle. I was happy and carefree and I watched as girls in my class got their periods, and then changed overnight, becoming somehow more beautiful. I looked forward to my menstruation and felt no shame or discomfort in my body, although I was beginning to notice a shift in the behavior of boys and men toward me.

I remember an event like it happened yesterday. I was in eighth grade and it was the year-end annual cultural fest at my school. I was in a play wearing my mother's transparent synthetic saree—brand new and from

Singapore. I was quite excited to wear it, but my teacher got mad at me for not wearing a bra under the blouse and for "shamefully" displaying my breasts to the public; she blamed my mother for the negligence. I was shocked. For the first time, I recognized and experienced shame and embarrassment around female nudity—my breasts, my legs, my arms, and my whole body. It was as if there was something wrong for me to be uncovered. This incident shifted and shaped my conscious presence in my body from feeling natural to being overtly self-conscious, especially in the presence of boys. I was angry with my mother for not warning me and my mother was surprised at my teacher's outburst, since she had felt it was too soon for me to wear a bra. After that, I refused to go to school until she got me the bra; that summer I also got my period.

My first blood. I had my first blood in my grandmother's house. I did not want anyone to be informed, other than my mother and grandmother. My mother taught me the use of the menstrual cloth, and asked me to take rest. On the third or fourth day, I insisted on going with my aunt and uncle on an hour-long journey to the city to watch a movie of one of my second cousins. On the way, I had an episode of intense bleeding. The back of my dress and the auto rickshaw seat was almost soaking wet in my blood. My aunt was shocked and extremely mad at my mother for not informing her about my first blood and for letting me come out of the house. I connected her anger to the inconvenience caused by my *bleeding* incident. However, looking back, I realize that she was angry with me for coming out of the house during my bleeding, as it was customary in her time for girls to remain indoors during their menstrual cycles. Following that day, my bleeding did not stop for months and I had to go through several doctor visits and medications to normalize my periods. This whole episode lasted for nearly a year, causing me a lot of mental and emotional trauma. My mother stood by me without ever letting me feel less of myself, never showing any signs of embarrassment around my blood. I never shared those challenges with my friends or teachers in school, feeling that it was not something people wanted to hear or talk about. However, my mother's positive attitude toward menstruation helped me have deep reverence for my blood.

Another experience of my body and nakedness happened around the same time. I was crazy about books, reading anything and everything. Most of my schools did not have libraries and those that did only had books for high school students, so when my mother mentioned having seen an old trunk full of books that belonged to my uncle, I was ecstatic to explore it. I discovered it carefully hidden under my grandfather's cot with over 30 books written by authors around the world. The book that caught my attention was *Never Love a Stranger* by James Hardly Chase, the only book with a newspaper wrapping carefully hiding the book's cover. Out of curiosity I unwrapped it and unveiled the naked body of a woman lying on her back; I was staring right at her breasts, nipples, and pubic hair. The rawness of the picture hit me hard and I quickly put the cover back on. I wanted to look and yet, somehow I could not look at the picture, feeling fear, shyness, and danger. My first thought was, "What if someone found me here with this book? Would I be seen as a bad person?" Slowly, as that feeling passed, I opened the cover and looked at the picture again. It was the first time I had seen a fully naked woman's body and it fascinated me. I had never seen my own body or that of any other woman in my family naked. In fact, until that day I had not thought of any woman's body that way, including my own. I put the cover back on the book and kept it close to me for days, reading it from cover to cover, including a lot of intensely passionate lovemaking. It opened me to a new world so different from mine—bold and free. In between readings I would open the cover and stare at the picture. It was my secret.

The faces of sexual abuse. Those 3 years in Kerala my father was not with us, and my relationship with boys and men began to shift. I had to travel along with my sister by public transportation for nearly an hour to get to school every day. I soon discovered how unsafe and uncomfortable it was to be in an overcrowded bus, as unseen hands crawled out of nowhere to touch my hips or my breasts or pinch me on the bottom. When I waited alone in the bus stop, college-going men would come in bicycles and hover —sometimes whistling a popular romantic Malayalam movie song, or having side conversations about romance loud enough for me to hear. I could have played along and laughed at the immature behavior of the boys and men, the way I saw many girls do, sometimes openly encouraging them—giggling, whispering to each other while eyeing the boys and sheepishly smiling at them. In my case, it just made me angry. I wanted to slap the boys for their stupidity.

When my father decided to move all of us out of Kerala to another state, I was relieved, thinking the problem was Kerala men. However, it was only when I moved away from Kerala that I appreciated the men of Kerala. Although they irritated me, I never felt unsafe there. Their boyish behavior was a constant hindrance, but outside Kerala I felt as if I had suddenly stepped into a world of vultures. It was everywhere: the purposeful dashing of strangers into female bodies, the unseen creeping hands grabbing at breasts and genitals, displays of male genitalia, shameful comments by men on the sidewalk. That behavior was neither boyish nor innocent, but scary and sick! I learned to sense sexual abuse like a sixth sense without even directly being in it. It came as a strong feeling of restlessness—every hair in my body stood up, my stomach churned and tightened, my heartbeat and breath shifted. I knew danger was in close proximity and every time I did not act on that feeling, I regretted it afterwards. I have sometimes screamed, slapped, and hit men to protect my body and those of other women in public places.

Surprisingly, I never shared any of this with my parents who seemed naïve to the sexual perverseness in the world. Once when we were traveling in a train and they were sleeping downstairs, with my sister and me sleeping upstairs, I kept watch the whole night because the man sleeping across kept reaching out to touch my sister and me in inappropriate places. I pretended sleep and then caught hold of his hand and looked him straight in the eye and said, "If you do this again, I will kill you." Although he did not do it again, I was shocked and angry that my sister had to experience it so young. These experiences brought a feeling of disgust and contempt toward my feminine body and sexuality, causing immense pain, shame, and humiliation.

My adolescent years in school. I thought school was a safe place. However, soon I realized that *once I was a bleeding adolescent female, no place was safe*. I learned from my female friends that some of the male teachers would pull their bras or pinch them in inappropriate places in class. Out of sheer embarrassment these girls chose to stay quiet. I never experienced any such incident personally perhaps because I had learned to protect my body just by the way I presented myself. There was a strength that came from within me that warned boys and men not to mess with me. I remember one specific occasion in 11th grade when I marched fearlessly into the principal's office to report sexual abuse by the male English teacher toward my girlfriend. In school, on one side was this sexual perverseness and on the other side was the pseudo morality of the male teachers.

Flirting, romancing, or any kind of outward display of intimacy or closeness among boys and girls was strictly forbidden. The students were expected to be *decent* and *proper,* meaning displaying behavior that did not involve affection, including holding hands, sitting or walking too close. A female student paid a heavy price for getting involved romantically with a boy in school, the male teachers could affect her grades, her friends could stop talking to her, and her parents could get notified, which was the worst. Many times a girl's name might appear alongside the boy's with obscene comments on bathroom walls and it was enough to shatter the reputation of that girl. In short, there was a model of behavior expected of girls; boys were never affected the same way. These double standards made me angrier.

Becoming a male-identified woman. Looking back I realize that I had to navigate and deal with all the challenges of becoming a woman by myself. I saw how girls were discouraged and even forbidden from engaging in passionate endeavors like free-form of dancing, singing, casual flirting, or any pleasing sensations or sounds or laughter, ecstatic experiences and feelings—all experiences natural to adolescence. Most girls had to resist or suppress these feelings and experiences. For instance, when my heart fluttered naturally at the sight of a boy, or when in the middle of the night I woke up to an ecstatic body experience tingling with passion and aliveness, or when I became aroused watching a romantic scene in a move—I feared it was wrong that these experiences of and in my body were not spiritual. It was sinful. I felt I could not talk to anyone including my mother for the fear of being judged and blamed.

I was beginning to realize that my feminine body and sexuality served no purpose outside marriage, belonging to a man, or becoming a mother. Although fully clothed, slimly clothed, naked, and erotic images of the Goddess adorned temple walls and palaces, these images did not have any relevance to the living bodies of women in my culture. I slowly began to alienate and disconnect from my feminine body—my breasts, nipples, pubic hair, genitals, physical sensations and my bodily discharges—as if my body did not exist. I dared not touch, look or innocently inquire about my body, or be deemed shameless, dangerous, animalistic, and most importantly non-spiritual.

My body language shifted. My shoulders stiffened. I began to slouch. My arms dropped close to my shoulders, my legs stuck together, my trust in men and even women shifted, and my male friendships were tightly guarded and restricted. I was still bold, outgoing, free, and open. However, I was alert all the time for myself and other women. I had many male friends, but intimacy was off limits. I disconnected from my body completely, losing the ability to be amorous, feminine, and sensual. I embraced and expressed my masculine energy in the world in terms of my clothing, body language, the tone of my voice, topics of interest, and my choice of profession—engineering. I lived a lot in my head, less in my feelings, and often suppressed the knowing that came from my body and sexuality.

I did not want to marry. On one hand, I was wary of the intention of any male I encountered, and on the other, I longed for the perfect lover and mate. As a teenager the mythology of Goddess Paravathi and Lord Shiva, and stories of their union fascinated me. Shiva, the ash-smeared graveyard-wandering dispassionate recluse not drawn by any worldly interests filled my heart. In high school and college I was drawn to romantic novels and movies, which portrayed the main male character as the tall, dark, ruggedly handsome wanderer totally dispassionate about women—the ideal Shiva, and these intimate fantasies dictated my worldly relationships of romance.

By the time I graduated from high school and got into a professional degree college for my bachelor's, I was totally opposed to the idea of an arranged marriage, and even more, I was opposed to the concept of the traditional Hindu wife. I observed the qualities of a traditional Hindu wife from images of women in the Hindu culture as portrayed by mythology, Hindi movies and mythological comic books. She experienced happiness in the obedient service to her family—her husband and her children (Leslie, 1992, pp. 15-65). Her husband was her rightful God and she was required to engage in severe fasting and austerities for the long life of her husband and children (Leslie, 1992, pp. 71-87). Every man other than her husband was like a son or brother to her. She was required to make sacrifices at every turn of her life for the well-being of her family, and a woman who lived her life like that was considered a good wife or *Pativrata*, meaning a chaste woman (Leslie, 1992, pp. 86-87). This role playing was unrealistic and unlivable by my standards because it seemed too restrictive and suffocating and even more so I did not see many Godly men in the society. It was only later in my life that I realized I had internalized the traditional Hindu wife without even realizing it at that time of my life.

I also did not want to marry a Malayali because the memories of the Malayalee college boys and their bold openness confronting girls in public places with love letters, sexual proposals, and erotic gestures were still fresh in my mind. Looking back now, I think the directness of the Malayali boys and men toward sexuality were in direct opposition to my own disconnectedness with body and sexuality. Their ability to see and recognize my erotic sensuality challenged my invisibility toward it, bringing up strong emotions of anger, hatred, guilt, regret, and shame toward them. Sadly, I had no awareness about this at that time. I had no one to talk to about it. The social culture I lived in then had no conscious ways of guiding me toward this awareness.

I recognized my sexual disconnect. Then at my first job—alone, independent, and free in Bangalore, I fell in love. He was shy, reserved, and quiet and came from a completely different cultural upbringing than mine. In a subdued yet romantic way he proposed—my longing for eternal romance was fresh and so was the desire to leave my matriliny to be with a man—and I agreed. Looking back, I realize that without even realizing it at that moment I gave myself up completely to him. However, as we courted there were numerous instances were my body and sexuality felt exactly like it did many times in the dark corridors of a train or bus or theatre—cornered, forced, and pushed into physical intimacy. I longed for togetherness and connection of the heart but most of the time I walked away feeling weak, unnoticed, and less of myself—as if only my physical body had received a response from him. My past experiences surrounding body and sexuality weighed heavily on my present. I could not walk out of the relationship for the fear of hurting him, and I did not know how to say *no* when physical intimacy was forced. I hoped if I could just cut myself off from the feeling of disgust in the body and surrender to his desires, I would be okay. We got married and came to United States in 1999.

We shared many beautiful moments together and a deep resonance in our spirits. However, in our bodies we were a mess. I longed for intimacy of the heart, and he only knew to connect through his physical body and its responses. Many nights I resented going to bed, seeing his advances as feverish and forceful—focused on getting his way and fulfilling his bodily desires, and in those moments he became a complete stranger to me and my sexual shadows from the past resurfaced. I would try to use humor and completely unrelated conversation to defuse my hatred and fear, but it made things worse—my body withdrew and tightened and my breath changed. Sometimes, I silently wept and most nights I lay awake, sad, and lonely. I was also overburdened with emotions of guilt and fear of not fulfilling the role of the traditional Hindu wife. When I tried to talk about it, my choice of words would hurt his ego and he would withdraw.

That is when I realized that I did not know how to step into my body and sexuality, how to lead him into or even out of his lust, how to indulge in pleasures of the body without feeling guilty and, most importantly, how to embody the dance of love (or *sringaram*). So I just pretended that physical intimacy was pleasurable. There was no one to confide in or talk to. I slowly merged with my insecurities, became a timid fearful mouse. My fearless directness was now replaced by avoidance and the inability to hold a person's gaze. It was like being caught in a nightmare without knowing how to wake up. Leaving him never occurred to me and, in fact, I did not even think it was an option. I prayed and prayed for both of us.

I found my spiritual teacher. Within 2 years of our marriage, on my mother's insistence I attended a 6-day workshop called the Art of Living Program. It was the most powerful spiritual experience of my life. I found my spiritual path, my purpose, and my spiritual Guru and friend in His Holiness Sri Sri Ravi Shankar, a world-renowned humanitarian leader, spiritual teacher, and an ambassador of peace (not to be mistaken with the Sitar Maestro of the same name). His work has touched the lives of millions of people around the world, going beyond the barriers of race, nationality, and religion with the message of a "one-world family" and my life's journey took on a new meaning. Through the grace of having a living Guru and the powerful yogic breathing and meditation practices he taught, I woke up out of a bad dream. This awakening brought a deep sense of expansion, connection, and self-love.

My trauma, shame, and disgust around the body dropped. I experienced a conscious knowing and reverence for my body and sexuality.

My playfulness and innocence returned. My laughter was loud and clear. For the first time I felt like the little girl I once had been—free, light, and in control. My body began to move and I danced without shame at the spiritual retreats. Everyone who knew me noticed the shift. I also got the opportunity to interact with women and men from around the world and noticed a different quality of freedom, intimacy, and friendship between married couples that was based on mutual respect and independence; most husbands and wives had interests independent of each other which they pursued without guilt and fear. I sincerely hoped and prayed that my marriage would embody that some day.

However, on January 14, 2010, in the most shocking, bizarre, and dramatic turn of events my marriage collapsed. It was a deeply traumatic experience. My spiritual path and the guidance of my Guru gave me immense strength. However, this experience made me question the very foundation of Indian marriages and the role of traditional Hindu wife. Through my closest friend and spiritual sister from Israel, Arielle Warner, I learnt about the Women's Spirituality Master's Program at the Institute of Transpersonal Psychology (ITP; now called Sofia University). After going through the website, I learned that two of the core faculty, Dianne Jenett and Judy Grahn, had spend considerable time doing research in Kerala on the Nayars. The cultural familiarity of the core faculty encouraged me in the decision to get my master's degree.

CHAPTER 5.

RELEVANCE AND EMERGENCE OF THIS STUDY

Theorist and activist educator, Judy Grahn, interviewed me prior to enrolling in the program. I was really moved by her love for the Nayar culture and the Goddess. She informed me that she and co-director, Dianne Jenett were really glad that I was entering the program. My thought process was—that's great but I am not here to explore my Nayar roots but to explore my purpose as a female on this planet. Little did I know then that spirit had a different plan sketched out for me, and embedded in that plan were the answers to my questions about the feminine body and sexuality. At ITP, I found myself heavily drawn to investigate my life in Kerala, and my Malayaliness. In every class and papers, I was drawing my experiences from my Malayaliness. It was not intentional but somehow only my Nayar identify existed in my memory. My longing and passion for Kerala—the land, the women, the men, the rituals, the food, the attire and everything returned. Fortunately for me, the women's spirituality program was the perfect organic soil to plant my seeds of inquiry into my indigenous roots. It challenged me in every possible way. I was forced to go beyond layers and layers of conditioning, perceptions, and hearsay to access my own knowing that came from my body, my memory, and my being.

My introduction to matriarchy. I was introduced to matriarchy in a course called Matriarchal Societies taught by author, Vicki Noble, also part of the Sofia faculty. I learned that most matriarchal societies are egalitarian, and gender domination based on hierarchies, classes, or castes are unknown to them (Goettner-Abendroth, 2005, 2007, 2009; Sanday, 2009). In these societies, gender roles are about maintaining balance; different genders and generations have their own value and dignity and are co-dependent on each other (Goettner-Abendroth, 2009, p. 1). I learned that many of these matriarchal societies exist even today:

> Some of these still existing matriarchal societies are the Mosou, Yao, Miao and Tan peoples in China; the Chiang people of Tibet; the Minangkabau of Sumatra; the Ainu of Japan; the Trobrianders of Melanesia in the Pacific; the Khasi and Garo in Northeast India, and the Nayars of Southeast India; the Bantu of Central Africa; the Akan and Ashanti peoples in West Africa; the Berbers and Tuareg of North Africa; the Arawak people of South America; the Cuna and Juchitecan societies of Central America; and, the Hopi and Pueblo people as well as the Iroquois people of North America; just to name the main ones. (Goettner-Abendroth, 2009, p. 20)

Through my 2-year graduate program, I was introduced to matriarchal ways of life, including relationships between men and women, mothers and daughters, brothers and sisters in the cultures and, most importantly, the space held in these cultures for female sexuality. In addition, I learned that most matriarchal civilizations revered and deified the feminine (Goettner-Abendroth, 2009, p. 24). This encouraged me to look at my own relationship with the Goddess. I realized that I grew up with numerous images of goddesses. I never felt separate from them. I never had to struggle with the thought that God was only male. In fact, I grew up knowing that God is in every creature, and that the Goddess is as powerful as the male Gods. I learned that this was not the experience of some of my other American cohort sisters in the program.

My Nayar Matrilineage. In the Women's Spirituality Program, I got an up close and personal insight into the past lives of the Nayar community of Kerala through the extensive work of my professors, Dr. Jenett and Dr. Grahn, and the various books and journal articles they introduced me to, especially those written by female authors (den Uyl, 1995, 2000; de Tourreil, 1995, 2009; Gough, 1952, 1955, 1961, 1965; Grahn, 1999; Jenett, 1999; Moore,

1988; Neff, 1995; Saradamoni, 1982, 1994, 1999). Through these scholarly writings, my Nayar matrilineal consciousness was awakened.

I learned that in the past the Nayar kinship organization was matrilineal, matrilocal and matrifocal. In the Nayar social organization all property and assets were understood to belong in principle to the females and inheritance (or property) was passed down the female line and the woman never loses her rights in her natal matrilineage (de Tourreil, 1995, pp. 43-44). The Nayar culture was centered and focused on its women, especially daughters, mothers, and grandmothers and it was the responsibility of the male head of the kin group to protect, provide, and care for them irrespective of the presence or absence of a biological father (de Tourreil, 1995, p. 44). The most fascinating revelation was that women and men continued to live in their respective maternal homes after marriage and the Nayar daughters usually stayed in close proximity of the maternal family following their marriages, sometimes never leaving their maternal homes (de Tourreil, 1995, p. 44). The husbands practiced visiting the wives in their maternal homes at night, leaving for their own maternal homes the following morning where they lived and exercised their responsibilities (de Tourreil, 1995, p. 44). These new discoveries propelled me to focus more intensely on understanding the rich heritage of Nayar matriliny and the life of a woman living within it.

Savithri de Tourreil's (1995) doctoral dissertation, *Nayars in a South Indian Matrix: A Study Based on Female-Centered Ritual*, described in elaborate detail the Nayar female-centered rituals around pre-puberty, puberty, and marriage. Through these rituals the maternal kin guided, acknowledged, and celebrated the daughters of the lineage, and ensured the fruitful blossoming of the female energy from a young girl to a sexually mature adult woman. In another paper, *Nayars of Kerala and Matriliny*

Revisited, de Tourreil (2009) shared that the prosperity of the matrilineage was connected to the birth of a girl child, as she was the propitiator of the lineage. Most importantly, I learned that the maternal uncle considered it his duty to punctuously carry out traditionally required ritual for all females at puberty and sometimes he even performed religious austerities and went on a long arduous pilgrimage for the birth of a daughter in the lineage (de Tourreil, 2009, pp. 207-208). I will present more detailed descriptions of the Nayar matriliny and its history in Chapter 7.

These different stories deeply impacted me. They came from the lived experience of women from the Nayar household. As much as I wanted to believe these stories, I could not because these stories had no connection to my lived experience as a Nayar woman. The Kerala I grew up in did not mention or talk about its matrilineal past. Even the Kerala I witnessed through the memories of my mother had no direct connections to matriliny. With deep sadness, I realized that I had never known the existence of female-centered rituals in my life. On closer examination, I also learned that none of my paternal or maternal cousins had experienced any of these female-centered rituals. Even practices like the visiting marriages were looked down upon in the present culture, not spoken, being associated with the uncivilized past of Kerala. Most of the younger generation was either ignorant of these practices or they did not care. Today, patriarchal marriages are the norm in Kerala; the woman leaves her natal home and lives with her husband upon marriage. The husband is expected to care and provide for his wife and children. Shockingly, these changes have taken place in the last century, and already the past has been wiped out of the memories of the present generation. The Kerala in my memory is no longer the Kerala of the present generation.

The fast changing face of Kerala. Briefly, I would like to highlight some of the positive and not-so-positive shifts I have seen happen in Kerala over the last 2 decades. Using the statistical publication (Chandramouli, 2011) of the Ministry of Health and Family Welfare, *Family Welfare Statistics in India*, I will highlight some of the positive shifts. According to this report, Kerala was and still is the state with the highest literacy rate (meaning almost everyone irrespective of caste or gender or economic status can read and write) in India with a higher number of women literates in comparison to men. Kerala also has the lowest female infant and child mortality rate in India. However, I found that the female infant mortality rate in Kerala has increased from 9 (per 1000 live births) in 2001 to 12 (per 1000 live births) in 2009, and I feel this needs further exploration. The life expectancy of women in Kerala is also the highest (74 years) in India and the average age of marriage for female in Kerala (22.7 years) is second highest to Jammu and Kashmir (23 years). In addition, Kerala along with neighboring state of Tamil Nadu have demonstrated the best maternal health and fertility rate among their women. These numbers clearly demonstrate that women in Kerala still have better opportunities in comparison to the rest of India.

However, in the last 2 decades I have also witnessed some not-so positive changes happen in Kerala. For instance, in the 3 years I lived in Kerala (20 years ago), I never saw slums or beggars. Families lived together and most families owned property that yielded an abundance of food and other supplies to live happily. People were simple, content, and shared what they had with each other. There was a harmonious co-existence between people of different castes and religions; whereas, the rest of India was burdened with religious conflicts. Kerala was also known as one of the cleanest states of India. Thievery, burglary was almost nonexistent. Women were protected by the culture: traveling and moving safely in Kerala. However, in the last 2 decades, I have witnessed families' selling their ancestral property (including my own parents) and moving to nuclear family dwellings like apartments or gated communities sometimes out of Kerala. Slums have popped up in many parts of Kerala such as Kannur, Kollam, and Trivandrum. Begging has also increased; I have experienced this firsthand. Thievery, burglary, religious and political conflicts have intensified. Again, the brutality of violence in all these incidents is shocking —killings in broad daylight without fear or concern for the passers by. Another trend that has overwhelmingly increased or should I say *penetrated* the nuclear homes of Kerala is cable television and Malayalam soap operas that promote intense violence, gossip, affairs, wife beating, alcoholism, and other negative influences on a mass scale. As if this were not enough change, I was shocked by the high suicide rates, and the rising issues of sexual abuse and domestic violence toward women in Kerala. Let me present some numbers to illustrate the intensity of these issues.

According to the official website of the Kerala State Mental Health Authority (KSMH), since 1995 Kerala has the highest suicide rate in India, three times the national average ("Suicide in Kerala," n.d.). In other words, Kerala contributes 10% of all the suicides occurring in India when its population only constitutes 3% of the national population. Although the suicides were more among males (74%), the attempted suicides were more among women, and sadly 78% of the suicides were among married people. There has also been an increase in the teasing, verbal and physical abuse, rape, domestic violence, pornography, and sex trafficking in Kerala. The flirtatious advances of boys and men lack the innocence and playfulness of yesteryears.

> Rape cases increased by about 80 percent and molestation cases by 188.9 percent, which is the second most reported crime in Kerala. Eve teasing, although is a less severe crime compared to other crimes, increased by 435.7 percent. Kidnapping is the least reported crime in the state. Only few cases were registered in the early 90s. But, it has increased during the past decade by 17 percent. Hence, cent percent

increase in total crimes against women has been observed in the decade (1995-2005). (Kumari, 2009, p. 22)

In 2004, *Malayala Manorama*, the largest circulated newspaper of Kerala, ran a series of articles, *(How) Kerala Behaves With Women* (Jacob, 2004). These articles were the firsthand experiences of six brave women newspaper reporters who traveled across the state, cities, and district capitals, unescorted. The physical abuse, trauma, and difficulties these reporters encountered shocked the entire state. In addition, the newspaper also conducted a survey of 1200 women who traveled frequently. Seventy-two percent of the women did not feel safe traveling, 60% had to put up with unruly behavior from men, and 61% of the women traveling after nightfall were more prone to a higher risk of abuse.

In an interview with rediff.com's Shobha Warrier, Kerala's well-known writer Paul Zacharia called Kerala a sexually starved state. Zacharia states,

> I have lived in Delhi, I have lived in Mysore. I have lived in Chennai but I have not seen such starvation anywhere and I have not seen people peeping into another person's affairs, especially the affairs of a man and a woman, at this level anywhere. (Warrier, 2010, para. 5)

He challenged the conservative attitude of the Malayalees to sex, and male-female relationships. This is a trend of sexual moral policing in which certain sections of society (mostly consisting of middle class men and sometimes even women) with the support of police in Kerala, have become enforcers of strict sexual morality for men and women, taking action whenever they suspect two people indulging in impermissible (as decided by them) sexual activities. This pseudo morality is applied to any male-female dyad seen together after sunset including husband and wife, father and daughter, or brother and sister. Leela Menon, a veteran journalist and social activist addressed this in one of her regular columns with *En-Malayalam*, an online news magazine:

> The morality brigade that is taking root in Kerala are on the lookout for couples who are out after sunset, unconcerned about their purpose, whether they are going on an urgent errand, or whether they are on the way to a hospital. Just recently Sugatha Kumari was telling me of a husband and wife who was standing at the bus stand around sundown. A gang walked up to them and questioned the woman who the man was. When she answered that he was her husband she was asked to show them her *tali* (wedding chain). Who gave them the right to invade the privacy of a couple, disregarding all social etiquette and norms of behavior? This is a question that is beginning to haunt the people at large especially the women folk of Kerala. Kerala is an educated community and women are as visible as men in all fields of work. This phenomenon is particularly irksome for girls who are working in the IT sector whose duties begin after sunset. The self-styled moral police who are illiterate in matters of law and ignorant of social realities assume that women's place is at home after sunset, that if they emerge out of their home after sunset it could only be for immoral activities. (L. Menon, 2011, para. 6)

In the last century, Kerala has shifted from a *sexually open, socially safe, mother-centered, joint-family matrilineal matrilocal life* to a *sexually uptight, socially unsafe, male-dominated, patrilineal patrilocal nuclear family culture*. As I looked at the rapid transitions in values around sexuality of the Nayar people, from *sacred* to *shameful* I could not help wondering if there was a direct connection to the shift from matrilineal to patrilineal social organization!

The Relevance of My Research Topic

Today, I see the younger generation of Nayar women drawn to western models of female sexuality (such as drinking, smoking, displaying their bodies, and more) to reflect their own independence and freedom. They are unaware of the rich Nayar indigenous cultural and spiritual tradition around feminine sexuality. Through this research I hope to give the younger generation of men and women something from within their own tradition to hold on to and work with. As a first step I decided to look back into my own life in search of memories directly or indirectly connected to the matrilineal past of Kerala, and that was when it dawned on me that I knew so little about my matriliny—its history, the female-centered rituals, and the lived experience of women like my mother, and grandmothers.

I realized that my mother did not grow up in a traditional Nayar matrilocal joint family, but instead lived with her father, mother, and siblings in a nuclear home. This happened to many women of her generation. My mother's complete lack of knowledge around any matrilineal practices is a reflection of the shift in the culture. However, most of my grandmother's generation was born in matrilineal Kerala and grew up in a matrilocal and matrifocal system. I also remembered that my grandmothers were extremely comfortable in the nakedness of their bodies without feeling shame. This could have been partly owing to the fact that they grew up bathing in the family pond with other women and men. Most Nayar ancestral homes had huge bathing tanks (like ponds) with separate entrances for men and women. Women would loosely tie a thin muslin cloth around their bodies and swim with their girlfriends. My mother and her sisters, on the other hand, do not know how to swim, and my sister and I do not either. All of us grew up in modern homes with bathrooms and without a family pond. That was a significant shift. I wondered what else had shifted in the last century!

In Malayalam, grandmothers are affectionately called ammamma (meaning mother's mother). I grew up having many ammammas within and outside the family. However, I never spent time hearing their stories. As this reality dawned on me, my mind exploded with questions:
  1. Was the life of my grandmother and her kin living in the North Malabar Nayar matrilineal family and social structure different from the social structure in which I grew up?
  2. Did it provide a safe and sacred space for them to express their sexual thoughts, feelings, and behavior?

3. How did they perceive their bodies and sexuality? How did the Nayar women from yesteryears respond to amorous advances of boys and/or men?
4. Were they guided consciously in that response?
5. Did this guidance help foster healthy sexual relationships between men and women?

Sadly my direct maternal and paternal grandmothers have passed on to the ancestral realm. However, I realized that there are still many grandmothers alive in my near and extended family with a rich collection of stories. Many are over 80 years of age, educated, active, and speak Malayalam fluently. Their memories are a treasure chest of precious information of yesteryears—of a matrilineal Kerala, which I have never directly known or experienced. As far as I know, no one has ever spoken to these ammammas, or even my mother, about their yesteryears. Their memories are disappearing with them. I realized that their stories might be relevant to any woman with a matrilineal lineage where the grandmothers are still alive. In that moment I decided that I would like to record the stories of my mother and grandmothers from my maternal and paternal family using the qualitative methodology of organic inquiry. Using semi-structured questions I would document the lived feminine experience of my mother and grandmothers, their relationships with body and sexuality, and the various factors that shaped or shifted those relationships.

PART III

LITERATURE REVIEW

"I realized that to understand the shift in Nayar matriliny across the ages, the relevance of its practices supporting female sexuality and the various cultural, political, and religious influences plagueing the culture of present-day Kerala, I needed a broader perspective spanning across time (from Paleolithic to present civilizations) and space (matriarchal societies across the world)."

CHAPTER 6.

MATRIARCHAL SOCIETIES OF PEACE

The present-day face of Kerala as well as India is overtly patriarchal. In fact, I have realized that the entire world is overtly patriarchal and male dominated. I began to inquire into the matriarchal origins of the world. Recently, in a conversation on Nayar matriliny with a scholarly male Nayar friend of my father, I was told that the Nayar men temporarily created that system to support the women, as most men in those times were away fighting a war. Although that argument did not make sense, I did not have any understanding around matriarchy or existing matriarchal cultures to comment. That is when I realized that I needed a global perspective on matriarchy spanning time periods and spread across continents. I needed to understand the key concepts of matriarchy prevalent in cultures around the world, and even more I needed to look at existing matrilineal and matriarchal cultures. So the next time the matriarchal ancestry of Kerala and even the world is refuted as a myth, I can respond with facts.

As I have already described, my understanding of matriarchy was deeply influenced by a broad array of literature (de Waal & Lanting, 1997; Gimbutas, 2001; Goettner-Abendroth, 2005, 2009; Hua, 2001; Noble, 2003; Taylor, 2002; Zak, 2012) introduced in a course called Matriarchal Societies taught by author, Vicki Noble, in my Women's Spirituality Master's Program. In this chapter, I will highlight some of the key principles around the social organization of matriarchal cultures followed by a closer look at two matriarchal societies from the Asian subcontinent and the various practices around female sexuality prevalent in these cultures.

Redefining Matriarchy

When I first heard the word "matriarchy" in my master's program, like many others I mistakenly assumed it meant domination (arche) by mothers or women (*matri*), a power-over relation of women over men. However, my understanding has shifted considerably after reading the work of Heide Goettner-Abendroth, foremother of the international Matriarchal Studies movement. The word arche in Greek means both "beginning" and "domination" (Goettner-Abendroth, 2007, p. 17), and thus matriarchy can be translated as "mothers from the beginning" (p. 17) because motherhood is a natural beginning; women do not need to establish mother right through domination as it happens naturally. However, fathers do not have a natural right to beginning and, hence, they have had to force their right through domination, thus patriarchy became "fathers from domination" (Goettner-Abendroth, 2007, p. 17). This interpretation of matriarchy and patriarchy brought a huge breakthrough in my own understanding.

Concept of Power in Matriarchy

Another idea with which most people struggle in regard to matriarchy is the concept of power of women over men. However, most matriarchal societies are gender-egalitarian in the sense that the "natural differences between genders and the generations are respected and honored, but the differences do not necessarily lead to hierarchies, as is common in patriarchy" (Goettner-Abendroth, 2007, p. 20). In these societies, genders and generations play an important role; men and women are codependent upon each other.

Based on our experience in a patriarchal social organization of the abuse of power—someone gives commands and someone else obeys them

—we associate a negative feeling with the concept of power because obeying is not a voluntary or inspired behavior. In order to make someone obey, the domination system needs an elaborate system of "enforcement staff or structure, such as the police, army, the laws, prisons, tributes or taxes to compel obedience" (Goettner-Abendroth, 2005, p. 27). Our modern-day patriarchal society is based on this principle. However, matriarchal social organization operates on the principal of balance and honoring "natural authority" (Goettner-Abendroth, 2005, p. 27) that flows between mother and child, grandmother and grandchild, brother and sister, sister and sister, brother and sister's children, and more and this natural authority is based on "between someone giving advice and someone else accepting it voluntarily" (Goettner-Abendroth, 2005, p. 28).

The Role of the Clan Mother

In most matriarchal cultures, the oldest and wisest living grandmother is known to have natural authority and is chosen as the matriarch. The matriarch along with her daughters, sons, granddaughters, and grandsons lives matrilocally together in a clan house with social organization based on kinship (Goettner-Abendroth, 2005, p. 28). There is a natural trust in her leadership based on her experience in raising most of the clan members. Her life wisdom is valued, and the entire clan entrusts the matriarch with maintaining daily affairs of the clan and resolving conflicts, disputes, and maintaining the peace within the clan. She is also the keeper of the clan's wisdom across generations. Most importantly, decision making in matriarchal cultures involves every member of the clan versus one person or a certain group of people like in societies of domination (Goettner-Abendroth, 2005, p. 28). This form of decision making is still practiced in many matriarchal clan houses for instance the Minangkabau people of Sumatra:

> In the beginning, the problems are discussed among all women and all men separately. They only stop talking when they have reached consensus. Then both groups meet to discuss the matter with each other again, keeping at it until all women and men agree. If they do not come to an agreement, then and only then will the clan mother make the final decision and tip the scales in favor of one side or the other. Because of her natural authority, this will be accepted not as her verdict but as the final conclusion of a discussion in which all members of the clan have participated.(Goettner-Abendroth, 2005, p. 29)

Motherhood in Matriarchy

In most matriarchal societies a woman is naturally considered a mother based on her innate qualities of nurturing and caring for a child (Heide Goettner-Abendroth, 2007, p. 21). Furthermore, matriarchal societies give women the freedom to decide whether they want to be biological mothers or not, and usually, the children within a clan address every adult female as mother, highlighting the principal of common motherhood of a group of sisters (Goettner-Abendroth, 2007, p. 21). In these societies women are visibly celebrated and acknowledged as mothers, different from the dominant patriarchal principle that wants to control female sexuality and the female womb. Matriarchal cultures are also matrilineal in the sense that social positions, property, and political titles are passed down the mother line, and also matrilocal because women live permanently in their mother's house and never leave even when they marry (Goettner-Abendroth, 2007, p. 22).

Marriages and Role of Women

Within matriarchal cultures, marriages are not between individuals but between clans and communities (Goettner-Abendroth, 2007, p. 22). The man and woman continue to stay in their respective mother's houses even after marriage. The man visits his wife in her home at night and returns to his mother's home the following morning, because his responsibilities are connected with his mother's house. In these marriages, the fathers do not have rights and duties over their children, as the children are part of the mother's clan. Men act as "social fathers" to the children of their sisters. These systems of "visiting marriages" are still prevalent to this day in cultures around the world (Goettner-Abendroth, 2007, p. 22).

Matriarchal societies place immense value on the role and position of women in the society (Goettner-Abendroth, 2007, pp. 21-26). The feminine principle is worshipped as the Creatress of the land and the earth is worshipped as the Great Mother. Women enjoy considerable freedom of movement, decision making, and independence in matriarchal societies. Many people have the false notion that in matriarchal cultures women make men do the entire job. This is a myth. Most existing matriarchal cultures clearly illustrate that women work as hard as men and sometimes even more so. The only visible difference between the two cultures is that in a matriarchal culture, women's contribution is valued, acknowledged, and sought by the clan members as opposed to patriarchal cultures, where women's contributions are often considered secondary and dismissed.

Female Sexuality in Matriarchal Cultures

Matriarchal cultures place a great deal of emphasis on the natural bodily cycles in the life of a female—her first blood, menstruation, consummation, pregnancy, birthing and menopause (Goettner-Abendroth, 2007, p. 24). Matriarchal men acknowledge these rituals and sometimes even play an important role in overseeing these rituals for their nieces (de Tourreil, 2009, p. 207). This helps build graceful intimate partnerships between men and women unlike those seen in patriarchal cultures. In addition, sexuality is considered a natural part of life, and there is no shame or stigma attached to it, and people's sexual preferences, sexual acts, and sexual fantasies are confined to their lives and considered intimately private and never discussed in public (Hua, 2001). This gives people living within these societies considerable freedom. I elaborate on this in the next section.

Tending and Befriending Instinct

I observed early on that my mother and father responded to stress differently in the sense that my father became completely distraught and unable to act in the moment, while a serene calmness dawned in my mother in moments of crisis as she took on the role of tending to the needs of the family, keeping up everyone's spirits. In the backdrop of this knowing, the scientific theory that generalized human response to stress as fight or flight did not make sense. Through my matriarchal studies course I was introduced to a landmark study conducted by renowned psychologist, Shelley E. Taylor. Taylor wrote that while fight or flight might be the response of men to stress, women respond by "tending and befriending" (Taylor, 2002, pp. 24) in moments of stress, and that this behavior was caused by the release of the social hormone called oxytocin in women while the male body released testosterone (pp. 20-28).

Based on the same theory, Taylor summarizes that fatherhood is more a learned behavior from observing mothers and the larger social context and perhaps less biologically guided (Taylor, 2002, pp. 29-34). While patriarchal social organization is predominantly centered on the importance of biological fatherhood (and marriage), in most matriarchal cultures this role is absent, and replaced by social fatherhood through the role of the maternal uncle. Also, a patriarchal marriage is more likely to benefit men than women, because most men are fed, clothed, and nurtured by their wives while for the wife the work hours continue beyond her work life affecting her health in the long run (Taylor, 2002, pp. 113-124). In contrast, in a matriarchal culture where men and women continued to stay in their respective homes tended and supported by their blood relations, it can be assumed that life expectancy of both the genders might have been high. These new theories based on biology, evolutionary psychology, physiology, and neurosciences strongly support the mother-centered social organization.

In the subsequent sections I will review two living matriarchal cultures to highlight the quality of life of women, men, and children in these societies. These cultures allowed me to understand my Nayar heritage in the backdrop of matriarchal values and the absence of patriarchal norms and prejudices. Following this, I will also investigate the origin of matriarchy in the Indian subcontinent.

The Kingdom of Daughters: The Mosuo Culture

Mosuo is a peace-loving matriarchal indigenous group living in Southwest China high in the Himalayas close to the borders with Tibet, on the shores of Lugu Lake also called Mother Lake with a population of approximately 30,000 people. The earliest records of the Mosuo people indicate that they are over 1600 years old (Gatusa, 2009, p. 240). Just like the people of Kerala, the high altitudes and tough mountainous terrains kept the Mosuo people out of contact with the modern civilization for a very long time. According to singer, Yang Erche Namu, until the late 1980s, the Mosuo people were virtually unknown outside Western China. This helped preserve and sustain their rich culture without influences of the modern-day patriarchal norms. However, unlike Kerala the matriarchal Mosou culture is still preserved even today. The matriarchal social organization of the Mosuo people of China, as articulated through various studies (Danshilacuo & Mei, 2009; Gatusa, 2009; Hua, 2001; Namu & Christine, 2003; Ruxian, 2009), gave me a broader perspective on the Nayar matrilineal system of living; in the absence of patriarchal norms and tenets, the Nayar community might have been like the Mosuo.

Social organization of the Mosuo. The entire matriarchal family of the Mosuo consists of all the matrilineal members—grandmother, mother, maternal uncles, and aunts (mother's brothers and sisters), children and grandchildren belonging to all the sisters—living together under one roof (Gatusa, 2009, p. 241). The Mosuo are matrilineal in the sense that the property is passed down the mother line to the daughters. The mother is the matriarch and chosen based on her intelligence, capability, and her impartial nature toward everyone. Once chosen, she is the deciding and uniting force of the family. Her opinion is valued and sought by the entire matriliny. She is in charge of the economics of the family—its well-being, fair distribution of food supplies, goods and wealth, and assignment of household tasks. Following her, the oldest daughter takes on the responsibility of the matriarch and, hence, the mother-daughter relationship is of great importance.

Roles and relationship of men and women. Men and women are considered equal. Usually the matriarch distributes the work based on people's special skills. Women's work is centered on the house, while men usually do the heavy work outside the house:

> Thus, women grow, cook, and distribute the food, while the male relatives engage in all the other outside activities such as house building, herding animals, trade and so forth and bring home whatever cash they make in the outside world. (Namu & Christine, 2003, p. 277)

However these roles are easily interchangeable if the situation demands it; there are no gender stereotypes around work. Religiously women and men's roles are also quite different. The women take care of daily prayers to the house gods and ancestors, while the men are involved in public religious rituals and rites. The Mosuo are simple, honest and hardworking people, and life is fairly peaceful—there are no quarrels, thievery, or stifles among the people. Violence toward women does not exist in the community and there is considerable safety of movement for children and women:

> We children could roam at our own will and visit from house to house and village to village without our mothers' ever fearing for our safety. Every adult was responsible for every child and every child in turn was respectful of every adult. (Namu & Christine, 2003, p. 69)

Among the Mosuo people, three relationships are completely absent: the father-son, father-daughter, and husband-wife (Hua, 2001). Comparing with other societies, we find that the husband-wife relationship is replaced to a great extent by the brother-sister relationship in the Mosuo way of life, and this translates to a strong bond between the brother and the sister's children (Hua, 2001, p. 145). In fact, during childhood, the brother-sister relationship is based on intimate friendship; as they enter into puberty and adulthood, it takes on a more reserved nature with focus on executing responsibilities toward the clan—that is, jointly providing for the sister's children and sustaining the economic stability of the clan. Because the sexual lives of the Mosuo social organization are focused around visitation, neither sibling, in most cases, would bring an outsider into the residence as a permanent member (Hua, 2001, p. 145). The brother-sister relationship in the Mosuo people is considered is lifelong and immutable in comparison to a matrimonial bond that is subject to change (Hua, 2001, p. 146).

Marriages of the Mosou. The Mosuo culture is most known for its unique system of marriage called visiting or walking marriage (Gatusa, 2009, pp. 242-244; Hua, 2001, pp. 185-236; Namu & Christine, 2003, pp. 275-276). The man and woman continue to live in their respective homes even after marriage. Every night the man leaves his mother's home to walk up to the home of his female friend, spends the night at her home, and in the morning he returns to his mother's home. Any children born through this relationship belong to the maternal family. The man does not have to provide for them. He helps raise his sister's children. Even today, men and women are free to choose their partners without any social or familial interference. The only time a relationship is interfered with by the elders is when the couples are maternally related in any way. Marriages are also not influenced by economic, political, and religious factors allowing relationships to be purely based on "erotic love and affection" (Gatusa, 2009, p. 242). Separation is easy—if a relationship breaks or fails, it does not affect the lives of the children who are with the woman's family.

Interestingly, there is no concept of a father in the Mosuo social organization. In fact, most children grow up without knowing their biological father, because neither the woman nor the man ever tells their children about the father (Hua, 2001, p. 228). The Mosuo believe that their way of visiting marriages maintains the harmony of the clan by not compromising the natural bond between brother-sister, and mother-child, within the clan:

> Because sexual relationships are assumed to be limited in time, because they take place outside working hours, and because they do not engage partners economically, love affairs don't intrude on the family's economic life or compete with the brother-sister and mother-children bonds that are at the effective core of the family. (Namu & Christine, 2003, p. 276)

Most Mosuo people have tried marriage when the Chinese government forcefully attempted to modernize and wipe out their ancient culture, but within a few years after the end of the Cultural Revolution, they returned to the old ways of visiting marriages (Hua, 2001; Namu & Christine, 2003). They realized that patriarchal marriage did not work for them, because it demanded a compromise between the partners in the name of maintaining family name, economic stability, property and other things, resulting in the man or the woman having to give up something; in most cases, this something was romantic love and almost always it was "(female) sexual freedom and pleasure" (Namu & Christine, 2003, p. 279).

Sexual etiquettes of the Mosou. The Mosuo follow strict sexual etiquettes between consanguineal (related by blood or birth) relatives. For instance, it is forbidden for consanguineal relatives to engage in any type of sexual talk, allusion, joking, or even singing or humming of love songs, or bathing, or accompanying each other at night (Hua, 2001; Namu & Christine, 2003). Even in the matriarchal residence these strict rules apply. While the old people and children under the age of 13 may stay in the main house, the adult men are strictly forbidden from sleeping under the same roof as their adult sisters. While adult women have their own bedrooms to entertain their male guests, "the adult males are strictly required to sleep at their lovers, or if they don't have lovers, in one of the outhouses or guest rooms if the family has those" (Namu & Christine, 2003, p. 275). Furthermore, in order to give people freedom around their sexual engagements, the community as a whole follows certain codes of conduct:

> Although women and women are free to choose their lovers and to maintain sexual relations for as long or short a time as they desire, what a woman and her "friend" (azhu) do in the privacy of her bedroom, is left to individual discretion. If a couple decide to make their relationship public, they can spend time together with each other's relatives, but their romantic involvements cannot be discussed in front of the family members of the opposite sex, including their own children. (Namu & Christine, 2003, p. 275)

These protocols helped the Mosuo community maintain the sacredness and openness around sexuality without invoking jealousy, shame, and lust among members of the clan or community. At the same time, this etiquette allowed the natural and timely blossoming of sexuality in children based on their natural cycles and for the Mosuo to exist as a community without fathers in which "people often learned about their fathers indirectly, or they might not have known at all" (Namu & Christine, 2003, p. 275).

Sexual freedom of women and men. The woman in a Mosuo culture enjoyed the freedom to choose a partner as well as separate from the partner if needed without any prejudice or shame. Many people who look at Mosuo people from the outside perceive their culture as one of free love and free sex. However, from my reading, I understand that Mosuo people do not care so much about sex. Their relationships are based on finding true love and sometimes women and men stay in the relationship for their whole lives. In fact, I was deeply touched by the Mosuo men's understanding around love when the woman he loved did not reciprocate his feelings:

> If a woman is loved by two men at the same time, the one who is not chosen does not hold ill feelings, because he loves her sincerely and holds no grudges, as he makes no demands of his love. He may get a chance later on if he is patient enough. He gains something just by loving, even if his desire is not fulfilled. (Gatusa, 2009, p. 242)

In the Mosuo culture, women are the "legitimate figures of family authority, managers of family wealth, co owners of family property, caretakers of ancestors, and owner of their own bloodlines" (Namu & Christine, 2003, p. 278). In contrast, in a patriarchal world the focus is on the man with the woman seen as subordinate to him. This makes everything associated with man clean and holy, while woman becomes associated with uncleanness and sin. These tenets are completely absent in the Mosuo people (Gatusa, 2009, p. 243).

Mosou female-centered rituals. Like other matriarchal cultures the Mosuo also celebrate the natural cycles in the life of a woman in a sacred way: birth, adult initiation rite, pregnancy, and consummation (Gatusa, 2009, p. 244). Most interesting is the adult initiation rite performed for a female at the age of 13, which welcomed her into womanhood and was marked by her receiving the traditional Mosuo skirt (Hua, 2001, pp. 180-181). In most families, this skirt was passed down several generations from mother to daughter. The girl wears it at different festivals to attract a male suitor. It proclaims her coming of age. All the maternal relatives and neighbors attend the ceremony and the ceremony involves sexual teasing and adoration of the girl:

> All the while, as she was dressing me, Cilatsuo commented, "Look at those eyes, they are like stars in the sky. Look at this face; it is round as the moon. Look at her breasts, they are like ripe peaches." She spoke of my waist, my buttocks, my thighs while I felt at the same time embarrassed and proud. (Namu & Christine, 2003, p. 121)

It is important to understand that there is no shame in this narration; rather the girl felt "embarrassed and proud." Following the initiation ceremony, the girl is usually awarded the status of a woman, which gives her special privileges of having her own separate room to receive men when she wanted. The intimate bond shared by women within the Mosou culture involved sexual teasing, encouragement, and support to pursue visitors. Author and singer, Yang Erche Namu, illustrates this in the personal account of her initiation ceremony:

> My big sister was sitting on my bed, waiting for me, and soon her friends were knocking at the little window and we let them in. They were in a happy mood, "Namu, don't let too many men into your room!" they joked. "Too much love is bad for your eyes," another warned. "Actually too much love makes it harder to get pregnant," someone corrected her. And another pretended to look inside my shift to see if I was ready for love, "Are your nipples pink?" She asked. She was very funny and everyone laughed. At last I was a grown woman; I was just like my sister and her friends, and it all felt so good and so embarrassing. (Namu & Christine, 2003, p. 122)

The openness of sexuality in their conversation is something I have never experienced in my life with other women.

Today, China is promoting the Lugu Lake and the Mosuo people as its top tourist destination. Arrival of outsiders to observe, study, and even temporarily live with the Mosuo is impacting their culture. Many Mosuo people have ventured into the tourism industry and are making more money than ever before. This has brought many modern amenities like television and refrigerators into the Mosuo homes. The young men and women of Mosuo are being lured by the gleam and glitter of the outside world, many of them leaving their culture behind in search of newer pastures, but soon to find out how different the outside world and its ways are. Many return back to the comforts of Mother Lake. In the backdrop of patriarchal norms, Mosuo culture offers many lessons for the betterment of modern civilization.

> The Moso have made an extraordinary cultural choice—they have sacrificed neither sexual freedom nor romantic love nor economic security nor the continuity of their bloodlines. Instead they have discarded marriage. What they have gained is a society where all the essentials of existence (food, affection, property and family lines) are birthrights established by the most evident fact that it is the maternal tie. And interestingly from the perspective of family continuity, not only women but also men find fulfillment in this say of life, which frees them from anxiety of ensuring descendents—with multiple sisters, Moso families are almost guaranteed a next generation. (Namu & Christine, 2003, pp. 279-280)

Mosuo culture has seen its share of influence by foreign cultures like the Han dynasty, and the "marriage movement" by communist China (Gatusa, 2009, p. 245), and survived. I hope the younger generation of the Mosuo can find ways to adopt modernization without compromising the traditional values of their culture.

Sexual Education in the Girl's Dormitory

In most matriarchal indigenous cultures, adolescent initiation ceremonies into sexuality were common; for girls it was considered a must. These ceremonies facilitated the blossoming of an adolescent into a sexually mature adult socially and culturally valuable, and ready to embark on new responsibilities. In fact, the tribal societies of North East India, namely the Adis, Noctes, Zemi Naga, Tangsa, Khampti, and Apatani people of North East India had formalized institutions called youth dormitories where cultural and sexual knowledge was imparted to the youth throughout their adolescent years.

Almost every tribal village in the North East region housed a male and female dormitory. As soon as a girl (or boy) reached 13 years of age, she (or he) was moved into the dormitory house. In the Zemi Nagas tribe, this separation began as early as 8 years of age (Mann, 1996, p. 116). During the day, the girl assisted in all the household duties of her home, but at night she slept in the dormitory system. In the absence of a separate female dormitory, the house of a widow or the oldest woman in the village became the space to house the adolescent girls. An older experienced girl from the tribe usually headed the female dormitories and was responsible for training the younger generation in cultural heritage, such as folk dances, folk songs, and folklore. The girl's mother trained the girl in the arts of spinning, weaving, and household chores. In many tribal societies, the dormitory system helped preserve a higher age of marriage for girls (Mann, 1996, p. 120).

Most importantly, the dormitory was the place to give the boys and girls practical training into the "mysteries of life, in addition to the social and communal life, to the mysteries of sex" (Mann, 1996, p. 115). In fact, the girls began their romantic life in the dormitory through courtship with the boys from the male dormitory. This was supposed to help the girl in her ability to interact with boys, learn the art of love, and find her mate for life. It was something like a modern-day dating system, only without the patriarchal moralities around body and sexuality. Although the girl was free to invite any boy into her dormitory, she was strictly forbidden from visiting the boys' dormitory system except for some special occasion of feasting or dancing. In some tribes the girl continued to stay in the dormitory even after her marriage and was visited by her husband till he had his own place or when the girl had a baby, whichever happened first. Sometimes the dormitory also served "the purpose of bridal home, though temporarily" (Mann, 1996, p. 115). In my own experience as youth mentor and educator, I can see immense value in the system of the dormitories. It is a brilliant concept, allowing a practical space for young people to get to know each other and learn the art of love. These systems allowed for "pent-up psychological tensions" to be released so that females could be their natural selves, and it avoided "abnormal sexual activities" among the youth (Mann, 1996, pp. 120-121).

The dormitory systems began to collapse a couple of decades ago through "conversion to Christianity" (Mann, 1996, p. 119). Christian morality associated considerable shame and stigma with female sexuality. In many tribal villages the church had started to control these dormitories with the sole purpose of separating unmarried boys and girls from each other and restricting their movements and associations with each other. This completely defied the original purpose of the dormitory systems:

> The very purpose and aim of dormitory, mixing of young men and women freely, is defeated by the all-encompassing impact of Christianity, education and modernity. They denounce the old way of wooing and choosing the marriage partner by the tribal, hence underrating of dormitories and more so of girl's dormitories on immortality ground. (Mann, 1996, p. 119)

Many people with their newly acquired sense of civilized morality considered the dormitory systems primitive and immoral (Mann, 1996). In the backdrop of rising sexual violence, teen pregnancies, sexual bullying, rape, and objectifying of male and female sexuality, I feel that these dormitories were anything but primitive and immoral. In fact they helped cultivate positive relationships between boys and girls:

> Before the vices like female infanticide, child marriage, forced marriage, widow problem, sati (bride immolation), dowry, prostitution, selling of girls, eve teasing, rape (which are the boons of the so-called civilized non-tribal society) get entrance into the interior tribal settlements, which is likely in the absence of dormitory institutions, something is to be done about the preservation of such useful cultural institutions. (Mann, 1996, p. 122)

I have not been able to locate any article on the dormitory systems in North East India within the last 2 decades, so I do not know if this system is still practiced. Maybe it has become a memory in the minds of the older generation. I hope this research study inspires tribal daughters from the present generation of North East India to reclaim these cultural institutions through the memories of their mothers and grandmothers who witnessed and lived in these dormitory systems.

Changing Position of Indian Women

In December 2010, I made a trip to Kerala to better understand my matriarchal Nayar roots. In that travel, I had the opportunity to stay with a revered saint from Kerala, Swami Nirmalananda Giri Maharaj. He has given several talks on Kerala: the sacred groves, the ancestral worship, and most importantly on mother-centered cultures. I asked Swamiji about the matriarchal origin of Kerala, and he responded, "Not just Kerala, the whole of India was Matriarchal," and continued on to other conversation. He never elaborated on that remark, but he sowed a seed of inquiry in my mind. This section is an exploration of the matriarchal origins of India and the shifting faces of women's roles in India through the work of various scholars (Altekar, 1959; Dube, 1988; Fane, 1975; Flood, 1996; Gupta, 1997; Holdrege, 1998; Jayakar, 1990; Johnsen, 1994; Kinsley, 1988; Kishwar, 1994; Leslie, 1992; Saraswati & Saraswati, 2007; Smith, 2003; Young, 2002).

The earliest recorded history of civilization on Indian continent is found in the archaeological sites of Indus Valley which recently (Khandekar, 2012) has been re-estimated to go back to 7380 BC to 6201 BC, thus making it older than the civilizations of Egypt and Babylon. This civilization was most noted for its elaborate architecture of ceremonial swimming tanks, huge water systems of canals and drains, technologically superior domestic tools, and a highly sophisticated lifestyle. Most importantly for my purposes, the archaeological remains of this ancient civilization contained an abundance of female figurines depicting women with exaggerated hips, full thighs, bare breasts, and elaborate hairstyles in comparison to the male figures that were very few; suggesting the importance of the female principle in the Indus Valley civilization (Amazzone, 2010; Fane, 1975; Jayakar, 1990). Also, most of the female figurines were independent of a male consort (Fane, 1975). In addition to figurines, numerous seals with images of male phallus (lingas) and vulvas (yoni) were also found in the Indus Valley (Fane, 1975). The disappearance of the Indus Valley civilization is clouded in several hypotheses and is subject to severe debate on the Indian subcontinent. It is too controversial and complex to address in this study.

The earliest references to the Hindu woman on the Indian subcontinent are found in the written records of the Vedas, which are assumed to have written between 1200 to 800 BCE known as the Vedic Period (Altekar, 1959; Flood, 1996; Kinsley, 1988; Leslie, 1992; Smith, 2003; Young, 2002). Although this period documented a patrilineal society, in the early Vedic period, there was considerable "complimentarily between men and women" (Young, 2002, p. 5) despite some degree of male dominance. Family was the center of religious life, women's role as mother and wife was revered, and the principal goals of life were centered on progeny, prosperity and longevity. Gods were mostly male in this period with the exception of few goddesses like Usas (goddess of dawn), Saraswati (personification of the major river of this period) and Prithvi (the Earth) (Young, 2002, p. 5). The middle and later Vedic periods show the emergence of a hierarchical social organization based on caste systems, which made categories of pure and impure based on the body—organs above the navel considered pure and those below considered impure—and further connecting purity and impurity with bodily sensations, bodily fluids, and bodily discharges.

> Natural bodily processes and functions such as eating, sleeping, urinating, defecating, sexual intercourse and menstruation are considered impure. The bodily secretions associated with such processes, including urine, feces, semen, menses, saliva, phlegm and sweat, are similar classified as inherent impurities of the human body. (Holdrege, 1998, p. 365)

Thus, a woman with her monthly bleeding cycle, receiver of semen in her body, and bleeding as a result of giving birth got associated with the impure body and, hence, needed to observe strict pollution rituals. Her body and sexuality attained higher status only in association with a male—father, husband or son—and in the context of a monogamous marriage. This restricted the movement of women, especially those belonging to the elite upper caste—they could not participate in rituals if menstruating, they had to wait to eat after their husbands, they could not have inheritance, and so forth (Young, 2002, p. 8) and by the later Vedic period (400 BCE to 400 CE) there was a steep decline in the status of women:

> Whereas once their womb was understood as the fertile field, now it became but a vessel for male seed. Whereas once their fertility was emphasized, now their impurity was underscored. Whereas once they were married only when mature (after puberty), now they were married before puberty. Whereas once they had real input in the choice of a marriage partner, now they were marginal to the process of arranged marriages. Whereas once both daughters and sons were viewed as important, now sons were not only highly preferred but daughters came to be viewed as serious liabilities. (Young, 1992, p. 9)

This period also saw the emergence of goddesses and epic heroines that modeled the role of the ideal wife represented with an ascetic sexuality controlled and connected to the husband. This led to the idea that it was necessary for women to marry and express their sexuality in safe ways and under male supervision and authority (Kinsley, 1988, p. 203).

I feel that the concept of the traditional Hindu woman was culturally and religiously constructed to fit the patriarchal social organization of India. Her actions, behaviors and expressions were wrapped around the "shoulds" and "should nots" dictated by ideologies postulated in religious scriptures. Within the context of this patriarchal social organization, woman were given certain duties (serving the husband, nurturing the children, observing austerities like fasting for the families welfare, engaging in prayers and rituals, upholding traditional values, and more) and within the sincere execution of these duties, she was allowed to experience herself as a powerful agent respected by all and worshipped as the Goddess (Leslie, 1992). These roles required her to fulfill the virtues of "chastity, subordination, submission, tolerance, endurance, self-control, and last but not least, self-sacrifice" (Gupta, 1997, p. 90). However, when she chose to deviate from this path as the daughter, mother or wife, she became the target of severe criticism, condemnation and wrath from society, often from women themselves.

The Nayar Malayali woman was quite different from the traditional Hindu woman I observed outside of Kerala, and she represented the matriarchal values of Kerala. As my understanding of matriarchy has grown I am inspired to look at my own life in search of matriarchy and matriarchal values.

My Matriarchal Reflection

To me the most fascinating truth about matriarchal cultures is the positive meaning, sacredness and freedom attached to feminine sexuality and its relevance in the lives of men and women in the culture. Even in the absence of a conscious matriarchal culture in Kerala, I see matriarchy reflected in the lives of the men and women of North Malabar.

I recognize matriarchy in the privileges I received as a girl and the appreciation reflected in the eyes of my parents, uncles, aunts, grandparents, granduncles, grandaunts, and everyone else in my extended maternal and paternal families.

I recognize matriarchy in my father's pride for his daughters, and his firm belief that his daughters could accomplish great things in life.

I recognize matriarchy in my father's closeness to his maternal family and the excitement that came over him every time he planned his trip to visit them.

I recognize matriarchy in the empowering explanation of menstruation by my mother—it is a privileged embodied experience of a girl, and one that makes her powerful. In spite of my painful cramps, I cherished an intimate kinship with my blood, as opposed to the feelings of disgust shared by many of my non-Kerala Hindu friends.

I recognize matriarchy in my freedom to return back to my mother's home anytime unannounced, the knowing that I am welcome there—roaming freely in the paddy fields, playing hide and seek among the trees, waking up leisurely in the morning, eating to my heart's content, and demanding with authority the preparation of my favorite dishes and sweetmeats.

I recognize matriarchy in the closeness I experienced with my maternal family as compared to my paternal relatives—the periodic sharing of information between my mother and her sisters and brothers, the intimacy shared between all the mother's sisters children, the comfort and easiness I experienced in my maternal aunt's (mother's sister's) home and my insistence every summer vacation to spend more time at my maternal grandparents' home.

I recognize matriarchy in the auspiciousness and beauty associated with being a girl or a woman. Any festival or occasion, women led the way. I remembered during vacations when I walked through the fields with my father, older women from other homes would appreciate my sister and me, telling my father how fortunate he was to have been blessed with such beautiful goddesses, and personally I saw it in their eyes—a deep appreciation of me as a girl.

I recognize matriarchy in my parent's complete support and understanding through the difficult phases of my marriage and separation. They never made me feel guilty or alone.

CHAPTER 7.

WOMEN'S SPIRITUALITY

Although I saw numerous images of popular Hindu goddesses (such as Sita, Lakshmi, Durga, and Saraswati) in public places—on sidewalks, in temples, in shops, and more—the sexual aspect of these Goddesses was missing. Each one appeared married to a male God and was presented fully covered, wearing a traditional Indian silk sari wrapped around every part of Her body with only Her feet, arms, and face visible—Her nudity invisible to the eye. In fact, like many other girls of my generation, I did not associate sexual intimacy, menstruation, and eroticism with the Hindu goddesses.

However, in Kerala, the Goddess Bhagawathi appeared in a completely different image with Her nudity accentuated—Her full breasts displayed in grandeur, and She stood in the inner sanctum of the temple alone without a consort. I had no context from which to behold Her and did not know how to respond to Her, as She invoked feelings of discomfort in me. Although many temple walls, both in Kerala and outside, had erotic male and female copulation images carved or painted on them, there was shame and stigma attached to looking at them, and I recognized as a child the discomfort of adults around these images—they wanted to rush past without looking at them, lest their character be judged negatively. I sensed this even more outside of Kerala. These different opposing images of the Goddess deeply affected my own relationship with the nakedness of my body and the sexual aspects of my being. At the same time, I had no global perspective of the Goddess and did not know of Her ancient existence.

The two years of my women's spirituality master's program gave me the foundation to understand female spirituality, sexuality, and the shift around its perception and expression over thousands of years. I will briefly review some of the key concepts and principles that guided me in that knowing and supported my research study.

Archaeomythology

My research study is deeply influenced by Archaeomythology, an interdisciplinary approach formulated by Lithuanian archaeologist Marija Gimbutas. Archaeomythology is dedicated to cultural research with a particular emphasis on the beliefs, rituals, social structure and symbolism of ancient societies (Marler, n.d.).

I was introduced to Archaeomythology in a course of the same name at Sofia Institute taught by my professor, Vicki Noble. I understood that the evidence of a culture's matriarchal history usually lies in the local art forms and folk traditions that have continued as a substratum underneath the foreground patriarchal culture. The revolutionary work of Gimbutas was based on this discovery, bringing to light the Goddess civilizations of Old Europe from the Neolithic period (8th to 4th millennia BCE). The course provided me with the methodology early on in the program to understand the rituals, symbols, beliefs, and goddess culture of the North Malabar region of Kerala, and trace its transition from matriarchy to patriarchy.

Using this theory, I was able to recognize, compare, and understand symbology across time (Paleolithic through present times) and space (across continents and land mass) and map it to the present-day culture of Kerala. I was able to recognize many matriarchal elements in the present-day life of North Malabar, such as serpent worship, existence of numerable sacred forests, ancestral sites, and offerings at these sites, harvest festivals, ritual costumes, goddess worship, and more. I incorporated some of these elements into the making of my body map (an experiential art project for the Archaeomythology coursework). By recognizing these matriarchal elements in the culture, in spite of its morphed appearance, it was possible for women like me to reclaim and embody it.

Metaformic Theory

Metaformic theory (Grahn, 1993, 1999) postulated by poet, feminist, and co-director of the Women's Spirituality program, Judy Grahn, is another discipline that has deeply influenced the way I connect to my body, my menstrual blood, and feminine sexuality. I have to say upfront that it is difficult to explain the vastness of this theory in a few sentences.

Metaformic theory is based on the idea that what differentiated the ancestral human consciousness from primates was the entrainment of the female menstrual cycle with the lunar cycle (exactly 29.5 days) resulting in human females bleeding in seclusion as a group with the dark of the moon, followed by entrainment of the males to the lunar and menstrual cycles using parallel menstruation rites (Grahn, 1999, pp. 1-15). These steps pulled the human consciousness outside itself, establishing "an externalized languages of cultural containers, artifacts and gestural acts" (Grahn, 1999, p. 15) called *metaforms* that formed the basis of human social and cultural evolution. Based on the metaformic theory it is possible to trace connections between ancient menstrual rites of seclusion and the development of agriculture, mathematics, geometry, writing, calendar, horticulture, architecture, astronomy, cooking, money, and many other realms of knowledge in most cultures.

Today, most women do not experience the menstrual entrainment with the moon and rely on external information over the whisperings of their own bodies. I feel this has disempowered women and affected their knowing of the earth, the seasons, and natural cycles, and sadly, women are transferring this disconnection to their daughters and sons, creating whole generations of people disconnected from the rhythms of nature. In the backdrop of this disconnection, with menstrual blood perceived as dirty and impure by men and women alike, Grahn's metaformic theory offers an empowering alternative for re-establishing a woman's relationship with her blood and her inner bodily wisdom. Metaformic theory has walked with me every step of the way in this thesis, guiding my menstrual and lunar entrainment. I have shared it with many women.

Feminine Worship is Ancient

Through my master's program I learned that numerous images of the feminine have been unearthed in excavations around the world dating as far back as the upper Paleolithic (30,000-10,000 BC) era to the Bronze age (Bahn & Vertut, 1988/1997; Dowson & Lewis-Williams, 1994; Gimbutas, 2001; Noble, 2003; Sjöö & Mor, 1987; Stone, 1976). These images celebrated a woman's menstrual blood, her entrainment with the moon and natural rhythms; celebrated her as the life-giving, life-sustaining, and regenerating principle in the universe and represented her in innumerable forms of birds, animals, flowers, plants, trees, earth, wind, rivers, grains, rain, sun, moon, and just about every aspect of life. Furthermore, her naked body and sexuality were accentuated in many figurines with exaggerated breasts, vulvas and buttocks.

Most anthropological writers have focused on the evolution of the human male as a hunter gatherer, highlighting his inventions and adventures, while the human female was merely seen as an auxiliary in this male-dominated journey of evolution. However, there is ample evidence today to support the fact that women contributed immensely to the evolution of humanity. They were the first users and domesticators of fire, the first potters, first weavers, the first textile dyers and hide tanners, the first to gather and study medicinal plants; the origin of language is also attributed to the communication between the mother and child (Sjöö & Mor, 1987, p. 7). Lunar markings on cave walls and carved sticks have indicated that women made the first time measurements and calendars. In the Upper Paleolithic period nearly 30,000 years ago the only image of God that adorned the inner walls of caves, carved on rocks and, in the later Neolithic, sculpted in clay, was that of a woman.

> It shows with clarity—in the solidarity of stone and bone—that the first 30,000 years of *Homo sapiens'* existence as dominated by the celebration of the female processes: of the mysteries of menstruation, pregnancy, and childbirth; of the analogous abundance of the earth; of the seasonal movement of animals and the cycles of time in the Great Round of the Mother. (Sjöö & Mor, 1987, p. 8)

I also learned that goddess worship was not restricted to India but that a vast expanse of civilizations across the world worshiped the goddess: Ireland, Lithuania, Scotland, Wales, Britain, France, Iraq, Iran, India, Saudi Arabia, Lebanon, Jordan, Israel (Palestine), Egypt, Sinai, Libya, Syria, Turkey, Greece, and Italy as well as on the large island cultures of Crete, Cyprus, Malta, Sicily and Sardinia, Africa, Australia and more (Stone, 1976; Sjöö & Mor, 1987; Gimbutas, 2001). Furthermore, She was celebrated and known by numerous names around the world: Inanna, Ishtar, Isis, Tiamat, Gaia, Hera, Artemis, Athena, Aphrodite, Demeter, Persephone, the Great Goddess of Anatolia and Rome, and more (Baring & Cashford, 1991; Dexter, 1990).

Another way in which I engaged with the ancient Goddesses was through the practice of tarot reading, using the circular deck of Motherpeace cards co-created by Vicki Noble and Karen Vogel in 1981. The hand-drawn colored vibrant pictorial images in the 78 cards of the Motherpeace combined art, history, mythology, folklore, philosophy, and religion and embodied the spiritual and feminist perspective from ancient to present times (Noble, 1983, pp. 1-14). Through these cards I engaged with the ancient matriarchal consciousness of our planet (Noble, 1983, p. 8) and in the process celebrated the feminine principle as a spiritual practice.

Women and Sexual Hominization

Usually in conversations, I heard that men are evolutionarily superior to women and that the purpose of a woman is to satisfy her man, bear him children and never entertain any sexual desires of her own. I believed it to be true until I read about *sexual hominization*. I was familiar with the term hominization from my biology class in high school that described the process of our primate bodies becoming human. Sexual hominization, according to artist and author, Monica Sjöö, and her collaborator, Barbara Mor, is the transformation that happened in our sexual characteristics and functions as we evolved from primates to human, and interestingly is "almost exclusively the story of the human female" (Sjöö & Mor, 1987, p. 10).

It appears that male sexuality has not evolved much since the first primates mated. The revolution in human sexuality resulted from the evolutionary changes that happened in the female body, namely development of the menstrual cycle (allowing the human female sexual activity at any time), development of the clitoris and vagina (providing enhanced orgasmic ability in the female), change from rear to frontal sex (providing enhanced love making and connection between the sexes), and lastly, the development of breasts in the female (enhancing her potential of sexual arousal; Sjöö & Mor, 1987, p. 11). It is only in the human female that sexuality and reproduction are separate; the only purpose of the clitoris is erotic stimulation and stress release (Sjöö & Mor, 1987, p. 10). Contrary to this, the male penis—simultaneously procreative and erotic—is the carrier of both semen and sexual arousal. So based on anatomy, it can be concluded that the male sex organs have a purely reproductive function, but not the female (Sjöö & Mor, 1987, p. 5). In the human female, sexuality is not restricted to reproduction or procreation alone but could be a recreational activity; "It can happen for emotional bonding, for social bonding, for pleasure, for communication, for shelter and comfort, for personal release, for escape—as well as for reproduction of the species" (Sjöö & Mor, 1987, p. 11). Recent studies on the social life of the bonobos (member of the great ape family) as the "make-love-not-war" (de Waal & Lanting, 1997, pp. 108-114) primate (because of their use of erotic encounters to resolve tensions within the clan) has shed new light on the role of sex in human society and negated established theories the origin of human aggressiveness (de Waal & Lanting, 1997, p. 2).

I have realized that sexuality is an integral part of my feminine existence. It is beyond the act of sex; it is the pulse of the universe and flows unceasingly through my body and I cannot step into my power by ignoring and denying my relationship with my body and sexuality.

CHAPTER 8.

NAYARS OF KERALA

For centuries, the Nayar matrilineal kinship in Kerala has fascinated historians, anthropologists, archaeologists, writers, poets, religious leaders, and many travelers. In the last couple of years, I have made a sincere effort to understand the origins of Nayar matriliny and the various influences on it over the years through my connection to the land, my memories, and through the works of numerous male and female scholars (de Tourreil, 1995, 2009; den Uyl, 1995, 2000; Devika, 2008; Fawcett, 1901; Fuller, 1976; Panikkar, 1900; Gough, 1952, 1955, 1961, 1965; Grahn, 1999; Jenett, 1999; A. S. Menon, 1978, 2008; Moore, 1988; Neff, 1995; Panikkar, 1918; Saradamoni, 1982, 1994, 1999). Although the exact origins of Nayar matriliny are clouded in many unknowns, it was firmly established in the social culture by the time Europeans began arriving regularly on the Kerala coast in the 1500s (Jeffrey, 2005, p. 648).

Geographically Kerala, also called the Malabar Coast, is located on the Southwest peninsula of India, She is bordered on the east side by the Western Ghat mountain range and on the West by the Arabian Sea. Until the coming of modern transportation these eastern mountains prevented large-scale migrations, and also wars and invasions in the North of India, from penetrating Kerala. However Kerala had an active sea contact spanning over 2,000 years, and had contact with civilizations around the world:

> Kerala was already in touch with the civilizations of Babylonia, Assyria and Sumer (Mesopotamia) a few thousand years before the Christian era began. The Egyptians used Kerala spices for their perfumes, and for mummification. Later on, Phoenicians, Arabs, Greeks, Romans and Chinese entered into trading links with Kerala. The trading items include such as spices as cinnamon, cardamom, ginger and turmeric,

as well as ivory, peacocks, and monkeys, and increasing quantities of pepper, which was steadily becoming Kerala's trading item. (den Uyl, 1995, p. 56)

In this chapter I would like to trace the history of Nayar matrilineal kinship in Kerala, along with its salient features.

The Matriarchal Sangam Era

The earliest documented history of matrilineal Kerala can be traced to the first 5 centuries of the Common Era, called the Sangam Era or Chera Era. Sangam Era was known to be the most economically and culturally prosperous period of Kerala, although it was steeped in war. Marion den Uyl (1995) describes the social life in Sangam Era in great detail in her book, *Invisible Barriers,* crediting Kerala historian A. Sreedhara Menon as her main source. For this study, I used two of Menon's works, *Cultural Heritage of Kerala* and *Kerala History and Its Makers,* published in 1978 and 2008 respectively.

The Sangam dynasty spread from the land of present-day Kerala across Tamil Nadu and was divided into three kingdoms of the Cholas, Pandyas, and Cheras. The Chera kingdom is roughly approximated to present-day Kerala. These three kingdoms shared a common language and culture, but seemed to have been constantly in war with each other. Most importantly, this period was devoid of any caste or class systems. There were "no social dividing lines and barriers to separate the various tribes and communities" (den Uyl, 1995, p. 57; Menon, 1978, p. 11). This is in contrast with the fact that until the beginning of last century, Kerala had the most complicated caste and class system. But in the Sangam era, these different clans (called *kudis*) of people co-existed peacefully with each other. In fact, there is evidence from that time that clans like the *Paraya, Panan, and Kuravas* who later got classified as the lowest classes, were important poets, ministers in the king's palaces (den Uyl, 1995, p. 57). The Hindu Vedic fires, rituals, and rites had not yet permeated the culture.

Although there is no evidence of a solidified form of organized religion in this period, there is evidence of goddess worship (den Uyl, 1995, p. 57). The two main feminine deities of the Sangam period were Kottavai, the goddess of war and Kali, the goddess of death. Additional forms of the goddess like Mariamma and Bhadrakali were also worshipped. Ancestor worship was practiced in addition to the worship of natural elements like trees, animal spirits and stones, and every town and region also had its own gods and goddesses. Even today, in the villages of Kerala, the remnants of these earth-based indigenous practices can be seen and felt. The reasons for the end of this period in Kerala are not clearly known, and even little is known about the 3 centuries that followed this period.

In the Sangam period, everyone had a right to education, especially women, who had the freedom to choose any profession, including that of a musician, poetess, or dancer (den Uyl, 1995, p. 59). Women were not just wives and mothers, but actively participated in the society as "artists and skilled manual workers" (den Uyl, 1995, p. 59); they also held "formal, public positions of power" (p. 59). Marriage was not a necessity—women married when they reached adulthood and enjoyed a profession (den Uyl, 1995, p. 59). There was no concept of dowry. On the contrary the groom was required to pay a bride price (den Uyl, 1995, p. 59). The *Gandharva* form of wedding, allowing men and women to freely engage in the art of love and choose their life partners, was the most popular form of union. Polygamy and polyandry were common. There were no social taboos around widowhood, divorce and remarriage. A woman also had the freedom to reject a lover if she did not want to be with him anymore (den Uyl, 1995, p. 59). Clearly, the Sangam Era illuminates a time when women moved freely with many more options available to them than that of the *chaste devoted wife*.

The Matrilineal Kinship of the Nayars

The reasons for the end of this period in Kerala are not clearly known, and little is known about the 3 centuries that followed. Around 800 AD, a new Chera dynasty emerged extending beyond the present-day borders of Kerala. This was a prosperous period during which Hinduism was established in Kerala. By the end of the 10th century, a long period of war broke out between the Chera dynasty and the neighboring Chola kingdom. It was during this war period that the land-owning matrilineal warrior caste thought to be the ancestors of the present-day Nayar community first came into the forefront (den Uyl, 1995, p. 63).

The *marumakkathayam* system. The Nayars were described as the swordsmen, the military caste of the Southwestern coast of India, and they practiced the *marumakkathayam* system of social existence, meaning inheritance by the sister's children as opposed to ones own sons and daughters. Although it is no longer practiced in Kerala, *marumakkathayam* still informs the relationships of many Nayar families. Within the *marumakkathayam* system, a group of kin spanning several generations, all tracing descent from one common ancestress, lived together in a clan house called the *taravad* with social organization based on kinship.

> The basic configuration of a *taravad* residential unit would consist of a woman, her sons and daughters, the sons and daughters of the daughters, and so on. The spouses of Nayar men and women were not normally part of such a household. (de Tourreil, 1995, p. 42)

The fundamental features of *marumakkathayam* system in Kerala consisted of the three basic institutions of the traditional Nayar *taravad*, the marriage system which is reported to have permitted polyandry and polygamy, divorce and remarriage, and inheritance where descent was through the female line (Saradamoni, 1999, p. 62).

Matrilineality was at the core of the *marumakkathayam* system—property belonged to the women of the lineage and it was passed down the female line to the daughters. This meant that the daughters had full rights to the property, while the eldest male member of the family (the maternal uncle) was the caretaker and protector of the property and of the affairs of all the members of the *taravad*. Unlike classical matriarchal models in which the oldest woman is the matriarch, in the Nayar model the decision maker of the *taravad* was the oldest maternal uncle or brother, addressed respectfully as the *karnavar*. The *karnavar* did not own any private property; anything that he possessed was generally earned out of the incomes of the joint estates under his management (Panikkar, 1900, p. 19) or through his own private business or job, just as in the case of my maternal grandfather. Most *karnavars* consulted with the oldest women in the family—their mother, grandmother or an older sister—in decision-making when needed. My own granduncle (on my mother's side) visited my grandmother (she was the oldest) throughout his life almost every week, and also consulted with her in personal and financial matters, and the same was true of my maternal grandfather.

Importance of natural relationships. Another interesting aspect of the *marumakkathayam* system was the importance of blood relationships over those formed through marriage. Marriage between the members of a *taravad* was strictly forbidden. The most valued women in the life of a man were his grandmother(s), mother, sister(s), and niece(s), and the most valued men in his life were maternal uncle(s) and his nephew(s).

> Nayar men had obligations toward their own mothers, mother's brothers, sisters, and sister's children rather than their own offspring. Being an uncle or a brother rather than being a husband or a father

played a role in the construction of their male identity. (den Uyl, 2000, p. 185)

Similarly the most important men in the life of a woman were her maternal uncle(s), including the *karnavar*, her mother's brother(s), and her sons, while the most important women in her life were her grandmother, mother, maternal grandmother(s) and aunt(s), sister(s), and daughter(s). Equally important in the Nayar culture were the uncle-niece, mother-son, mother-daughter, and brother-sister relationships. A son's loyalty never shifted entirely to his wife even after his marriage (Gough, 1961, pp. 344-345). The uncles were responsible for carrying out the pre-puberty, puberty, and marriage rituals for their nieces (de Tourreil, 2009, p. 207) and it was a common practice for a *karnavar* to undertake austerities, such as fasting or pilgrimage, in order that female offspring might be born to his sisters (de Tourreil, 1995, p. 46). A mother and daughter shared an intimate bond with few secrets, and the mother was responsible for grooming the daughter in the ways of the *taravad*, such as "cookery, household duties, child-care, manners, morals and minor agricultural work" (Gough, 1961, p. 346) as well as in the "the art of love" (Gough, 1961, p. 346). Within the kinship, a man's duty toward his sister was second only to that of his mother; he was expected to protect and care for them, and in return the sisters reciprocated with strong devotion to their brothers "over their husbands even" (Gough, 1961, pp. 352-354).

Female-centered rituals of the Nayars. Owing to the fact that any female in the lineage was considered to be the "purveyor of prosperity, fertility and good fortune" (de Tourreil, 1995, p. 48), a great deal of emphasis was placed on the natural blossoming of the female from a girl into a sexually mature woman through several obligatory rites of passage rituals. Since this constitutes the main topic of my research, I have included this as a separate chapter.

Sexual freedom enjoyed by women. Within the *marumakkathayam* system, patriarchal marriage was nonexistent. The union between a man and women was called by different names, such as *sambandham* (relationship), *podamuri* (cutting of the cloth), and *kidakkura* (sleeping together). These ceremonies did not have the "faintest shadow of a religious element" attached to them (Gough, 1955, p. 48), but simply facilitated the "union of female and male for enjoying sexual activity and to bring forth children for the woman's *taravad*" (de Tourreil, 1995, p. 101). Through the course of any of these relationships, the woman and man continued to live in their respective *taravad*s, with the husbands practicing visiting rites similar to those of the Mosuo (de Tourreil, 1995, p. 108). That is, the husband would visit the woman at night, spend the night with her at her *taravad* and in the morning, return back to his own *taravad* to execute his duties as brother to his sisters and uncle to their children.

The institutionalization of husband or father did not exist in the *marumakkathayam* system, and children born through these unions belonged to the woman's *taravad*, and were protected and cared for by them. All that was required of the woman's partner was that he acknowledged the paternity of the children and provided customary gifts to the woman on important festivals (de Tourreil, 1995, p. 103). Partnerships could be dissolved from either side without any difficulty at any time. The *karnavar* or other significant kin also had the power to call of this relationship if it was not in alignment with the prosperity or status of the *taravad*.

Any man or woman had the right to say *no* to a relationship and "no *karnavar* or mother or grandmother or brother could force a young man or woman to continue to have relations with a partner against his/her will" (de Tourreil, 1995, p. 105). Although in North and Central Kerala, women left their natal homes to accompany their husbands following their union a woman still retained her rights in her *taravad* and could choose to go back anytime (Gough, 1961, pp. 398-400).

Women seemed to have enjoyed considerable sexual freedom within the *marumakkathayam* system, because there was no inherent need to control their sexuality, which was associated with auspiciousness and the prosperity of the *taravad*. This had a significant impact on the social organization and meaning of marriage, sexuality, and motherhood:

> The absence of the "need" for control over female sexuality contributed to the relative sexual freedom enjoyed by women within *marumakkathayam*. Furthermore, this sexual freedom meant more than just the absence of restrictions on her freedom of movement, or forced arranged marriages, chaperonage, or guarding of virginity. It meant that beliefs concerning the nature of men and women, maleness and femaleness, which are connected with such institutions, did not develop among the matrilineal castes in Kerala. (den Uyl, 1995, p. 85)

Also, unlike what happens within a patrilineal Hindu social organization, the daughter in a Nayar *taravad* did not have to be *given away* in marriage, and if she so desired, she could stay celibate in her maternal *taravad* all her life without any prejudice (de Tourreil, 1995, p. 109).

As English education became more widespread, these ancient matriarchal practices were criticized, which—in the long run—resulted in the dismantling of the *marumakkathayam* system and the establishment of monogamous marriage rituals. After that the daughter had to leave her home following the marriage, living with her husband or his family; her father became the decision-making authority in her life, while her duty was understood to be in the service of her husband.

Religious, Cultural, and Political Influences

Kerala has seen numerous religious and cultural influences, including Christianity, Judaism, Jainism, Buddhism, Hinduism, and Islam (Menon, 1978, pp. 11-21). In spite of these different religions existing in the culture, there was no religious animosity between the people of the various religions and everyone co-existed peacefully as good neighbors in the yesteryears of Kerala (Fawcett, 1901; Fuller, 1976; Gough, 1961; Menon, 1978, 2008; Panikkar, 1918).

However, as Hinduism gained power in Kerala around the 5th century, there was a decline of Buddhism and Jainism. By the 8th-century CE, Hinduism along with the caste system was firmly established in Kerala. The people of Kerala were divided into classes, with the ritually high ranked Brahmin Namboothiri possessing large powers of oppression and domination over the numerous sub-castes, including the Nayars in Kerala:

> All the domestic concerns of the Nairs, all their social intercourses, all their liberty of thought and action are regulated by the arbitrary will of the Brahmin priests. Not one of them, in their true religious capacity, is allowed to move his little finger except on consultation with the Brahmin priests; and disobedience to their orders is often visited with their displeasure and the resulting deprivation of their means of livelihood and banishment from society. (Panikkar, 1900, p. 12)

People's trade and occupations became linked to caste, and many local sects like the *Panas, Vetas, and Kuravas* who once occupied a high social status were relegated to the lowest ranks of the social ladder (Menon, 1978, p. 14). The concept of pollution came into existence, forbidding the lower castes from touching or even crossing paths with the upper castes (Panikkar, 1900, pp. 152-176; Gough, 1961, pp. 312-313; Menon, 1978, pp. 270-275). With the establishment of caste systems in Kerala, women's freedom became considerably restricted. They were forced to enter into relationship only with men from the same or upper caste men, and had to declare the caste of the father so as to ensure that the child did not belong to a lower caste. The caste systems also influenced the establishment of complicated feudal systems controlled by the upper castes and breakout of war between various feudal lords in Kerala.

The arrival of the Europeans—Portuguese, Dutch, British, and French—further complicated the social structure. Toward the end of the early 18th century, invasions from the east headed by Islamic king, Tipu Sultan, disrupted the political structure and the system of land holding in the northern half of the Malabar Coast; the Nayars were the special targets of these attacks (Menon, 1978, p. 277). The legends of North Malabar recount numerous stories of terror, rape, and destruction caused by the Tipu Sultan's army in North Malabar. Many were forced to convert to Islam.

In 1792, the British East India Company conquered the Muslim invaders and with the support of local small rulers assumed the government of Malabar, thus establishing British rule in the Malabar region. With British rule in Kerala, and English education becoming more widespread, the basic features of Nayar social organization were further questioned and criticized, and there were several attempts to reform Nayar institutions to align with modern patriarchal values. These attempts in Kerala resulted in the establishment of the Cochin Nair Regulation (1919 to 1920), legalizing customary marriage and declaring the wife and children as being entitled to maintenance by the husband or father, followed by the Cochin Nayar Act (1937 to 1938), which brought about the complete disruption of the Nayar matrilineal form of inheritance or splitting of the *taravad* and property. Men could now individually own land and property money (Menon, 1978, p. 299). This further compelled the husband to maintain his wife and children as opposed to those responsibilities belonging to the woman's *taravad*:

> Thus, though a woman may now for the first time own a house and land independently of either her *taravad* or her husband, she looks to her husband rather than to her brothers for further economic support.... In particular the legal rights and obligations of the mothers brother have almost lapsed, and the father has become the moral and in part the legal guardian of his children. (Gough, 1952, p. 81)

These oppressive reforms caused many Nayar families a lot of grief. Families were pitted against each other, as they had to break up jointly owned property—brothers against sisters, nephews against uncles, and sons against their mothers. Members from the same family fought each other in court for years over land and property. The change favored monogamous marriages, leading to the gradual disappearance of visiting marriages (de Tourreil, 1995, p. 111). Nayar couples began to live in separate houses, as the authority of the *karnavar* and maternal kin also diminished. Nayar fathers became more and more involved in the duties of raising children and gradually earned most of the authority and decision making powers (de Tourreil, 1995, p. 118).

In the initial days, Nayar females used to retain their mother's *taravad* name. However, today most women take their husbands' names. For example, although my mother was able to retain her *taravad* name, I only inherited my father's name and his caste; my name has no reflection of either my paternal or maternal *taravad* name. In this modern system, although legally women have the right to choose their partner, it is not exercised and furthermore, separation and remarriage have become uncommon and many times the woman is expected to "put up with the disturbed family life" (Renjini, 2000, p. 22). Today, Nayars are patrilineal. However, the maternal ties as well as the bond between sister-brother, mother-son, and mother-daughter can still be strongly felt in the social culture.

Nayar Female-Centered Rituals and Festivals

Within the matrilineal *taravad* of yesteryears practicing *marumakkathayam*, a daughter's femininity had been directly connected to the prosperity and fertility of the maternal lineage (de Tourreil, 1995, p. 46) and thus her blossoming from a young girl into a sexually mature woman was of great significance to all the maternal kin. In fact, a Nayar female's maternal kin namely her mother, grandmother, and aunts consciously prepared her into this knowing through various female centered rituals:

> A Nayar female has ritual performed when she is born, when she approaches puberty, at the onset of menarche, at marriage, during pregnancy and parturition and when she dies. There is a sequence to those rituals, which accomplish the transformation, in clearly marked stages, of a young girl into an adult, sexually mature woman with the attendant rights and responsibility. (de Tourreil, 1995, p. 51)

These rituals facilitated the development of a woman's sexual knowing and expression in the world of relationships. In this study I am most interested in understanding these female-centered rituals through scholarly work and interviews with my mother and grandmothers. Most of the scholarly literature on Nayar matrilineal social organization was written by western scholars such as Fawcett (1901), Fuller (1976), Gough (1952, 1961, 1965), Moore (1988), Neff (1985), and Uyl (1995, 2000) in addition to Nayar male scholars such as Panikkar (1900), Menon (1978, 2008) and others. It is only in the last 3 decades that Nayar women scholars like Saradamoni (1982, 1999), Savithri de Tourreil (1995, 2009), Renjini (2000), and many more have contributed their voices to the scholarly writing. I was particularly interested in these women's writing as it reflected their lived experiences in the culture.

Nayar female-centered rituals were classified as obligatory and non-obligatory rituals around rites of passage, auspiciousness, femaleness, and more. The three obligatory Nayar female-centered rituals were the pre-puberty ritual of *tali-kettu-kalyanam* (the tying of the tali or amulet around the girl's neck), puberty ritual of *thirandu-kalyanam* (menarche or first menstruation ritual), and the *sambandham* (sexual relationship) ritual, and some of the key non-obligatory rituals were festivals like *thiruvathira* and the North Malabar *pooram* ritual. The themes of female eroticism and beauty were apparent in each of these rituals, and each ritual highlighted or accentuated a key aspect of female sexuality that facilitated the *blossoming* of the Nayar female into a sexually active woman. (Moore, 1988, p. 268; de Tourreil, 1995, p. 84)

The pre-puberty ritual of *tali-kettu-kalyanam* involved the tying of the tali (or amulet) around the girl's neck. This ritual accentuated the *prosperity-bringing auspiciousness* associated with female sexuality, honored the girl as the Goddess of the lineage and celebrated the prestige and prosperity of the *taravad* (Moore, 1988, pp. 257-263). The menarche (*thirandu-kalyanam*) ritual protected her and also celebrated her coming into sexual womanliness (Moore, 1988, p. 263). This ritual publicly announced the girl's sexual readiness so as to attract eligible sexual partners for her (de Tourreil, 1995, p. 84). These two rituals empowered the girl into the final ritual of *sambandham* or sexual activity. The *sambandham* ritual was connected to the act of procreation and bearing children, especially daughters to carry on the lineage. The non-obligatory rituals of *thiruvathira* and North Malabar *pooram* were centered on appeasing the sexual God of Kerala, Kamadevan.

My interviews with my mother and three grandmothers highlighted three rituals around female sexuality: the obligatory menarche ritual and the non-obligatory rituals of *thiruvathira* and *pooram*. In the next section, I will describe these rituals in more detail to provide the readers a better understanding prior to the Narrative chapter.

The Shift From Matriliny to Patriliny

In the last decade, incidents of suicides, sexual teasing, verbal and physical abuse, rape, pornography, sex trafficking, and domestic violence have increased in Kerala. I was interested in understanding these problems against the backdrop of Kerala's matrilineal past. Today, Nayars in Kerala identify themselves as Hindus, a dominant gender hierarchal social organization favoring men. Within such a system, the only model that provided the husband emotional security was that of a dominant male and the submissive role of the wife (Uyl, 2002, p. 101). However, these new roles were in direct conflict with the matrilineal Nayar gender roles.

In the matrilineal Nayar system, the roles prominent in the life of a man were those of son, brother and uncle, without him having to individually provide for his children. Similarly the most important men in a woman's life were her maternal uncle, brother and son, and she played the roles of daughter, sister, mother, and grandmother. She had no particular duties toward her husband. Her children were the responsibility of her maternal kin. However, in patriarchal Kerala, the men stepped into the *new* role of a father, husband and breadwinner, and the Nayar woman stepped into the role of a wife, fully dependent on her husband and mirroring the qualities of obedience, chastity and purity. A man's inability to provide for his wife and children got associated with shame and failure, leading to low self-esteem, and further causing psychological and emotional struggles, along with the maladaptive practices of drinking alcohol, smoking cigarettes, and even domestic abuse. Furthermore, the rise in western images of male aggressiveness toward women and objectification of the female body and sexuality through media, movies, and popular culture is also contributing toward relationships based on domination and violence in Kerala. There is an urgent need to redefine roles of maleness and femaleness in the new social organization of Kerala based on the matriarchal past.

PART IV

NAYAR FEMALE-CENTERED RITUALS

"The maternal or paternal aunt carrying the oil lit nellavillakku from the girl's room led the procession. The menstruating girl walked behind the aunt carrying the vallukannadi (or mirror) in her hand. The other women from the family closely followed the menstruant carrying different things."

CHAPTER 9.

THIRANDUKULLI : THE OBLIGATORY MENARCHE RITUAL

A girl's first blood has a "strong rite of passage quality, demarcating a permanent and irreversible transformation in the girl's status" (Moore, 1988, p. 263). The various steps involved in the *thirandukulli* ritual in Kerala empowered a girl into this experience without making her feel overly scared, disgusted, or uncomfortable in her body.

The three grandmothers I interviewed described the menarche ritual in great detail because of their direct participation in it as young women and their adult experiences of staging this ritual for their daughters, nieces, granddaughters, and grandnieces. In the ethnographic accounts of the menarche ritual by Tourreil, Moore, and Gough, it was always referred as *thirandukalyanam*; however, most grandmothers referred to the menarche ritual as *thirandukulli,* and *vayasu-ariyikucha*. I will first describe the ritual in elaborate detail followed by interpreting the meaning of the various steps involved.

Full ritual description through the interviews with my grandmothers. When a Nayar girl started her first blood, it was a moment of great importance in the family. She was asked to stay indoors and word was immediately sent to the women in her paternal and maternal families. It was only after the arrival of these women that the girl was guided into a separate room to begin her 3 days of seclusion. In some families, the mother guided the girl; in others it was the right of the girl's maternal aunt (mother's brother wife) or paternal aunt (father's sister). The female relatives arrived as soon as they received the message. Sometimes they would bring gifts in the form of food, money, or jewelry. The girl was treated as someone very precious. Jokes with erotic undertones were also shared with her. Once the girl was guided into seclusion, the women went back to their homes to return on the fourth day, when she emerged from seclusion to take her ritual bath. Participating in a daughter's menarche ritual was considered the rightful duty of the maternal kin, and if these rituals were not done appropriately or if someone from the family was not informed, it would lead to quarrels in the family. The girl stayed in seclusion in the room for the 3 days avoiding movement, sun, water, boys, and men, but she was never left alone. Food was brought into the room and if she had to leave the room, a close female kin always accompanied her.

The seclusion room was prepared with great care, first being swept and cleaned. In many homes, a mixture of cow dung and water was used to first ritually purify the space. Then the women mixed paddy (rice with husk) and grains of raw rice and spread it evenly on the ground. On top of it they placed a hay mat and covered it with a ritually laundered fresh white bedspread. I found a slight variation from this in the narration by one of the grandmothers, in whose menarche, the paddy and rice was placed on either side of her as she lay in between the mounds on a hay mat. In some affluent *taravads*, a thick woolen blanket was used instead of the hay mat. The girl sat or slept on this bed like an arrangement. She was also given a bell metal hand mirror, called *valkannadi,* to hold in her hand, which she was encouraged to look into it all the time. Toward the head of the girl was placed an oil lit bell metal lamp typical of Kerala, called *nellavillakku*. The girl's maternal kin made sure that this lamp burnt continuously in her room during the entire time of her seclusion. At night, the girl's mother or grandmother slept next to her in a separate hay mat without touching her.

During the period of seclusion special attention was put on the diet of the menstruant. She was not allowed to feel hungry (as if she were a special guest) and so was fed sumptuously throughout her seclusion. Her care was the utmost priority of the womenfolk. Special foods with prophylactic qualities were prepared under the guidance of the oldest female in the *taravad*. These foods nourished the girl and helped strengthen her body. She was also given delicious sweetmeats like *neyyi-appams* (rice dumplings made of jaggery and banana deep fried in ghee or clarified butter), and *chakkarachorru* (sweet rice cooked with jaggery). The food was always covered to avoid the eyes of everyone and secretly taken into the girl's room. Everyone took responsibility to keep the girl happy and healthy during her days of seclusion.

On the third night the grandmother of the *taravad* instructed the *Thiyyan* (name of a caste) man to bring *kuruthola* or tender coconut leaves and a young branch of covered coconut blossoms. The fourth day in the early morning, the women prepared the menstruant for her ritual bath. Coconut oil and *talli* (a cooling paste made of Hibiscus flowers and leaves) were applied to the menstruant's hair, and warm coconut oil was applied to her body. The women prepared earrings, necklace, bangles, and hairpins using the tender coconut leaves, and adorned the girl with them, after which she was led in a grand procession to the nearly pond or river to be given the ritual bath.

The maternal or paternal aunt carrying the oil lit *nellavillakku* from the girl's room led the procession. The menstruating girl walked behind the aunt carrying the *vallukannadi* (or mirror) in her hand. The other women from the family closely followed the menstruant carrying different things—a bronze *kindi* (typical round shaped vessel of Kerala) with fresh coconut oil, the hay mat, plate and cup used by the menstruant during her seclusion, a tamarind branch, and the closed coconut blossoms. The washerwoman and the barber woman, both ritual experts, also accompanied the women in the procession. The women ululated loudly, announcing to the entire neighborhood the coming of age of their daughter. In some *taravads* a fresh *mundu* was carried over the girl's head held in the front and back by two women holding the ends of the mundu, which acted as an umbrella protecting the girl from the sun as well as bestowing a higher status upon her. In some affluent *taravads*, the girl was seated on an elephant and accompanied by musical instruments. One of grandmother's shared a unique custom in which any woman they met on the path was offered oil from the *kindi*. The women then put the oil on the top of their heads. This was the oil remaining from what was applied to the menstruant. I have not read about this in the literature.

On reaching the river, the women guided the girl into the water. Her adornments made from the tender coconut leaves were removed and thrown into the river. Then the women ritually washed the girl. To complete the process of ritual purification, she had to take three full dips in the river holding on to a freshly laundered piece of cloth, called *mattu*, brought by the washerwoman. The *mattu* was intended to protect the girl from danger, ward off evil and purify her. All the women ululated during this process. In exchange for the *mattu*, the washerwoman (or *Vannathi*) was given for washing the bundle of the bloodstained menstrual cloth along with the clothes worn by the girl during the 3 days. The girl's maternal kin also washed and cleaned the hay mat and other vessels used by her in the flowing river. After her bath, the girl was brought out of the river and dried by her maternal kin, whence she was instructed in the tying of the *onnara mundu* for the first time. Then she was dressed in ritually laundered fresh clothes brought by the higher caste washerwoman. The women teased her, nudged her, and sang songs to make her feel shy, and then played games with the girl to guide her into womanhood.

The most common game was one in which the girl's aunt or grandmother struck the covered coconut blossom forcibly on the ground three times while the other women cheered and laughed. This caused any tender or weak baby coconut blossoms to fall off. Then the women opened the coconut blossoms excitedly and counted the remaining blossoms inside. That number predicted the number of children the girl would give birth to in the future. The women took time to tease the girl about it. If nothing remained inside the blossom, the women warned the girl about the possibility of her having no children. In another game, the menstruating girl was shown two branches from the tamarind and mango tree, and asked to identify and pick the tamarind branch, known to be very strong and cannot be broken easily. So through this game the women instructed the girl to choose her man wisely—a strong reliable Nayar male from a good *taravad* as opposed to the weak and easily breakable branch of a Mango tree.

Once all the instruction was finished, the women led the girl back into the front yard of the *taravad* where preparations were made to ritually bless her. A wooden seat was set facing east and the girl was made to sit on it. The lit *nellavillakku* carried by the aunt was placed in front of her. Several items were placed in front of the girl—*urulli* (a traditional bronze cooking vessel), rice, *kindi* with water, and freshly plucked *thumba* (tiny white flowers). Then every female kin blessed the girl by putting rice on her head, sprinkling water and giving her money or gifts. Once everyone blessed the girl, the *thumba* flowers were put into the *urulli* and the ceremony was over.

An elaborate feast was prepared in the kitchen for the near and extended family. In many homes, the remaining rice from the blessing ceremony was used to make sweet jaggery rice and shared with everyone as a ritual offering. It was also customary to look at the alignment of the floating *thumba* flowers in the *urulli* (cooking vessel) to foretell the direction from which the girl would receive alliances for marriage. After an elaborate feast the menarche ritual came to an end.

From then on, the girl was required to observe the seclusion for 3 days followed by a ritual bath on her own every month. During her seclusion she was expected to stay separate. Most *taravads* had a room adjacent to the kitchen, which was the room of separation. She was advised to take full rest during her 3 days of monthly bleeding, without attending to any duties of the *taravad* including taking care of children.

The Goddess and the menstruant. Through her dissertation research study in Kerala, Goddesses are Metaformic Constructs, scholar and poet Judy Grahn demonstrated strong cross-cultural correlations between the menstruant at menarche and the Goddess in terms of involvement of nature elements (such as animals, birds, certain plants, trees, flowers), body decoration, body adornment, gestures (such as ululation), attire, sounds (such as ululation), bathing, food substances, ritual songs, ritual drawing, astrological divination and use of different materials such as lamps, umbrellas, and mirror (Grahn, 1999, pp. 124-215). In fact, she clearly says that Goddess rites can be seen as containing more exaggerating portions of the menarche rites.

The auspicious aspects of the ritual. The auspicious and celebratory nature of the ritual is evident every step of the way—paddy and raw rice, lit bronze lamp, special sweets, and the mirror. Paddy and raw rice are seen as symbols of auspiciousness and fertility all over India, and it is the prime cultivation for the people of Kerala. Rice means everything. In that light, to have a menstruant lie or sit on paddy and rice while bleeding makes her first blood pure and blessed. It doesn't defile or pollute the rice in anyway. A lit bronze lamp, symbol for auspiciousness, truth and sacredness, is present at every auspicious and important occasion of a Nayar family, and is also found at death next to the body indicating completion of a journey. Hence, the presence of the lamp in the menstruant's room next to her head is definitely auspicious, and at the same time acknowledges the completion or death of one phase of the girl's life, and the beginning of a ritually lit period. Sweetmeats like *neyyi-appams* and *chakkarachorru* are made only on very special occasions in the family. Their preparations at menarche point to the festive and celebratory nature of the first blood. Finally, the menarchal female is deliberately made to hold and stare into the mirror (*vallukannadi*) during her seclusion. The mirror is a symbol of the Goddess in Kerala. Most goddess temples greet the devotee with a huge mirror when entering and leaving the temple. Also, in oracular rituals the mirror is used to transform the shaman into a godly being. I have personally participated in a powerful process of *looking into the mirror* in the presence of my Guru. I cannot disclose too much about it, only that it was a life altering experience bringing to light past experiences, memories and a deep sense of self-love and adoration. I was fascinated to learn that the menstruant was made to look into the mirror in seclusion. It is like initiating her into higher knowing at this powerfully transformation phase of her life.

Preparing, acknowledging, and protecting the menstruant. A girl's first blood ceremony brought the women and even men from entire maternal and paternal family together. It is important to note that earlier accounts of this ritual did not mention the presence of the paternal family at the menarche ritual, pointing to a patriarchal shift in Kerala. However, the presence of near and extended family along with the their love in the form of words, gifts and teasing helped take the girl's mind off the fear and apprehension surrounding the blood and coming of age. It also helped develop a positive relationship with menstrual blood as a celebration rather than the feeling of being *cursed*. At the same time, the menarche ritual acknowledged the vulnerability of the girl, and great emphasis was placed to protect her from the influences of outside forces—evil spirits, boys, and men:

> The protective aspect is most pronounced when the girl is actually menstruating: she is immediately secluded in the house, and measures are taken to ward off dangers (for example, placing a piece of iron beneath her sleeping mat or an iron knife beside her). She is regarded as susceptible to entrance (hence possession) by extraneous beings. (Moore, 1988, p. 263)

The female is isolated and males have to avoid coming into contact with her . . . The manner in which a menstruous female may affect a male is plainly to the disadvantage of the latter (de Tourreil, 1995, p. 96). The girl's body and sexuality was also consciously protected. She was restrained from engaging in normal routine activities of going to school, moving freely around the house, playing, running around, and eating whatever she wants.

The women put extra attention on strengthening her reproductive health by what she could and could not eat. Extreme heat-producing foods such as chilli or pickles, and cold foods were avoided and different kinds of food with special prophylactic qualities were prepared for the menstrual girl:

> Indigenous understanding of the qualities of different kinds of food is at the back of these restrictions and recommendations. They are meant to make up for the loss of blood, regularize the menstrual cycle and flow, strengthen the reproductive organs, and in general, to contribute toward future fertility, to make the process of child-bearing

> smooth, and to restrain the girl's sexuality. Puberty celebrations and the special diet regulation seem to express the value restrained and controlled sexuality and of motherhood. (Dube, 1988, p. 14)

The food was also, secretly taken into her room covered with a cloth, due to the belief that when someone looks at food and salivates, they pass on their energy to the food. Avoidance of this for the menarchal girl shows the attention and care given to food preparation and deliverance. The first 3 days of the ritual emphasizes the protection of the girl as she is bleeding, and on the forth day she is ritually prepared physically, mentally, emotionally and spiritually to face her new life as a sexually active adult female. De Tourreil (1995) describes this process beautifully:

> Female kin bring her gifts, new clothes, food and jewelry to honor the life-producing power and eroticism that she now fully embodies. Sometimes there is singing and dancing around her. All these activities signal to the female that she is now at a highly valued stage of development. The special treatment and celebration enhance her self-image. No one thinks of her bleeding as a "curse." (p. 95)

By giving the first blood in a girl's life ritual meaning, her maternal kin have empowered her relationship with her monthly menstrual cycle in a sacred and intimate way, acknowledging her auspiciousness, celebrating her first blood, protecting her from outside forces, strengthening her body, and guiding her into a mature sexual knowing. By celebrating it publically with the conscious awareness of the women and men in the family, everyone is brought into the sphere of understanding, acknowledging and respecting menstrual blood.

Menarche ritual in the Indian subcontinent. Growing up I saw distinct differences in the attitude toward menstrual blood between my South Indian and North Indian friends with the experience of the South Indian friends more positive. Upon further inquiry, I found that celebrations similar to thirandukulli in Kerala had been prevalent in most of South India, and it consisted of common features such as:

> Seclusion of the girl for a certain number of days, *arti* to signify the auspiciousness of the occasion and to ward off evil to which a menstruating girl is believed to be especially vulnerable, serving her special food, informing the relatives and friends, giving the girl a ritual bath, presenting her with new clothes and accessories of beautification such as flowers, jewelry and bangles, and a feast which also serves the purpose of announcement of the event. (Dube, 1988, p. 13)

However, for most practicing Hindus of North India, with the exception of tribal and rural people, the treatment of the first blood was very different and not marked by any rituals:

> In most of north India the first menstruation is not marked by rituals. The event is taken care of by the mother and the female relatives unobtrusively and within the home. The observances relating to menstrual pollution are introduced quietly, often with the attempt that children and males in the family and outsiders should not notice them. (Dube, 1988, p. 14)

This difference could be because the North of India was influenced by patriarchal Hindu and Islamic moralities in addition to centuries of British rule, while the South of India was more shielded from these influences. Recently, my knowing of North Indian rituals around menstruation expanded through Apffel-Marglin's fieldwork in Orissa (North-East India). I learned about the unique festival of Raja Parba (*raja* meaning menses and *parba* meaning festival) that celebrated the menses of the earth, the sea, the goddess and women and was participated by everyone (except the Brahmins) irrespective of caste and religion:

> It takes place once a year in mid-June, when the monsoon rains make their first appearance, the earth and the Goddess and the sea are said to be menstruating for three days. . . . Men congregate on the hill of Haracandi, with all the men of one village sleeping and eating in the same tent for the four days of the festival. The women celebrate in the villages, where they take over the public spaces, the young girls swinging on gaily decorated swings (*dolis*) especially prepared for this occasion. (Apffel-Marglin, 2008, p. 257)

During this period no one (including men and women) was allowed to plough or do any work including household activities, sexual union—

everything was abandoned to honor the bleeding and rest of Mother Earth. It was believed that disrupting this rhythm of life would result in the "cessation of life, the cessation of continuity, and the negative shedding of men's blood, namely destructive war" (Apffel-Marglin, 2008, p. 263). Apffel-Marglin's fieldwork has made me realize that in the complex vast culture of rural India, there might be many rituals like Raja Parba undiscovered by modern civilization and yet, observed by the people.

Personal reflection. Although the occurrence of my own first blood was given no ritual meaning, my mother empowered me in embracing my monthly blood as a powerful happening devoid of shame and disgust. The only taboos I was instructed into by my mother were that I must not go into temples, nor light the lamp at the altar. She never forced me to go to school during those days if I did not want to or had too much discomfort. In my near and extended family of North Kerala, I do not know of any public celebration around menarche having been performed in the last 2 decades. Today, most cities and towns of Kerala are populated with educated nuclear families. In these homes, a girl's first menstruation is limited to the knowing of her parents and siblings. In most situations, her understanding is informed through friends, movies and TV commercials. She continues through the normal chores of life as though nothing has happened.

CHAPTER 10.

STORY OF KAMADEVAN: KERALA'S SEXUAL GOD

The legend of Kamadevan is closely connected to the festivals of *thiruvathira* and North Malabar *pooram*. The literal meaning of the word *kama* is desire, usually pertaining to love and sexuality, and *deva* means God or celestial being. So Kamadevan means the *God of playful love and sexuality*. During the *thiruvathira* and *pooram* festivals, the women of Kerala remember, celebrate and worship Kamadevan. These celebrations are unique to Kerala and have a sensual and erotic quality. In order to understand them, one must understand the story of Kamadevan. It is one of the well-known and popular stories of India and an integral part of the legend of Shiva and Paravathi. Shiva symbolizes the inertness or nothingness of consciousness, and Durga or Shakti represents the dynamic fullness of consciousness. Together they represent the whole—switching roles when necessary. Paravathi is understood to be the incarnate form of Durga. I grew up hearing numerous variations of the story of Kamadevan, but one in particular impacted me at a deep level: it was a narration by Linda Johnsen (1994) in her book, *Daughters of the Goddess*. I will narrate that story first and later share how it differs from the other stories:

The demon king *Taraka* was creating havoc in the universe because of the boon he received from the creator assuring that only the son of Shiva could kill him. After the self-immolation of his beloved wife Sati (another incarnate form of Durga), Shiva was desolate. He was engaged in severe penance and abandoning worldly life. Hence, the boon sought by Taraka made sense, because there was no possibility of Shiva ever marrying any other woman. However time passed and Sati was reborn as the most beautiful maiden in all the worlds, Paravathi. From childhood, Paravathi was an ardent devotee of Shiva and longed to marry him when she grew up. She knew the cave in the Himalayas where he was engaged in penance and would visit him every day with flowers and fruits as an offering. But nothing stirred Shiva from his deep meditative state. Kamadevan, the Lord of Love knew about Taraka's boon and wanted to help Paravathi, so he approached her and she willingly accepted his help to bring Shiva out of his penance. Kamadevan instructed Paravathi that the next time she visited Shiva she would place the flowers in his hands. At their moment of physical contact, Kamadevan would cast the arrow of love at Shiva hoping to break him out of his meditation. Everything went as planned. However, instead of a loving gaze, Shiva was enraged at being disrupted from his years of penance. Fire arose from his third eye and burnt Kamadevan to ashes, and Shiva returned to his meditation. Paravathi was devastated. Her desire to marry Shiva had caused Kamadevan his life. In that moment, she underwent a huge inner transformation or awakening, completely dropping her desire of marrying Shiva, deciding to instead to renounce the world and seek the highest. She smeared ash on her body and sat on the highest mountaintop in deep meditation. As the years progressed, Paravathi's meditations became intense and powerful. Nothing could stir her; she was determined to attain liberation.

In his deep meditation, Shiva began to sense the presence of an extraordinarily divine energy—subtle, sublime and brilliant. Shiva had never felt or experienced that energy before. When he realized that this growing field of consciousness was as powerful, perfect, and vast as his own, he wondered about the source of this energy, which forced him to open his eyes. His gaze fell on a most beautifully radiant dust-covered Yogini meditating on the mountaintop and oblivious to the world. Her body, mind, and spirit were in union with her higher self. In that moment, the great renunciate Shiva fell madly in love with Paravathi, resulting in their union. The entire universe celebrated. Out of this union was born Karthikeya who destroyed the demon Taraka. Paravathi restored Kamadevan back to life.

In every version of the Paravathi-Shiva story that I grew up hearing, Paravathi was portrayed as helpless, desperate, and weak following the death of Kamadevan. She was miserable for not having attained Shiva. Seeing her pitiful state, Shiva feels sorry for her and breaks his penance. He decides to grant her the wish of marrying him. But this story never made sense to me. Paravathi is the incarnate form of Goddess Durga. How could she be helpless? When I read this new feminist version of the story, it provided the missing link. I would like to quote the words of Linda Johnson—"In saving herself, Paravathi had saved the world. In mastering herself, Paravathi had mastered *Shiva*, a Sanskrit word that also means the supreme auspiciousness" (Johnsen, 1994, p. 93).

When I first read this story, I was hit hard by the fact that women give their power away so easily—she is either desperately wanting a man in her life or feeling like a loser without one. This story demonstrates that a woman, who has chosen to master her spiritual and sexual self, becomes instrumental in transforming her and the universe. This story also illustrates Paravathi's close association and friendship with the lord of love and passion, Kamadevan. Kamadevan's sacrifice is still remembered, celebrated and re-enacted by the women through the festivals of *thiruvathira* and *pooram*. The women of Kerala adore Kamadevan; they speak of him like an intimate friend who understands their intense longing for a lover. They seek his help in uniting with their beloved. Growing up, I never saw the significance of these festivals, but now I have a deeper understanding about them.

I recently learned that the worship of Kama was one of the most ancient spring rituals of rural India and the myth of his destruction symbolized his disappearance from the temple and household shrines:

> The legend of the destruction of the god of lust by the *yogic* fire of Siva's third eye symbolized the physical disappearance of the face and limbs of the presiding deity of erotic love from temple and household shrine. Kama became *Ananga*, the bodiless one, only remembered in the secret *vrata* rituals of women and in the saturnalian spring festival, the *holika*, sacred to Kama. (Jayakar, 1990, p. 85)

The spring festival of *holi* is one of my favorite festivals. It involves the throwing of colored water and everyone—men and women, young and old—participate. I had never heard the mythology of Kamadevan associated with the festival of *holi*, until I learned from author Pupul Jayakar that in rural India, *holi* was a celebration of playfulness of Kamadevan and it involved singing of obscene songs with erotic language and gesture followed by the worship of Kamadevan by the women. They applied sandalwood paste to his image and ate mango blossoms mixed with sandalwood paste (Jayakar, 1990, pp. 86-87). These festivals underwent significant changes with the emergence of Buddhism, Jainism and the rigid disciplines of Brahmanic authority in India, and its obsession over the annihilation of desire. However, in spite of the mythology of burning Kama, his presence could not be annihilated and his legend got fused with new emerging deities of the Sun, Siva, and Krishna (Jayakar, 1990, pp. 85-86). In light of learning about the association of *holi* with Kamadevan, I am hoping that the festivals of *thiruvathira* and *pooram* continue to stay connected with the mythology of Kamadevan and sexuality.

CHAPTER 11.

THE *THIRUVATHIRA* FESTIVAL

Thiruvathira was mostly celebrated in Central and South Kerala in the Malayalam month of *Dhanu* (December or January). Both married and unmarried women celebrated it. I found an early ethnographic description of this festival dating back to 1900 in the book, *Malabar and Its Folk* by T. K. Gopala Pannikar. *Thiruvathira* commemorated the death of Kamadevan, and was focused on the females of Kerala remembering Kamadevan, and enacting his tragic death:

> The popular conception of it is that it is in commemoration of the death of Kamadevan, the Cupid of our national mythology. . . . Kamadevan was destroyed in the burning fire of the third eye of Siva. . . . The memory of this unhappy tragedy is still kept alive amongst us, particularly the female section, by means of the annual celebration of this important festival. (Pannikar, 1900, p. 103)

In the recent times, the *thiruvathira* festivals are no longer celebrated in the way they were a century ago. Newer versions of the story focus more on Shiva than Kamadevan.

Full description of the ritual. This description of *thiruvathira* was written in a time when Nayar *marumakkathayam* (or matrilineal social organization) was still in practice. Women lived in their maternal *taravads* along with their maternal kin, while their husbands lived in their respective *taravads*, allowing women to freely engage in enjoyments of their pleasing. I am including the entire description as is, because it is no longer available in newer literature.

> About a week before the day, the festival practically opens. At about 4 in the morning every young female member of the Nair families with pretensions to decency, gets out of her bed and takes her bath in a tank. Usually, a fairly large number of these young ladies collect themselves in the tank for this purpose. Then all or almost all of these plunge in the water and begin to take part in the singing that is

presently to follow. One of these then leads off by means of a peculiar rhythmic song chiefly pertaining to Cupid (meaning Kamadevan). This singing is simultaneously underneath the surface of the water. Then the palm of the other is forcibly brought down in a slanting direction and struck against its surface. So that the water is completely ruffled, and is splashed in all directions producing a loud deep noise. This process is continuously prolonged together with the singing. One stanza is now over along with the sound and then the leader stops a while for the others to follow her in her wake. This being likewise over, she caps her first stanza, with another at the same time beating on the water and so on until the conclusion of the song.

Then all of them make a long pause and then begin another. The process goes on until the peep of dawn when they rub themselves dry and come home to dress themselves in the neatest and grandest possible attire. They also darken the fringes of their eyelids with a sticky preparation of soot mixed up with a little oil or ghee; and sometimes with a superficial coating of antimony powder. They also wear white, black, and red marks lower down the middle of their foreheads close to the part where the two eyebrows near one another. They also chew betel and thus redden their mouths and lips.

Then they proceed to the enjoyment of another prominent item of pleasure, viz. swinging to and fro, on what is usually known as Uzhinjal. These ladies especially derive immense pleasure from this process of swinging backwards and forwards, sometimes very wide apart so as to reach the other and higher branches of the tree. On the festival day after the morning bath is over, they take a light meal and in the noon the family-dinner is voraciously attacked; the essential and almost universal ingredients of which being ordinary ripe plantain fruits and a delicious preparation of arrow-root powder purified and mixed with jaggery or sugar and also coconut. Then till evening dancing and merry-making are ceaselessly indulged in. (Panikkar, 1900, pp. 103-106)

Interpreting the ritual. The most important aspect of *thiruvathira* was "till evening dancing and merry-making are ceaselessly indulged in" (Panikkar, 1900, p. 106). Although Panikkar did not describe the dance, I know from my mother and grandmother that the women danced the *thiruvathira* or the *kai-kotti-kalli* in the evening in a circle in the front courtyard of the house. According to them, at the center of the circle was placed a fully lit oil *nellavillakku* along with a plate filled with fresh native fruits, lit incense and freshly plucked coconut blossoms beautifully placed in a paddy laden bronze vessel. The entire family gathered to watch the women dance. The husbands of the married women were required to arrive at the *taravads* to partake in the evening festivities; failure to do so was "looked upon as a step or rather the first step on the part of defaulting the husband toward a final separation or divorce from the wife" (Panikkar, 1900, p. 106).

Today, *thiruvathira* or *kai-kotti-kalli* (or the dance of hand clapping) is performed at most cultural gatherings of Kerala. It is a very sensuous dance with a lot of hip and pelvic movements along with enticing eye and seductive head swaying gestures with women singing and dancing while clapping their palms in rhythm and moving round in a circle. The collective erotic sexuality embodied by the women is visibly mesmerizing.

The description of the water beating game enacted during *thiruvathira* festival is quite unique as well. My mother did not know about such a game. One of the grandmother's faintly remembered it during the interview. Through the water games and the act of swinging, the women reenacted their grief over the death of Kamadevan:

> The swinging process and the beating on the water, have each its own distinctive significance. The former typifies the attempt, which these maidens make in order to hang themselves on these instruments and destroy their lives in consequence of the lamented demise of their sexual deity, Kamadevan. It is but natural that depths of sorrow will lead men to extreme courses of action. The beating on the water symbolizes their beating their chests in expression of their deep-felt sorrow caused by their Cupid's death. (Panikkar, 1900, p. 107)

It is evident from the description that women embodied their love for Kamadevan through adornment, dance, and singing. I was fascinated to learn that there was a time when the women of Kerala openly displayed their devotion to Kamadevan and proclaimed their devotion to him proudly without any shame or prejudice. The entire week of *thiruvathira* was an occasion of unadulterated fun and entertainment for the women.

The present-day descriptions of *thiruvathira* found on the Internet and in popular books lacks the association with Kamadevan. Today, women fast all day long without eating any rice items, in order to please and seek blessings from Lord Shiva for their husband's long life. Kamadevan's death has become symbolic of the annihilation of sexual desires as the erotic sensual aspect of the *thiruvathira* festivals has been replaced by more controlled overtones of sexuality. Women mostly engage in severe fasting, going to the temple, praying and chanting. There is a heaviness and seriousness associated with the festival, which was not there in the past.

Personal reflection. Personally this narration brought back to me many summer memories spent swinging on the *uzhinjal* (or huge swings). Every summer my paternal uncle would set up the swing using a tight strong rope hung from a strong horizontal branch of a Tamarind or Mango tree. The base of the swing was usually made of a strong wooden plank on which I would sit firmly holding the ropes by my hand, while one of my cousins pushed me from behind. I used to do every possible acrobatic trick on the swing, from standing to sitting to double swinging and more. The higher the swing went, the more fun it was. Even when I was older I did it without anyone asking me to step down because I was now a *big girl*. Although I never participated in the *thiruvathira* festival, I can visualize the unveiling of the festival among the women—the excitement of waking up early in the morning, followed by a rendezvous in the family pond with the women folk, the leisurely engagement in water games, followed by dressing up for the festival, and then the hours of swinging—with kohl-smeared eyes, fresh set-mundu, jasmine flowers adoring their hair, and reddened lips—these women must have looked so beautiful.

CHAPTER 12.

THE NORTH MALABAR *POORAM* FESTIVAL

Pooram considered to be the equivalent of *thiruvathira,* is a spring festival celebrated during the month of *Meenam* (March-April) for 9 days in the North Malabar region of Kerala. Spring is also the time when all the beautiful sweet smelling flowers blossom in Kerala. The young girls and unmarried women observe *pooram* for the purpose of getting a handsome husband. I was not able to locate any elaborate ethnographic description of this festival in scholarly writing except for a brief paragraph (Menon, 1978).

During this festival, the young maidens of marriageable age prepared idols of Kamadevan, decorating him with beautiful spring flowers, offering him sweet delicacies and spending long hours with him. The girls hope that in return for playing the gracious hostess, a happy and satisfied Kamadevan would fulfill their desire of finding a passionate, handsome lover. For this study, I will describe the ritual based on the ethnographic description as witnessed, experienced and celebrated by my mother:

Full ritual description of the festival (from the interviews). The young maidens of marriageable ages in Nayar homes of North Malabar celebrate and worship the sexual god, Kamadevan for 9 days during the Puram festival. During these 9 days, the girls wake up early, have a bath, wear fresh clothes and then prepare small cow-dung dolls of Kamadevan. In the first 3 days, the dolls are made and placed next to the *taravad* well or pond, symbolizing the outside; the next 3 days they are prepared and placed at the far end of the courtyard; and the last 3 days the dolls are made and placed inside the courtyard, making it seem as if Kamadevan is slowly walking toward the house. Each doll is placed on a banana leaf or a small wooden stratum (specially made for this purpose). Every day the girl (s) decorate the idol with *champaka* flowers, offers water at dawn and dusk while the older ladies make the *kurava* sound (ululation). The last day or the 9th day, red mud or clay is mixed with cow dung and a big Kamadevan doll is made. The doll is then decorated with eyes, nose, and lips. A *nellavillakku* (bell metal lamp) is lit and placed in front of the Kamadevan and then Kamadevan's favorite dishes; *pooram ada* (sweet cake made of rice powder, grated coconut and jaggery, covered with green leaves), and *poora kanji* (raw rice prepared with grated coconut) are prepared and offered. Then the older women assist the maidens in offering water by having the girls sprinkle water over the Kama idols, after which all the nine idols of the Kamadevan are collected and carried around the house three times in a huge procession led by the older women with the maidens following them. The women ululate the whole time. Finally these dolls are deposited under the jackfruit tree, following which the women sing a song filled with longing to Kamadevan:

> Nerethe kallathe varanne Kama
> *(Kama, please visit us early next time!)*
>
> Puthilla Tarattil polle Kama
> *(Kama, please do go to the Puthilla Tarattu)*
>
> Putthilla Taratill pozhal Kama, aviduthe pennungal Eendola chuttu chathikkum Kama!
> *(Kama, if you go to the Puthilla tarattu then women there will feed you roasted palm fruits and cheat you)*
>
> Athukondu Puthilla Tarattil polle Kama.
> *(So please do not go to the Puthilla Tarattu)*
>
> Nerethe Kallathe Varanne Kama
> *(Kama, please visit us early next time!)*

With this song, the pooram celebrations come to an end.

Interpreting the ritual. The Nayar women celebrated the pooram for 9 days—adored and appeased the sexual God, and prepared their daughters to adore and appease the sexual God, seeking in return the mysteries of love and erotic sexuality. Although in the present culture, the erotic aspects of the festival are no longer evident, it can be assumed that when female sexuality was openly practiced, this festival must have had a different flavor. In an online magazine (Nambiar, 2007), I found a reference to the mythical origin of this festival which described that following the demise of Kamadevan, 18 virgins from heaven descended on earth, prepared the idol of Kamadevan, decorated it with flowers, and danced round it with varied songs and foot works and their female sexual energy revived Kamadevan back to life. The modern-day *pooram* festival is assumed to be an enactment of this mythology. Even today, the *pooram* festival in North Malabar is accompanied by the dance drama of *poora-kalli* (very similar to *kaikotti kalli*) performed exclusively by men. According to professor A. K. Nambiar, Secretary of Kerala Folklore Academy (Kannur), women might have played *poora-kali* in the past and somehow overtime it might have become the performing art of men (Nambiar, 2007, para. 4).

Personal reflection. I personally observed the pooram ritual and poora-kalli performances by men during the 3 years (12 through 15 years of age) when I lived in North Malabar with my grandmother. Sadly, I have seen the festival as well as the poora-kalli performances slowly disappear from the village life of North Malabar.

PART V

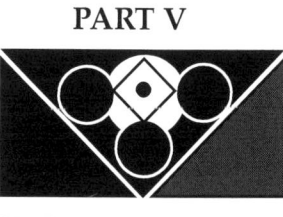

THE INTERVIEWS

"The men of that time were not like men of today. Married women were treated with utmost respect. They wouldn't even look at them. Even with women who weren't married, men wouldn't behave disrespectfully. Men had lot of discipline. There might be very few people who did things like that. The majority of men never bothered or even looked at women. Men won't even go where women were."

CHAPTER 13.

LETTING GO AND SURRENDER

Chthonic: The Roots Emerge

> When the ground has been prepared and the seed has been planted, the gardener must trust that what happens underground will be successful.... It splits open and roots begin to emerge which follow the rules of nature, not those of the gardener. Throughout the life of the tree, the invisible root system continues to grow in the dark and to affect what happens above ground.... Although the research begins with responsible intent and planning, the method is often called upon to evolve and changes over the course of the research because of synchronicities, dreams, meditations, intuition, body responses or other manifestations of the research muse. The researcher is urged to pay attention to expressions of inner knowing throughout the process of the research. (Clements et al., 1999, p. 34)

Chthonic phase of organic inquiry was most natural and known to me in spite of the unknowingness it embodied. Growing up in India, I am used to surrendering to the unknown, trusting the unseen, respecting the dark, and talking to the invisible. I have experienced the working of these forces since childhood. I trust in it more than I trust in information quoted, written and spoken by living bodies.

From the breakdown of my marriage to my coming to the master's program to my visiting the archaeological sites of Malta to cognizing the Yoni Mandala—everything has directed me to the topic of female sexuality. Strangers have trustingly given me rare books highlighting female sexuality rituals and images from Hinduism. Even through my travel in Kerala, I was guided with remarkable precision. I would like to illustrate one example of that.

As soon as I arrived in India, I spoke to the three grandmothers I had planned to interview to determine their consent to participate. I immediately realized that two grandmothers could not participate. For privacy reasons, I will not reveal their identities. One grandmother had poor physical, mental and emotional health. However, the other grandmother's decision to not participate came as a pleasant surprise. She was the most educated, most traveled, English speaking and modern grandmother. While speaking to her on the phone, I had realized that she was very hesitant and fearful of participating in a study around female sexuality. I was a little disappointed, as her behavior was in direct opposition to my perception of her as an empowered embodied female. Later my mother and I visited her. To my surprise, she completely avoided any conversation about my study or interview during the visit. Her response offered a deep learning for me, reaffirming the panic and fear felt by so many educated modern Indian women (including myself) around our bodies and sexuality.

I was still short of two grandmothers. Instead of panicking, I decided to pray and surrender to the will of the universe. I woke up early morning remembering, Yashoda *ammamma*. I have known her to be a very open and strong woman. When my mother spoke to her over the phone, she was enthusiastic about participating. I was still short of one grandmother for the interview. My first stop in Kerala was attending an ancestral ritual at my mother's ancestral *taravad*. I kept telling my mother that I would find my third grandmother there, refusing to search any further.

We visited that *taravad* the evening before the ancestral ritual. I was sharing with few of my distant maternal aunts from that *taravad* about my study and interviewing grandmothers. They jumped most enthusiastically at the mention of grandmother. The mother of one of the aunts was the oldest living *karnavarathi* (wife of the *karnavar*) of that *taravad* nearing the age of ninety. The women enthusiastically told me that she would be the most ideal person for the interview, and that she was supposed to attend the ancestral ritual the next day, when I would be able to ask her. The enthusiasm, joy and openness of these women were compelling. In that moment, I knew in my heart that she would be my third grandmother. As it turned out she was the first grandmother I interviewed.

My biggest struggle involved having to explain female sexuality and body connection to my co-researchers. Malayalam language does not have the proper vocabulary to embody the meaning I intended. My mother and I did our best in translating from English to Malayalam. On the night of the ancestral ritual, I realized I still harbored fear and doubt of being judged and misunderstood by the women. I did not want this to impact my interview, so I prayed to the Goddess and my ancestors to free me of this feeling. The very next moment, the eldest granddaughter of the *taravad* called me into a room. She excitedly asked me, "I am told that you are doing some research. Everyone says it is about the ancestral ritual. I have a feeling it is something else. Could you talk more about it?" She spoke fluent English, and seemed well read, educated, and a modern working woman. I breathed a sigh of relief and blurted out, "I am more than happy! It is so good to explain to someone in English." Then we spoke for hours about the Nayar culture, matriarchal civilizations, embodied feminine, sexuality, and everything. Soon a small group of young women assembled around me in the room. There was excitement and wonder in their eyes. The women congratulated me on undertaking a study like this. I was interrupted by one of the aunts that it was time for the interview, so I said goodbye to the women and walked out feeling confident and empowered! There was no trace of fear or doubt in my mind. My prayers were heard and acted upon promptly. That conversation with the women empowered me not just for that interview, but also for every other interview I did afterwards. It was a gift from Bhagawathi herself!

Relational: Growing the Tree

> A thin, sun-starved white stem with one leaf unfolds above ground and the gardener sees the progress of the plant for the first time. (Clements et al., 1999, p. 43)

This was visually my experience as I listened to my mother's voice—traveling through the pathways of her memory as she unfolded the gems of her life, never having shared or spoken with anyone before in such an intimate way. As my mind visually projected my mother's memories, every cell in my body felt blissful, alive and seen. My fears disappeared and I was completely present in wonder. It connected both of us in an intimate way, and for the first time I felt not alone in my experience, but seen and acknowledged. I felt honored and grateful!

> Although the researcher may begin the work alone, she or he finds co-researchers who can describe their own experience of the topic. The researcher and the co-researchers work together in face-to-face interviews to allow the stories to emerge complete with details. Each story is an articulated branch growing from the main trunk where it joins with the researcher's core story. (Clements et al., 1999, p. 43)

Every interview impacted me in a different way. It was as if my experience and awareness around female sexuality had expanded leaps and bounds. Every story I heard became a part of me—living and breathing in me. At the end of every interview, I touched the feet of the co-researcher—my mother and the grandmothers. They blessed me by touching my head. Every time I looked into their eyes, I saw a deep sense of appreciation, gratitude and pride. Their stories had found a new meaning for their children and grandchildren. Most importantly, they had impacted my life story in a profound way.

The Interview Setting

The comfort of my co-researchers was of utmost importance to me. I made sure that every interview was conducted in a setting comfortable to the co-researchers—my mother and the three grandmothers. The co-researchers signed the consent forms prior to the interviews. I was given permission to audiotape and videotape every interview by the co-researchers. In fact they were excited about everything and supported me throughout.

Initially I thought that the interview setting would consist of the grandmother, my mother, and myself. However, I soon realized what a phenomenal moment this was for females in the family, including the daughters, daughters-in-law, granddaughters, and even great granddaughters. So I decided to let everyone be present at the interview site. Just like me, some of these women were hearing these stories for the first time. They were excited and enthusiastic and joined in the conversation. The only time I interrupted was when the family members got too excited and spoke over the grandmother. They were quick to understand and act upon my gesture without feeling offended. I will always cherish the excitement, enthusiasm and belongingness shared in these interviews. I have directly experienced the support of the community of women and have tried to convey the atmosphere in my narration.

I am presenting each interview in the form of a narration that includes my question to the co-researcher, their responses, and my own mental and emotional reflections that surfaced during the interview as well as during the transcription. Each narration begins with a brief history of the co-researcher followed by a description about her relationship to me. I have used the letters "D," "M," and "G," in alignment with my topic, *The Rising Daughter* (D), *The Silent Mother* (M), and *The Fading Grandmother* (G), to designate the voices of the researcher, my mother, and grandmother respectively. I have used "S" to represent my sister and "W" to represent the collective voices of the women.

CHAPTER 14.

BALAMANI AMMA
MY SILENT MOTHER

Figure 1: My Mother, Balamani and I, before the interview

My mother, Balamani (see Figure Above) grew up in a small town called Cherukunnu in the Kannur district of Kerala. She was born to K. P. Paravathi Amma (her mother) and K. O. Kammaran Nair (her father), both of them the eldest siblings in their respective taravads. Paravathi Amma was Kammaran Nair's third marriage. His first marriage was through a sambandham practice that is rarely mentioned in conversations in the family, although he had a son in that relationship. Following that he had a second marriage in which he fathered five children; his second wife passed away when his youngest daughter was 6 months old. Subsequently, he married Paravathi Amma, my maternal grandmother, although she was nearly 20 or 25 years younger than he. It is difficult to understand the story of my mother, without knowing my grandmother and grandfather; hence, I will narrate their story first.

My grandfather, Kammaran Nair was a well-reputed karnavar of a well-known and prosperous taravad. He was respected in the community for his righteousness and spirit of giving. As a karnavar (oldest maternal uncle) he took care of many acres of matrilineal land and supervised all the taravad activities including paddy cultivation, care of the coconut and mango groves, construction and maintenance of the taravad buildings, and more. He had four younger brothers and two sisters and he was responsible for the lives of all these people, their children and his own children.

He had worked as a sub-registrar in the Kannur district. When he married my grandmother he was 45 years of age and nearing retirement. She moved into his taravad, in order to care for his siblings and the children from his previous marriage. Together they had six children of their own—three daughters and three sons. My mother, Balamani was their fourth child, and by the time she was born, most of the children from his second marriage were married and settled. When the marumakkathayam system was legally dissolved in Kerala and the joint property had to be divided between the members of the taravad, my grandfather bought a separate piece of land and constructed a home on it for his wife and children in Cherukunnu (not too far from his own taravad) and then moved them there. He divided his matrilineal property among his siblings without taking anything for himself, and this act of generosity is remembered to this day by some of his siblings. The land and home he built for my grandmother was accomplished through his work income.

My mother and her siblings grew up in this house and lived off my grandfather's meager income and later his retirement pension. They did not experience the prosperity of my grandfather's taravad as they grew up. The fading marumakkathayam system was based on values of simplicity, cooperation, living within one's means, and respect for life in general. In direct contrast, the emerging modern private property and British education system, to which his children belonged, was based on an evolving consumerist culture, individual freedom, and progress. This difference alienated the children from their father in many ways. They could never fully understand or connect with his way of life or thinking.

My grandmother was caught in between these two colliding worlds. She centered her life in taking care of her husband and children, rarely visiting her maternal taravad for any family functions or festivals. As I began this study I thought my grandfather's patriarchal conditioning was responsible for my grandmother's separation from her own matrilineage. However after having several conversations with my mother and her step-siblings, I realized that there were many contributing factors, including years of property dispute and friction among my grandmother's matrilineal kin. My grandfather and my grandmother's brother had initiated the legal process for my grandmother to get her rightful share from her maternal taravad when it was divided. This friction was one of the reasons my grandfather did not want her visiting her maternal taravad because every time she did, she would return hurt and sad.

I knew that my grandfather rejected the Nayar rituals central to taravad life. I could not understand how a spiritual person like my grandfather did not value the earth-based family traditions any more. During conversations with my mother and her sister, I discovered that in those days traditional family rituals such as ancestral theyyam (an ancient ritual art form particular to the North Malabar region) ritual had become occasions of flaunting family prestige and money, having lost their true meaning. I am sure participating in these rituals caused my grandmother grief, because she had fewer resources and was judged by her family for not having enough. When she attended these rituals, it often led to arguments in the house. My grandfather resented the growing obsession and greed in the culture and disapproved of his family participating in or hosting any such ritual in the house as a means of demonstrating wealth or status.

My grandfather's age also affected his relationship with his children. He was quite old and had retired by the time he had children with my grandmother; his relationship with his children was quite formal, without displays of affection or love. Somehow my mother got to know him more closely. Maybe her relationship with him grew when she stayed home for 6 years before getting married to my father. My grandfather had a lot of respect for my father and they were close, which gave my mother more opportunities than her siblings to know my grandfather. I remember him clearly. He used to make a special malt drink for himself. The malt powder was delicious to eat on its own but my mother would never let me eat it. However, every time my grandfather prepared the drink, he would call out to me. I would run to his room and extend my hand. He would joyfully put a spoonful of the malt powder in my hand. My mother could never say anything to that. I also remember him playing with my sister who was hardly a year old. He adored us. We are the only grandchildren who got to spend time with him. My grandmother was not the overly loving kind of grandmother who smothers grandchildren with kisses and hugs. I also felt many times that she loved her son and grandsons more than her daughters and granddaughters. I have learned to love my grandmother through my mother, who was there for her in every difficult situation of her life.

My mother, Balamani, was married at the age of 21 to K. Govindan Kutty (my father), a soldier (traditional occupation for most Nayar men) in the Indian army. My father was a young, handsome, open, and fun-loving man. Within a year of their marriage, my mother gave birth to me, and 5 years later, she gave birth to my sister. She supported my father through our travels to different cities and states of India. From only knowing how to read and write Malayalam, she learned to converse in different Indian languages, interacting easily with people from different cultures, castes, and ethnic backgrounds. In my view, she was the perfect companion to her husband, perfect mother to her children, and a compassionate friend to everyone who came in contact with her. Today, she has stepped up to the role of the co-researcher in the same way sharing her life, her memories, and past relationships with me. Her enthusiasm and childlike innocence have supported me throughout this study.

Today, my parents live in Vijaynagar, a small town in the Bangalore city of Karnataka, India. My mother is 62 and my father 69. They are the most active people in their age group. A typical day in my parents' life begins at 5:30 AM, and attains completion close to midnight. My mother, always on her toes, is the glue that keeps the family together. She cooks fresh breakfast, lunch, and dinner every day, takes care of everything in our lives —buying everything needed for the house, cooking, cleaning, finances and money management, monitoring timely payment of bills—everything, and she keeps the extended family (on her side as well as my father's side living in different cities of India) connected to us. In addition to all this, she is an active member in the apartment where they live, paying close attention to people's lives and helping as needed. She is secretary of the Vijaynagar Nayar Society's Women's Chapter in Bangalore. She has an active spiritual path (same as mine) and is deeply engaged in service activities through it. Her inner strength, patience, and perseverance directly contribute toward my father's success in the world.

Just like my mother, my father also has a very busy life for a retired man. He is on the Executive Committee of the Karnataka Nayar Society, secretary of the apartment they live in and also the Vijaynagar Nayar Society. Both my parents taught my sister and me, by example, the true meaning of taking responsibility, and my mother definitely is the one who has inspired our attitude of service and compassion. She guides my father through conflicts, calms his anger, keeps his health in check, and supports him in matters of the world. Our home is the most active place in the building—the phone is always ringing, people show up unannounced, children from the apartment pause for water, and many other things in motion. The number of hats my mother wears in one single day is simply beyond my comprehension. She does all that with a calm, peaceful composure. I have hardly ever seen her get angry. My father's helplessness can be seen every time my mother travels without him.

I interviewed my mother in my sister's apartment in Vijaynagar. She and her husband live on the second floor of my parent's apartment. We chose my sister's quiet apartment at around 6 pm for the interview so as to avoid any disturbance. My sister and I promised to take care of dinner for the night, so that my mother could give the interview in peace and relax afterwards. My mother and I dressed in traditional Kerala attire. My mother helped me wear the set-mundu, and she wore the Kerala saree: cream with golden embroidered border. My sister lit the big bronze nellavillakku at her altar in the living room. I placed my cowry shells and my mother placed her mother's glasses on the altar. We arranged our chairs next to the altar facing each other. My sister sat next to me with the video camera. My mother was comfortable, composed, and confident about the video recording. Usually I have seen women concerned about their appearance in the video. She did not ask me that question even once. I turned on the audio recorder, did some sound checks, and then gave it to my mother. We were ready. I took a deep breath in, savored the moment and with a smile, read out loud the first question in Malayalam.

> D: How did your relationship with your body and sexuality transform as you blossomed from a young girl into an adult woman?

My mother began to speak and I felt like I was dreaming. Her voice soft, gentle, and confident flowed through the room:

> M: As a small child, I don't remember very much. But maybe after 5 or 10 year old is what I remember more. In that age, there were no responsibilities. There was nothing much to think about. Everything was taken care of by amma (mother). It was a good time. Most time was spent running around and playing. Then go to school and come back.

It was wonderful to picture my mother as this little girl running around and playing. I wanted to know more about her life. Did she live with her father? Did she have connections to her mother's taravad?

> M: Yes. Yes. I lived my father's house. I would go to school and come back from home. My mother's taravad was close to my school. We would visit everyone, see everyone, go to people's home and play—I think I used to like all that very much. Once I remember from my house in Cherukunnu after school in the evening instead of coming home, I went to the taravad without telling anyone. I think Januechi (Grandmother's younger sister) was staying at the taravad then. Her daughter was my age, around 10 years old. So we used to visit them often. So after school I went directly to their house in the taravad. Everyone in my home was worried. I remember my father bringing me home. He was very mad at me for going without informing everyone. I think he even beat me then. That was the only instant I remember of my father getting angry.

I always pictured my mother as an innocent naïve girl. I could never imagine her wandering off on her own to visit her aunt. She reminded me of the numerous instances where I wandered off after school without informing my parents. My mother continued:

> M: Otherwise there was not any strictness growing up. "You can't do this. You can't do that"—I don't recall ever being told any of that.

> I roamed around freely is what I remember about my childhood. After that when I was 15 years old. I think when I completed SSLC (10th grade) . . . that is when I got my periods. Even then I never felt anything wrong or not right with my body. It felt very natural when it happened.

My parents practiced this in my childhood as well. My sister and I were never told, "You can't do this." I was happy to hear her begin the conversation around menstruation. I was curious to hear her experience, as we had never spoken about it.

> D: Did you know "what happened" when you had your periods?

> M: No, I didn't know. I was very afraid when it happened. Till then even when my body was changing and everything, I didn't feel anything wrong, it felt natural. But when I got my periods, I was very scared. It came at night. I was so scared the whole night. . . . "How will I tell this to my mother." It was my constant thought through the night. The whole night I was thinking and I couldn't sleep. In the morning when I woke up I told my mother.

This is another place I am extremely grateful to my mother. When I was in fourth or fifth grade, the commercial for sanitary napkins was everywhere in print. It showed girls playing basketball or talking together in groups, and next to that image would be the pack of sanitary napkins. Then one day, I saw them in my own house. I was curious, so I walked into the living room to both my parents and asked for an explanation for the sanitary napkins. At first my mother was hesitant and then on my persistence, she decided to tell me. There was a silent exchange of looks between my father and mother. It was like my father was telling her, "You better tell her. She is not going to stop asking." So, at a young age, my mother explained to me about menstruation as a privilege that only girls had—a privilege that made a girl a woman and gave her the ability to become a mother. Her explanation was so empowering that from that day forward I waited for my first blood. The day I had it, I screamed in excitement from my bathroom. I did not have to go through the fear of seeing blood. I felt sad that my mother had to spend the whole night awake and worried about her blood. It must have been a horrible feeling to go through. I could not wait to hear my grandmother's response.

D: What did ammamma say?

M: Ammamma said it is all right. Then she told me how to use the cloth. She tied a thread around my waist and showed me how to use the cloth for the periods. Then I knew what it was. I knew that women used to get periods because during that time a washerwoman would come home. Like there was a washerwoman who washed normal clothes, there was a particular caste who came to the Nayar homes when women had periods. Vannathan was the caste, which washed normal clothes, and then there was the caste called Vannan. The women from this caste would take the blood cloth used during periods, wash it and bring it back. That was my memory.

M: In those days the blood cloth was not thrown away. It used to be collected and kept tied in a bundle. Even the dress we wore during periods, everything was kept together. These women would come and take everything. They would take the clothes to a river, wash them, dry them, clean them, fold them and bring them back. So for 4 days during period, we stayed separate without doing anything.

I was glad to know that my grandmother took good care of my mother and did not make her feel bad about herself. The caste group called Vannan and Vannathan also fascinated me. I never knew about them. I could never imagine anyone touching my blood stained clothes other than myself in my own privacy around my blood. I did not know how to respond to this system that was built around a whole group of people cleaning and washing my menstrual clothes. Imagine every month someone coming to these huge taravads to collect the blood stained clothes of the menstruating women, including the clothes they were wearing and sleeping in, and then washing them, neatly folding them and bringing them back—it was beyond my comprehension. These Vannan women were considered as lower castes, and were never allowed to enter the Nayar homes. I was curious to know about any rituals my mother observed during this time:

D: When you had your first periods, did you have to go through any ritual?

M: There was no ritual that I remember but I think I had to stay separate without doing anything. I don't have a lot of memory around it. There was no ritual performed, because my father didn't like any rituals. I think because of that maybe no ritual was done.

I was hoping that my mother had experienced some ritual around her first blood, so I was a little disappointed. However the greater question was—Did the absence of the ritual affect her relationship with her blood?

> D: But, you had no negative feelings about it?

> M: Not at all! I had no negative feelings around my periods. My mother told me and then I stayed separate for 4 days without doing anything. I think many of my relatives came to visit me during that time. My mother told many relatives and then they came—Januechi (My mother's sister) and then some other relatives came to see me is what I remember. I don't have too much memory about then, but I recall that many relatives came to see me. After 4 days, I bathed and then there were all these people who were there. Women from my father's house had also come. I don't recall any elaborate rituals being done. If we need to know more, we should ask Januechi ammamma. She would remember.

I was amazed at my mother's complete trust in her mother and her natural comfort with menstruation. Her mother told her it was ok and that was good enough for her. I was happy to know that in spite of my grandfather's strictness, my grandmother did send word to her younger sister (Januechi) and other women in the family about my mother's first blood. In fact, I met Januechi ammamma during this trip, and I asked her about it. She did not remember all the details, but recalled that many relatives came on the fourth day to celebrate my mother's ritual bath and emergence from separation. They brought her gifts and sweets to eat. It made me happy to know that my mother did, after all, have a first blood ceremony.

> D: Do you remember it as a nice moment?

> M: Yes. It was a nice moment. That is what I remember. When I first saw the blood I was scared, but then it was nice. I don't remember anything bad or not nice about that moment. I felt that it was a natural transformation that happened to women. Other than that I had no negative feelings around it. I think I felt very shy with everyone being there.

Though my mother's initial lack of knowledge scared her, the ritual made her feel comfortable—her happy feelings indicate a positive experience. When she said that she felt shy in everyone's presence, I felt maybe there was some erotic or sexual teasing that may have happened to welcome her into womanhood. She could not recall. I wanted her to continue.

> D: And after that?

> M: After that I became more responsible.

My mother said this so matter-of-factly that I could not stop smiling, like the next step after menstruation was becoming responsible. She said it like it was the most natural phenomenon. Maybe in her time, it was like that. However, I wanted to know what she meant by that.

> M: After 10th [grade], I was staying at home then so I had more responsibilities around the house. My sister was small and she was going to school. I was then the bigger one, helping my mother with all the household chores and taking care of everything in the house. It was during that time; I joined a stitching class and would go there.

This was common in North Malabar in those days—as soon as a girl got her periods, she was pulled out of school. Post-10th grade was considered higher education and required going to a college. Most colleges required travel and additional finances, and it was not considered safe for girls to travel. Although my mother was exceptionally good at school, she chose to stay at home learning stitching and embroidery because my grandmother had no additional help. I recalled in those moments the various embroideries she had made in the past. She has a very steady hand. It was difficult to distinguish between my mother's stitch and the sewing machine. I realized that I did not know enough about her stitching experience—where did she learn, how far was it from her house, and how did she travel to the class?

> D: [Curiously] You went alone to the stitching class?

> M: [Surprised at my question] Yes of course. I used to go alone. Also, even when I was studying I had gone to Kannapuram (name of a neighboring town) to learn stitching on my own. Even during

> festival time we used to go everywhere to pluck flowers—as far away as the water source at the end of the town—with other girls.

This was news to my ears. Kannapuram is a neighboring town, and requires considerable walking from my mother's house. Today, that entire area is filled with modern shops, homes, and roads. During her time, she said it was full of paddy fields and ponds with water lilies, separated by simple mud pathways. I was amazed that she roamed all over the place on her own, and her father never opposed or stopped her. I always got the impression from my uncles and aunts that my grandfather was overly strict. Was he really that strict after all?

> D: For all that your father never stopped you?

> M: No. Never.

The feminist in me got reawakened at this point, and I had to ask the next question:

> D: As a girl, "I don't have freedom," did you ever feel that?

> M: No. I never felt that as a girl that I didn't have freedom. I used to go all the way to Kannapuram to learn stitching at Gomez Teacher's house. Maybe my neighboring friend, Jhanu used to accompany me sometimes. Gomez was the headmistress of our school. Then sometime later, she started a balawadi (Children's nursery) near my house. After finishing household chores, I had free time in the afternoon. During that time I used to go there to learn stitching.

This was a breakthrough in my knowing—my mother never felt that she did not have freedom. True freedom comes from within and it seems like my mother experienced it. That explains the freedom and ease she displayed throughout life in speaking with strangers, traveling and managing alone. Thanks to her and my father, I definitely experienced it in my own life as well. My mother continued telling me about her life at the balawadi or the children's nursery:

> M: During that time, there was an annual function in that school and they staged a play. I also acted in that play. It was the story of Noor-Jahan and Jahangir. I wore saree and played the part of

> Noor-Jahan. My sister was then in Singapore and I wore one of her sarees. There were lot of cultural activities happening there and I remember that I was involved in it. Being there was really entertaining for me, and everyone there used to like me a lot. It was a lot of fun there. After 10th [grade], I spent 5 or 6 years there.

These are moments when a daughter wants to stand up and jump and scream out of sheer excitement—my mother acted in a play; she played Noor-Jahan, the most beautiful and powerful Empress of the Mughal dynasty, married to Emperor Jahangir, the fourth ruler of the Mughal Empire from 1605 until his death in 1627. Jahangir loved his queen immensely and was known to consult with her on all matters of state. In fact, she was known to be the power behind Jahangir. These social and cultural engagements of my mother have helped me to understand her differently. It is clear that she spent 5 to 6 years going to the balawadi, engaging freely there. Her parents never questioned her on what she did there. Most importantly, I noticed that there was no hurriedness to get her married. As I was thinking about this, she naturally started talking about her marriage. It was a timely transition:

> M: In 1972, I got married. I had passed 10th grade in 1966. I think it was during the time when I was at home that my mother had some real help, as I helped in household chores. My sister went to college for 5 years. She never had time to do anything at home. That time, we also had a sewing machine from Singapore at our home. I used to stitch. So sometimes my mother would tell me, "I will take care of the kitchen, why don't you go and do your stitching."

This briefly describes the close mother-daughter bond in Nayar homes. In spite of the fact that my mother was my grandmother's only help, she encouraged her to get some free time for herself, allowing my mother to engage in something she loved that gave her a sense of accomplishment. I was beginning to understand my grandmother in a new way.

> D: You had a good relationship with your mother?

> M: Yes. I did. I was a real good help to my mother.

I have always known my mother to share a close bond with her mother. She showed up every time my grandmother needed her, consciously or unconsciously. I have the same deep bond with my mother. I would do anything for her. The mother is a powerful presence in the life of a Nayar daughter. I have seen this reflected in the lives of my cousins and Malayali friends. My mother was speaking about freely moving around in the village. I could not help wondering about her safety.

> D: That time when you went out, was there any eve teasing (a euphemism used in India for public sexual harassment of women by men), boys commenting or passing remarks?
>
> M: No. There was nothing like that I remember. If boys spoke to us, we responded and spoke with them. There was nothing like if you saw boys, don't talk to them. There was nothing like that. Like there were homes in front of ours. There were boys and men there. They used to talk to us all the time freely and we also engaged in conversation freely. It was very normal and natural to do that. There were no restrictions about anything. There was nothing like, that is a boy or that is a girl. But boys coming to our home, we talking and laughing with them aloud was not encouraged. If my father saw that, he would get angry. That was the only time I felt some restriction. Otherwise, it was fine. I have even gone to see movies with my male cousin . . . both my sister and me. Even that time when we came back, my father didn't say anything. But after few days he did mention, I think, "What is the urgent need to go watch a movie with a male cousin?"

On one side I saw that my mother had the freedom to speak to boys and men in the neighborhood, and yet there was disapproval of public display of intimacy between genders like watching a movie together or walking together or holding hands. It made sense to me. In the marumakkathayam system, sexuality was a private affair. What men and women did in the confinements of their homes was nobody's business. But with modern education and the European influence of romantic freedom between men and women, sexuality was entering the public domain. Was this public display of sexuality what men like my grandfather disapproved of? Did they think that pulling sexuality out into the public arena would take away its sacredness? Were they worried that this freedom would corrupt the minds of their daughters and sons? I will never know.

As my mother was speaking, I recalled a comment made by my mother's younger sister about their father—he never let us visit the local temple. I wanted to know if that was true.

> D: Where you allowed visiting the temple?
>
> M: Yes. For birthdays we used to go to temple. I never had to ask anyone. One of my closest friends used to live right next to the temple. So for everyone's birthday I would wake up early, have a bath, then go to the temple office and make the offering for the payasam (sweet rice porridge prepared with milk). After that I would go spend time at my friend's place. Around noon, I would get the payasam from the temple and come home.

This again shows the freedom my mother had. She never had to ask anyone. Going to the temple required considerable walking—easily 10 to 15 minutes, and yet she was never stopped from going on her own. She had the freedom to move about on her own. Present-day Kerala is not so safe for women. I was curious to know how it was then.

> D: Was it safe then?
>
> M: Of course! I used to go alone every time. It was very safe. I always went everywhere alone. I don't recall taking anyone with me for safety reasons. There was no restriction about that. By then my father was also aged.

I only experienced this feeling of safety within the perimeters of the army camp. But once I stepped outside the Army area into the public, I had to be alert most of the time—ready to defend myself from an attack or abuse.

> D: What do you remember about your marriage?
>
> M: Marriage was like a part of life. That was what I thought and saw around me! When you become old, you get married and then you have children. It was what we saw happening. So it was all a natural part of life. So when marriage time came, relatives would bring a proposal.

My mother's words made me realize that life, as she knew it, were quite simple. It was the complete opposite of my experience. Life was complicated! I did not want to marry. I wanted to work, get a job, and be independent. I was caught up in finding the perfect romantic mate. My education made me question the purpose of marriage, and the role of a wife. If that were not enough, I was in conflict with my own body and sexuality. My mother's innocent comment touched me deeply. She continued talking about her marriage:

> M: I remember someone from my father's family brought a marriage proposal for me from someone whose wife had passed away. I think it was my father's sister's son. His wife had died and then they wanted to marry me. My father did not agree for that marriage for me.

I was beginning to appreciate my grandfather deeply. He truly cared for his daughter's well being. Most of my negative feelings about my grandfather were formed by the judgment projected onto him by others. I was beginning to shift. My mother continued:

> M: Many proposals came then. Then it was my friend and classmate, Leela who brought the alliance for her husband's brother, your father. She was the main reason our wedding happened. She told my family, I think. That is how one day your paternal grandfather and your father showed up at our home to see me. I had just recovered from typhoid then. My father knew your father's father well through the court. When they came, my father was not home. I was actually so tired from the sickness that I couldn't even stand. I was inside. What I remember is that your grandpa was really funny [she laughs remembering] and his son, your father, was with him. My mother did most of the talking. I was sitting on the floor inside.

I was really thrilled to hear these stories of my paternal grandfather making a visit in the absence of my mother's father. My grandmother's interaction with him clearly shows the authority women enjoyed. They were not confined to the inner quarters of the house, but interacted openly and freely with men. In the absence of my grandfather, she was the one who engaged in conversation with the groom and his father. What really amazed me was that my mother was not forced to dress up and parade in front of the groom, as is customary in most Hindu marriages. It was true that my mother was sick, but in many patriarchal marriage systems, the girl's physical health is not a hindrance to this ritual. There seemed to be no urgency in getting the daughter married, and hence, there was no need to objectify her. I was curious to know if my mother got to see and speak with the groom and his father.

> D: Did you see them?
>
> M: Yes. They came to the door looking inside to see me—both father and son [she laughs remembering]. They asked me something I think. The son looked really smart—your father [she laughs]. He wore a nice shirt. I used to always remember him in that shirt later on. He spoke so nicely. He looked really handsome.

It was wonderful to hear my mother speak about her innermost feelings, as she shared these memories with us for the first time. I was glad to hear that my father and grandfather spoke to my mother, and my mother answered them without any fear or apprehension. She was extremely natural and comfortable. This differs so much from the present bride-parading tradition where the woman is made to feel so uncomfortable. In fact she is expected to be an epitome of a modest bride—gaze to the floor, shallow voice and shy. My sister and I felt a deep pride in listening to my mother's sharing. I wanted my mother to share her feelings:

> D: Amma, what were your feelings?
>
> M: My feelings were good. I really liked him. Later I don't know who spoke to my father. I don't remember all that. After a few days, your father's mother and your father's young brother came to see me. Ammamma (my father's mother) walked around the house, and the property, the courtyard and everything. Your grandmother liked to see the property and the outside. Your uncle was very friendly, and praising his brothers.
>
> Throughout this sharing my mother kept laughing, remembering these images in her mind. My sister and I could feel her happiness and joy. It had been such a positive moment for her, and we saw that she cherished and enjoyed those moments. These memories reaffirmed the fact that my mother did not have to dress up and show herself off. She was valued for the person she was and she interacted freely. The fact that my paternal grandmother visited my mother reaffirmed many things for me about the status of a woman. My father's home is quite far off, more than an hour by bus. My paternal grandmother had the freedom to undertake this long

journey with her son in a bus without her husband. That she did not fear to undertake this journey confirms the fact that this was not the first time she traveled alone. More importantly, her visiting my mother after my grandfather and father had already seen my mother, demonstrated that her opinion of the bride mattered in the decision making.

D: Was ammamma nice?

M: Yes. She was very nice. I really liked her. I walked with her through the property.
I think it was after that was when the wedding was decided. Your father sent a letter to my father asking for my picture [we all laughed thinking about that]. Then your uncle had to take me to the main city to a studio to click a picture. That is how I have that solo picture of me. Then we sent the picture to your father.

My mother's marriage was only decided after my paternal grandmother approved of my mother, showing her importance within the family. My mother freely moving around with her without any fear shows my mother's confidence in herself. I was also thrilled to learn of my father's request of my mother's picture. He was and still is such an extroverted person. Later my father told me that he wanted to show my mother's picture to his army friends. In fact, he wrote the letter himself to my mother's father. I was surprised that my maternal grandfather granted his request. He did not consider my father's request ungentlemanly. On the contrary, he allowed my mother to go to the town dressed up in a saree to get photographed by a complete stranger. I was getting a completely different perspective of him. What I was most interested in knowing is whether my mother's opinion of the boy mattered. Did she have the freedom to say no?

D: Did anyone ask you if you wanted to marry papa?

M: I don't remember but I think my friend Leela must have asked me and that my agreement must have been indirectly communicated to my family or something. I don't remember exactly.

D: But if you hadn't liked the guy, you could have told. You had that freedom?

> M: Yes. Definitely. Definitely I had that freedom. It was because I liked the alliance, I got more involved in it. So yes!

I was relieved to know that my mother had the freedom to say no. Her opinion mattered. What she shared next reaffirmed this even more.

> M: How I know this is because sometime before, there was the talk about exchange marriage—my elder brother and me both going into a family. I refused to do an exchange marriage and told my father that my brother doesn't have to compromise or get married to someone for me. My father agreed and never asked me after that for an exchange marriage.

Exchange marriages were common in North Malabar. As de Tourreil (2009) explains, exchange marriage was "two marriages arranged at the same time in a matrilineage which involves another matrilineage simultaneously in two marriages" (p. 209). It could be either two sister-brother pair or one sister-brother pair on one side and an uncle-niece pair on the other side. That is a female and male from one matrilineage exchanged in marriage to a male and female from another matrilineage respectively. De Tourreil points out the reason for this—"If any member of the conjugal unit is not treated with consideration and respect by the partner, there will be, or could be, negative 'fall out'" (de Tourreil, 2009, p. 209). My mother had witnessed the pain and displeasure caused through exchange marriages in the family, especially with Januechi (my mother's maternal aunt). It was wonderful to hear that my mother had the freedom to voice her opinion to her father and that he listened to her. I have a feeling that exchange marriage was intended to secure the life of the daughter of a particular matrilineage when women started moving out of their own houses into their husband's house. However, it put unnecessary strain on the bond between brother and sister, sometimes even leading to conflicts within the family. The sister-brother bond, and also the bond between sisters, is very strong in Nayar community in comparison to other cultures. There is more intimacy, friendship and sharing. The sisters are devoted to their brothers and vice versa, even after their marriages. This bond is encouraged and held high in the culture. I can say that my mother's closest friend is her sister. There is an unspoken bond between them, beyond feelings and words, reflected in my relationship with my aunt and her children.

Although the interaction between the brother-sister pair is more formal, this invisible bond still binds them closely. They protect and support each other in spite of the conflicts brought in by their respective spouses. I think this bond has been affected deeply by the patriarchal shifts, and has caused considerable mental and emotional trauma for women and men alike. I wanted my mother to speak about this bond:

> D: How was the relationship between siblings?
>
> M: Because my father was strict there was not too much show of affection or talking or laughter in the house. My eldest brother was a very simple person. I think he suffered the most because of my father's strictness. There was never any overt display of affection from my father toward any of us. What we saw was that any of my father's nephews who came home always stood behind my father when they spoke—never showing their face to him. Though my brother stood in front and spoke to the father, they never sat in front of him or engaged in any hearty conversation. Before it was like that. We never went in front of the father or uncle when we spoke. It was quite formal! Our sibling relationship was not very free. We spoke with each other but there was not too much freedom. With my younger sister, I was more like the older one. With my other brother I used to be freer. I remember I used to participate in flower kallam (or mandala) competition, and I knew the girls from my brother's class. They were good friends of mine and knew me as my brother's sister. So there was lot of freedom then that way.

It is easy to judge my grandfather for his strictness and formal nature but his role was extremely complex. He was the karnavar to his entire matriliny consisting of his six siblings and their children. His parents died very young and so he was a father to his entire family. He had five children from his second marriage, and six with my grandmother, his third marriage. He single handedly was responsible for the well-being of this entire group of people. That is a huge undertaking in itself. Last year, I visited my grandfather's only surviving kin—his youngest brother. He was over 80 years old. When I asked him about my grandfather, he started crying. His devotion and love for his brother was obvious, as he kept saying again and again that his brother was his God, his father, and everything! My grandfather's maternal kin adored him in a way that his own children never did. This shows the challenges men experienced balancing their matrilineal and patrilineal relationships. The role of a karnavar was more natural to my grandfather than the role of father or husband. His strictness and distance, especially with his sons, could have come from that. His age also defined that relationship. He was nearing 60 by the time my uncles were young men. However that strictness affected the level of intimacy and sharing between siblings in my mother's house. I was trying hard to understand my grandfather. It was time to bring the discussion back to interview. I wanted to know about the interaction between men and women outside the context of family:

> D: Did you go to a co-ed school?
>
> M: Of course! We only had co-ed school then. We were 10 girls and rest 20 or 30 were boys. We used to talk to boys and everything. We were friends. Teachers were strict. Without any reason just sitting with boys and gossiping was not done. Anyway we never saw anything like that growing up! We didn't know that.

There are many things in this sharing which clearly demonstrate the freedom boys and girls enjoyed in their interactions with each other based on friendship and innocence. The innocence with which she said "We didn't know how to be different with boys" touched me deeply. Another thing that came as a surprise to me was that she went to a co-ed school. I was under the impression that my mother attended an all girls school, because for as long as I remember my mother's village only had an all boys school and an all girls school. I was surprised to learn that this split into gender-based schools was a recent development. There could have been numerous reasons for this shift. The changing images of sexuality, and increased portrayal of love and romance in the popular Malayalam movies, could have influenced the public interaction of boys and girls in schools. This may have prompted the need to separate them in the public domain. Also the establishment of the Catholic Convent and hospital by the Christian missionary in Cherukunnu could have contributed to this shift. Now that we had gone through the various stages of my mother's life, I felt it was the right moment to bring the discussion back to her relationship with her body and sexuality.

> D: Now I will ask you once again: How did your relationship with body and sexuality transform with marriage and everything?
>
> M: Actually sexuality and sex after marriage was not very pleasing because I didn't know what came after marriage. One thing was that about sex I had no knowing but I loved your father's home atmosphere. I had my friend, Leela with me. They had a servant at home who did everything, and they didn't allow me to do anything. Your father's parents were really nice. It was a lot of fun. Your father was also very nice. But then you listen to your husband and go with it. I never had anger or sadness around it. Then it became natural.

My mother was clueless about what came after marriage. I am sure she meant sex and being intimate with a man. She was never guided into that knowing. In the matrilineal taravad of yesteryears, on the other hand, the mother and other matrilineal women had taken a personal interest in instructing the daughters in the arts of love, maintaining their appearance and physical attractions (Gough, 1961, p. 346). However, when a woman left her matrilineal taravad to live in her husband's home, she was completely on her own. From 4 AM in the morning till midnight she was slogging to get work done. She had no time to engage with her daughters intimately. This disrupted the flow of wisdom from mother to daughters. My mother was lucky that she could move into this experience naturally. It definitely was not natural for me. The media and the society informed my sexual awareness. I was disconnected from my bodily wisdom and, hence, could not access it. Since we were on the topic, I asked my mother about female-centered rituals:

> D: Do you remember participating in any female-centered rituals? Can you describe what they were like? How did you feel?
>
> M: I don't remember participating in any ritual. There was the Kaman ritual, which was for girls only. We did that every year for young unmarried girls.

The only festival she remembered was the pooram (also known as the Kaman ritual), which was celebrated by young girls in pre-puberty. I remembered it from my time living in Kerala. She did not remember the exact details of the festival, but tried to gather as much information she could from her own memory. I have elaborately described this festival in the female-centered rituals chapter, so I will omit it here. During my 3 years in Kerala, I saw this festival celebrated in my maternal uncle's wife's home, but neither my mother nor my grandmother ever forced or encouraged my sister and me to participate in this ritual. The younger sister of my aunt was unmarried and she made the Kama dolls, offered water, put flowers—she did everything. I would go to watch her. She did not know the deeper meanings of the festival, did it to get a good husband. I had no inclination to participate in a ritual that got me a good husband. I thought of myself as a modern and educated girl whose final destination was not being a good wife. My mother was aware of this, and she did not want that for me either, so this festival had no value for us. I feel differently now knowing it was about sexual empowerment in a woman. Sadly, there were not older women at the time to explain this to my mother or me.

> D: How come we never did any of this when we were in Kerala!

> M: I thought you did it when we were in Kerala. Maybe not! Even when we did it as children, my father used to get mad because for a particular flower we had to go to our neighboring home. Then grandmother in that house used to scream at us for plucking flowers from her tree. My father could hear that and then he would say, "Stop all this. For a Kaman here you don't have to go begging for flowers from other homes." And I think because of that and also, we growing up my mother stopped doing it.

During the interview, my mother did not recall if she celebrated this festival with us. However, later in a conversation she asked me, "Do you think you would have found this ritual meaningful then?" That is when it hit me that I would not have found it meaningful. She had known that and did not want us to feel forced to do it. She also explained that even in her days the social culture of Kerala was shifting. With property laws coming into place, and land getting distributed, people became more mean and selfish. They feared sharing with others, lest they did not have enough. I wanted to understand if my mother saw the meaning in these rituals.

> D: When you met papa, did you remember these rituals you did to get a husband?

> M: Not really. We never really made the connection. We did these rituals innocently. My mother was also so busy with six children. No one had the time to explain all the details of why we are doing the ritual. My grandmother died when I was very young so I don't remember spending any time with her. Usually your grandmother is the one to explain these rituals to you but my grandmother wasn't there to explain anything to me.

The loss of this tradition in our lives saddened me deeply. I knew it was time to step away from the female-centered rituals to the next question.

> D: Did you bathe with your maternal kin in a pond or kullam? What was it like? What conversations did you have? Were women shy around their nakedness or comfortable in their bodies?

This question was very important to me because I harbored a lot of shame around nudity and my body. I was keenly listening to my mother's response.

> M: I don't remember going to a pond or kullam to swim. But maybe sometime I went to our taravad kullam. I had gone there after my 10th to learn swimming. I tried few days but didn't learn. My father never said don't go or anything. I went alone to learn swimming. I think with my elder sister I went to the temple kullam to bathe for 41 days as part of a prayer. I don't recall us taking off our clothes. Women had a separate side, and it was a huge kullam and with the wet clothes on we went into the temple and prayed. There was no fear of boys or men passing comment or anything like that.

> D: Did you see women naked?

> M: Yes. It was all normal and natural. The conversations were normal just like usual. It was all very comfortable.

My mother's usage of the words normal and natural again and again fascinated me. Her responses seemed to be triggered naturally from within her body without the active participation of the mind or thinking or reasoning. However, in my case there was more reasoning involved in every action. I wanted to understand more about her relationship with her body.

> D: Was there any brassiere at that time?

> M: There was something called bodice which we would stitch at home . . . from white cloth, and we could tie it in front. I used to stitch it myself. Then we also learned to make straps and the tailor used to stitch it.

I was amazed to hear that women designed the garment for their breasts themselves. It was like designing clothes. Unlike me, they felt more connected to their breasts in a natural way. I never thought of my breasts as mine until a few years ago. They were something attached to me as opposed to being a part of me. I never looked at them or adored or touched them growing up, never even acknowledged them in an intimate way.

> D: When did you start wearing it?

> M: I never wore it until I was like 18 or 20 years old.

Now I understood why she never asked me to wear a brassiere so young.

> D: Was there any discomfort or shame in the body?

> M: There was nothing like that. It was all very natural.

My mother response was empowering for me. She spoke her words with confidence. I wanted to know if this awareness was reflected in her relationship with boys and men.

> D: How did the girls or women respond to the flirtatious advances of boys and men? Was talking to boys and men outside the taravad allowed?

> M: I don't remember any boys like that in the neighborhood. School was over for me at 10th grade. I got my periods after that. Only at functions or festivals we might have seen boys. I remember boys from my father's house that used to touch me. I remember one cousin like that. I think I got mad at the behavior. I never cared much for that. Sometimes I remember smiling back if I liked the person. That is all. It was all very innocent.

Her innocent response fascinated me, as it was so different from my experience with boys and men. My response, conditioned and clouded by the various images from media and magazines, had been far from natural.

My mother continued to share about boys and men in a way that she has never ever shared with us before.

> M: I remember there was this person who was the brother of one of our neighbors. He used to visit from out of town. Before my marriage, when I would be outside washing clothes, this person would stand there looking at me with a sheepish smile on his face. He would sometimes whistle standing there. I used to find that behavior very funny and wonder—"Is there a screw loose in his head?" I never gave it much importance.

Here is where the English language fails to express in its entirety my mother's response. She used the Malayalam word *illakkam* to describe the man's behavior. I translated it as a screw loose in the head, but that is not the literal meaning. The word is funny and the way she said it, my sister and I burst out laughing. We had never heard our mother speak like this before. She was basically telling us that she had been oblivious to what he was doing. I am sure this person from out of town was influenced in different ways of flirtatious behavior, such as whistling or winking at the girl, which was unfamiliar to my mother! I had always assumed these behaviors where natural instincts. Now it hit me that they were socially constructed through media, literature and other influences. My mother continued her sharing:

> M: Then there were these other neighbors. I really liked the men there. They reminded me of the Malayalam Film stars like Prem Nazir (famous Malayalam movie Actor) with great personality. They never misbehaved even once like staring or talking cheap or anything. I would always see them right next to our home. They were men of really good character. We never had occasion to talk about men or boys.

This is a direct indication of how Malayalam movies were beginning to influence the romantic fantasies of a young girl. Prem Nazir is the complete personification of the ideal romantic hero—the gentle lover, ideal husband, son and brother. He never mistreats women, never cheats on his lover—the perfect man. My mother must have only seen a handful of movies, but they had already begun to influence her expectation of men. I wanted to know if physiologically she experienced any changes in her sexuality, and if that influenced her interactions with boys or men.

> D: Did you experience feelings in your body or hormones or anything during adolescence? Feeling love. Feeling attracted to someone!
>
> M: No. I never experienced anything like that. We were often told not to speak unnecessary with boys or flirt with boys so there was no such occasion to engage with boys. It felt like having no discipline to engage in activities like that. I would often hear my father scolding people . . . his sister's children . . . for engaging in activities like that. Everyone feared him . . . even in the village . . . women engaging in unnecessary activities with men . . . he would speak angrily about that.
>
> D: So in the culture you grew up, was sex or women enjoying sex seen as something bad.
>
> M: Do you mean before marriage?
>
> D: Doesn't really matter.
>
> M: Before marriage maybe . . . after marriage I never felt like that.

Apparently, a girl was able to freely engage with boys before reaching puberty, but after that, her sexuality was the taravad's most important asset to attract potential suitors, who brought with them honor and prestige for the taravad. A woman's sexuality was therefore guarded and protected by the men in the family. In the marumakkathayam practices of earlier times, sexuality had been a private affair, taking place in the darkness of night, inside the inner compartments of the taravad. Every time a Nayar woman went out of her taravad, older men or women accompanied her. With education, modernization, and a concept of equality with men, girls stepped out into the public domain, demanding the right to engage with men publicly, and a new social culture began to emerge which was not held in high regard by men like my grandfather. For the first time, I have begun to see that their strictness might have been more out of respect and protection for the women. I cannot say that it was true for all men, but it might have been true for my grandfather and men of his generation. I wanted to know if the strictness around her sexuality influenced her relationship with it.

> D: Did you experience shame around the body growing up? Because I had that experience.
>
> M: I never had that experience. Never. Even after the marriage. Feeling shy was there but there was no shame. Like if we women had to change dress together, I felt shy but no shame.

I was in awe of this response and told her, "I never had that experience."

> D: Did you see women not wearing anything on top?
>
> M: Yes, there were older women. They would just have a thin muslin cloth loosely thrown over the upper body. Women who were like 60 years or older!

It hit me that my mother was 60 years old right now. I wanted to reflect that back to her and see her response.

> D: Like your age now, correct!
>
> M: Yes.
>
> D: There was no problem in the culture.
>
> M: No. Sometimes children would be playing with their breasts. They would not be scolding them or anything. It was not a problem. It was quite normal.

Simultaneously, my sister and I started laughing on hearing this. I think we both had a picture in our head of grandmothers doing chores, while their grandchildren are playing with their exposed breasts. If I saw something like this today, how would I respond to it? I have no idea. But it sure has expanded my thinking around nudity and shame.

> D: Was eroticism or flirtatiousness encouraged or seen as something wrong?
>
> M: It was not like you can't do that, but somehow it was about discipline. That is what I would think.

I was really curious to know how this discipline was enforced.

> D: Even if no one directly told you, you must have heard or observed about the discipline in the culture, right!
>
> M: Yes. "Girls shouldn't go and flirt with boys," I would often hear my father say that. Even with my male cousin when we were overly free and laughing, my father has asked "Why [do] we need to be so overly flirtatious?" My mother never said anything. It was always my father.

I wondered about the mother or grandmother's role in educating the daughters into self-discipline around sexuality. How did they guide their daughters into safe guarding their sexuality from unwanted visitors, or the reverse—attracting those whom they wanted to be with?

> D: Flirtatiousness was not a value encouraged in the culture. Women talking freely with men were not seen as a positive thing, right!
>
> M: Yes. It was strict that way.
>
> D: Was this the same for all women from all castes?
>
> M: No. Women who were from low castes, they had lot of freedom. They even had instances of women finding partners on their own and getting married. The men in those homes weren't too strict. They didn't have too much discipline enforced on them.
>
> D: Was it true for all your Nayar friends?
>
> M: Yes. As far as I can remember! Some of my friends were connected to the temple, some were Tamil Brahmins—they all had a lot of discipline about their interactions with boys. Everyone had discipline, even the Ezhavas. I feel there was more freedom in the Harijan (considered a lower caste in India) community.

The upper castes had the need to control female sexuality to maintain caste purity and purity of the offspring. However, lower caste women paid a heavy price for their freedom in the form of sexual exploitation by men from the upper castes. I could see that formation of the caste system had deeply influenced the freedom of women irrespective of strata of castes they belonged to.

> D: Did girls have the freedom to choose their life partners?
>
> M: Not really, but then their opinion was asked and it was listened to. If they didn't like the guy they could say that. We trusted that our parents wanted our best. I never felt that the parents just wanted to get the daughter married off.

Within the framework of maintaining caste purity, then, the Nayar woman still had the right to say no if she did not like her suitor, and her decision was supported most of the time. Surely, this could only happen because daughter was not seen as a burden, but rather as a valuable asset and propitiator of the lineage.

> D: Did you experience the emotion of *sringaram* in your life? Was their encouragement in the arts like music or dance?
>
> M: In my family there was nothing like that. But when I came with your father, I felt there was more encouragement for all that and even the feelings of sringaram came with your father.

Sringaram is the word closest to sensuality that I have been able to find. It was wonderful for me to hear that my mother found more freedom in her womanhood with my father. I was still wondering about my grandfather's first marriage, which was a sambandham practice.

> D: Could you talk about your father's first marriage?
>
> M: My father had a son in his first marriage. He used to visit this house, which had these beautiful women. There he liked one of the women in that taravad. So he decided to have a sambandham with the woman there. He used to visit her often. She became pregnant and had a son through him.
>
> D: Do you know when was that?
>
> M: Maybe 90 years from now that son must have been born. During his relationship with that woman, my father somehow came to know that the woman was having a relationship with another man. That day my father walked out of that taravad and left that

woman. He never went back to visit her after that. Her son really disliked my father, because my father never did anything for that son of his. That taravad was very rich and prosperous, so they weren't dependent on my father anyway. I think after some time that woman married someone else. That was how my father was. We never had a relationship with that brother.

One of the great granddaughters from this family is currently a famous Malayalam film actress. That is why that relationship has resurfaced in our family. I hope I can reinitiate the relationship back with that family and heal the wounds of the past. My mother was beginning to get restless about dinner and other things that she needed to do, so I decided to step into the final question:

> D: Have you noticed a change in the images of female sexuality over the years?
>
> M: I feel today you have the freedom to think, as you want and also act as you want. We didn't have that.
>
> D: But you did say earlier that you had lot of freedom.
>
> M: Yes. I did. But I didn't have the freedom to go to college. For that we had to go in a bus far away with men. My father didn't want that for us. When my sister went to college, my father said, "Oh now! Boys and girls need to go in the bus together side by side touching each other." He was very opposed to that. You have that freedom. We don't know what you do or what your life is outside the home. You are allowed to do that. Your situations are different. What you do, and what you tell us—we don't even know if it is true! It is in your hand whether you want to take your life in a positive or negative direction. In our time, it was not like that!

It seems to me that although I had more freedom than my mother, the formation of my relationship with myself was unnatural and deeply influenced by the world—disconnecting me from my own wisdom and knowing. In my mother's time, paradoxically, although her freedom in the world was restricted, she naturally experienced her empowered self and matured into a woman—strong, compassionate, gentle, and wise. She guided me into that wisdom without using many words.

D: You never restricted us with anything.

M: I never thought like that. Your father also was very caring and loving. So my life was very nice. Everything was very good [she laughs]. Your father gave me so much freedom. He let me do things on my own without depending on him. Like when I was pregnant, first doctor visit he came with me. For all the subsequent visits, he would drop me at the doctor and then go back to work. Then I had to do everything on my own. But most men are not like that. They made their wives completely dependent on them.

D: You interacting with other men also papa had no objection, right!

M: Yes. There was nothing like that.

Since I had not experienced this freedom in my own marriage, which was a problem, I wanted to make sure that my mother appreciated this freedom she had:

D: Not every woman has that freedom.

M: Yes. That is true. We were very mature. I used to feel very fortunate to be with your father. Imagine going into a house where I didn't know anyone. My sister had many problems like that. Your father's family was very nice to me. Your grandfather [my father's father] was very free. In the morning he would teasingly ask questions, like "Did you have a good night's sleep?" There was a lot of freedom, which I didn't have in my own house. My brother in laws inquired about me. I was never allowed to work. My mother in law never interfered in anything. I felt very fortunate! At the same time, my father in law was also strict. He didn't like anyone lying or deceitfulness in people. He would name it and call it out.

Now that we have had such a long discussion about the body and sexuality, I wanted to go back to my beginning question:

D: What is your relationship with body?

M: From a girl to a woman, becoming a wife, becoming a mother. It all felt very natural—a journey of maturing. There were no negative feelings around it. Every change seemed very close to nature and the earth!

In the last couple of years, I had arrived at the knowing that women's blossoming from a girl to a mother was closely connected to nature, and the earth. I never expected my mother to voice it so effortlessly, "Every change seemed very close to nature and the earth." I did not even know she was aware of this connection. It was a moment of such joy and accomplishment for me. I had begun with apprehension as to where this interview would lead, and it had ended beautifully. I could see the pride in my mother's eyes and that she appreciated this whole process, which had brought us together in a beautiful way. In a couple of days, we would be making our trip to Kerala to interview the grandmothers.

CHAPTER 15.

MADHAVI AMMA
THE FADING GRANDMOTHER

Figure 2: Madhavi Amma (center) sitting with her daughter (on right), her nieces and my mother (leftmost)

Madhavi Amma (see Figure Above), was the first grandmother interviewed, after meeting her at my maternal grandmother's *taravad* where I went to witness the ancestral ritual. Although this was my first time attending this ritual, my relatives spread across lineages of seven generations were arriving from different directions for this occasion.

Madhavi Amma, the oldest living *karnavrathi* (wife of the karnavar) of the *taravad* arrived with her daughter and son. Madhavi Amma is tall and walks like a queen—upright and straight. Her big bright eyes shine with enthusiasm and light up on seeing familiar and unfamiliar faces. She seemed to know everyone present at the ritual, and those she did not know, she made it a point to meet. She wore the traditional off white Kerala saree. From a distance, I never would have guessed that she was nearing 90 years of age. Within moments of meeting her, I told her about my research and she was excited to be interviewed. Throughout the interview, she spoke with passion, her eyes lighting up as she remembered events from the past, her voice becoming louder. Sometimes she would her clap hands in excitement. She was completely centered in herself, unmoved by all the chaos around her. I enjoyed every moment I spent with her and her family.

Madhavi Amma grew up in a nuclear family with her father, mother, and three older brothers. Being the youngest daughter of her household, she was most loved and cared for in the family by her father and brothers. At the age of 14, she married the oldest son (23 years old) of a noble and well-known *taravad* called Kizhakke Pandarathil (K. P.). He had two brothers and a younger sister names Ammu, who was born after the *karnavar* of that *taravad* (her maternal uncle) had spent 20 years fasting and performing strict austerities. When *marumakkathayam* was in existence, in the absence of a daughter there was the possibility that the *taravad* and the property would change hands to the next female and her children in the lineage. Thus, Ammu was the favorite of everyone—especially her brothers.

When Madhavi Amma came by marriage into that *taravad*, Ammu was only 3 years old; her mother passed away when she was 7. Madhavi Amma, only 20 years old at that time, became a mother to Ammu, and also assumed the role of the *karnavarathi* for the entire *taravad*—a huge undertaking for a young girl. In due course, she had two children of her own—a son and a daughter. When her husband, the *karnavar* died, Madhavi Amma returned to her maternal home as was customary, and the Kizhakke Pandarathil *taravad* was given to Ammu *ammamma*, who had eight children—four sons and four daughters. Upon her death a decade ago, the main taravad and the adjoining property were divided among her children, most of whom lived on the property in separate homes. The main *taravad* house now belongs to her oldest daughter, Satyabhama. There is immense love and togetherness between Madhavi Amma's children, Ammu *ammamma*'s children, and the children of her siblings since they all grew up together in the *taravad*. Today, Madhavi Amma is the oldest living relative of that *taravad* and is treated with utmost honor and respect. Her presence is a must at every event or festival. I felt honored to meet her and hear her story.

I am maternally related to Ammu *ammamma* and the Kizhakke Pandarathil *taravad*. Four generations ago, the Kizhakke Pandarathil *taravad* had four daughters, one of whom was Ammu *ammamma*'s great great grandmother. The other three daughters were adopted into three different *taravads* spread across Kannur district. It was a common practice in those days within the Nayar matrilineal social structure to adopt young females from a different *taravad* when faced with the prospect of extinction of a lineage (de Tourreil, 2009, p. 207). One of the daughters adopted was my great great great great grandmother. We did not know about this until 4 years ago, when my mother's younger sister consulted an astrologer about the challenging marriages experienced by the daughters in our matrilineage—my great grandmother, grandmother, my eldest and youngest maternal aunt, daughters of my eldest aunt, and myself. The divination revealed that my matriliny had abandoned the ancestral mother of the lineage and her conscious absence had manifested as the withdrawal of auspiciousness and abundance from the daughters of her lineage. Since none of us knew of an ancestress that had been abandoned, my aunt had to do a lot of research; in the process she unearthed the fascinating story of adoption of my great great great great grandmother from the Kizhakke Pandarathil *taravad* into our *taravad*. For more than 200 years, the Kizhakke Pandarathil *taravad* housed an ancestral shrine for one of its *karnavars*. This *karnavar*, by way of his nobleness and compassion, was elevated to the status of the Gods. Every year the shrine witnessed a *theyyam* ritual in memory of this ancestor called the *Dharma Daivam theyyam*. It was customary for all the matrilineal kin connected to the ancestress of the original Kizhakke Pandarathil *taravad* to witness and participate in this *theyyam* ritual.

Theyyam is a powerful ritual performed mostly in the North Malabar region of Kerala that provides the sacred space for Gods and Goddesses to manifest themselves in the bodies of men and, in rare cases, women, and also to interact with their devotees. In case of the ancestor *theyyam*, the ritual brings a particular *karnavar* back to life in the body of the *theyyam* performer. Then the ancestor inquires into the welfare of every maternal kin—one person at a time—offering blessings, fulfilling wishes, and offering specific life wisdom to some. The entire family connected to the *taravad* comes together to witness this ritual. As part of my research, for the first time my mother, sister, and I all gathered (along with my maternal uncles and aunts) to witness this ancestral ritual at the Kizhakke Pandarathil *taravad*. Although I was meeting many of my family from the Kizhakke Pandarathil *taravad* for the first time, the comfort and familiarity I felt with the women, men and children at Kizhakke Pandarathil *taravad* was effortless. They knew my grandmother and all her children by name. The appearance of these women and men, and some of their mannerisms, reminded me of folks from my mother's family. I felt like I was waking out of sleep and continuing as though nothing happened.

The rituals for the *theyyam* began at 3 PM and were expected to go until 5 AM the next day. The main Dharma Daivam *theyyam* was to commence at midnight followed by the *taravad* Nageni Amma (the serpent mother of the land) *theyyam*. No one slept the whole night, although there were moments when I could not keep my eyes open. Many relatives were tired and took naps during the breaks. However, Madhavi Amma was awake and active throughout the ceremonies—moving around the house, talking to women and children until everything came to an end. Madhavi Amma was there only for the night so I had no choice but to do my interview that night in this most active and chaotic environment.

We had two hours before the commencement of the Dharma Daivam *theyyam*. One of the daughters of the *taravad* offered us her home for the interview. My mother, my mother's sister, my sister, and I accompanied the grandmother to the house along with five other women, the grandmother's daughter and four of Ammu *ammamma's* daughters. It was impossible to conduct this interview with any fewer women, and fortunately some of the other women chose to sleep instead. Once the interview began it was difficult to stop the women from prompting or talking or volunteering questions on their own. There was laughter, excitement, and uninterrupted chaos with everyone wanting to talk, share, and ask questions. As we all sat down for the interview, I was praying inside that the interview would proceed without interruptions, but as it turned out, the questions and prompting by the women were very helpful. They stepped in where I could not or did not remember or was hesitant to ask. They were all enthusiastic and supportive of my study and the entire atmosphere was celebratory.

I began by giving a brief description of my study—why I was doing it, how I arrived at the topic, and what it meant for women around the world. My mother helped me translate the topic of my study in Malayalam. I encouraged the grandmother to speak openly and freely, stressing that there was no right or wrong, good or bad answer, and that I was interested in her experience. Everyone was doubtful if the grandmother understood what I was saying. I asked her directly if she understood what I meant by *female body and sexuality*. She nodded confidently and even repeated it for me in her words. She knew exactly what I was talking about better than any of the women. With a prayer in my heart, I began:

> D: How did your relationship with your body and sexuality transform as you blossomed from a young girl into an adult woman?
>
> G: I was the youngest daughter in the family. I had three older sisters and two older brothers. I was the youngest. I was brought up with immense love and vatsalyam (meaning adoration). In the evenings my father would come home with a little alcohol. He would sit in the verandah. I would prepare Betel leaves and Arecanut and give it to my father. I would also make hot water for my father. That way after nicely pleasing my father [her eyes widened with excitement], I could ask him money for my school [she laughs mischievously, the other women joined in]. I studied till eighth grade. There was lot of necessities in the school, which needed money. If I directly ask for money, no one would give me. So by nicely pleasing my father, he would give me money. Like in school the cloth man would bring cloth for everyone. The teacher would cut the cloth and give it to every student. So I needed money to buy my share of the cloth. I could give the money only if I got it from home.

Just this introduction told me a lot about this grandmother. At such a young age, she had been clever, smart, and skillful in her dealings, and most importantly, she was brutally honest and fearless. She did not care about the responses of the other women, because her daughters and nieces found everything she said extremely amusing and were hysterical. Madhavi Amma continued uninterrupted.

> D: Ammamma, how old were you then?
>
> G: I must have been like 10 years old.
>
> D: Ammamma, were you living in your father's house then?
>
> G: Yes. I was with my father—my father and mother.

This is when I realized that Madhavi Amma was living with her father, and not in her mother's home like in the *marumakkathayam* system. It was different from my maternal grandmother who grew up in her mother's *taravad* without the constant presence of a father. Her maternal uncle had been the strongest male presence in her life. I asked Madhavi a*mmamma* about it.

> D: So ammamma, you were not living in your mother's house like in the marumakkathayam system.
>
> G: No. I was living with my father.
>
> W: Amma's father and mother came from another town by selling all their property there. Then it was only her mother, her father, brothers and sisters living together.

Madhavi Amma answered each question and waited for my response. Her answers were concise and to the point with no extra information provided. I appreciated the presence of the other women because they elaborated on her answers.

> D: You didn't have any relationship with your mother's home?
>
> G: No. I didn't. I never even visited that village.
>
> D: How come you didn't have any relationship with your mother's family?
>
> G: My father married my mother. Then my mother had us. My father brought some land, built a house and we all lived there.
>
> W: In those days, there was no means of proper transportation. Traveling was difficult especially for women.
>
> W: Women never went outside their taravad. So once someone moved away it was difficult for the family to visit or stay in touch.
>
> W: It was a different time from now.

The women's responses were giving me an idea about Kerala of the past without modern amenities like car or buses. I also realized that I needed to start asking explicit questions to get more explicit answers.

> D: Ammamma, do you remember participating in any female-centered rituals? Can you describe what they were like? How did you feel?

Malayalam language is tricky when translated from English. Grandmother first looked at me kind of confused, until the women prompted her with the names of the female centered rituals around first blood, *vayasu-ariyikucha* (meaning age or *vayasu,* made known or *ariyikucha*) ceremony. Grandmother nodded in understanding and continued:

> G: Yes. I had the ceremony around 13 or 14 years of age. It was when I was studying in school. That time there was a dance program in my school. I was in that program. Because of that the school sent the peon to my house to inquire why I didn't show up for school
>
> W: [Explaining to me] Because for 4 days she didn't go to school.
>
> G: [In a complaining tone] And because of that everyone came to know[all the women start laughing].

I learned that grandmother had her first blood around 13 or 14 years of age and in those days, the 4-day rite of passage ritual associated with the first blood was perceived to have far more learning potential than education; school was more like a pastime. Yet I found it interesting that Madhavi Amma was upset about everyone in her school knowing about her bleeding. Was it shame that I sensed in everyone knowing! Did she enjoy the ritual of *vayasu-ariyikucha* or did she see it as something that took her away from her school and friends? I was curious to find out.

> D: Ammamma, do you remember the rituals they did during that time?

All the women started asking her to explain.

> G: Yes. I do.
>
> D: Could you tell me about it?
>
> G: That time without touching you were made to sleep comfortably in a separate room. In the morning, in an urulli there was kept rice,

and water and then there is something called vallukannadi (long handled brass mirror) that which the theyyam uses. With that they stirred the urulli, which was kept on a thira (a wooden stand). Then they kept the Nellu Katir (fresh flowers of paddy) on the center of my head [she points toward her head] and they sprinkled water.

D: Was this done at the end of 4 days?

G: This was done on the first day as soon as it was known that the girl is menstruating. Then without having to feel hunger, I was fed my favorite foods.

Grandmother's description did not have a beginning or end. It had been over 7 decades since she had experienced her menarche ritual. She spoke about it like it had just happened yesterday—easily and casually without too much thought. However, her choice of words fascinated me—she was "made to sleep comfortably" and "without having to feel hunger" was fed her favorite foods—clear indications about the positive influence of these rituals that provided the girl with the best care physically, mentally, and emotionally—preparing her for womanhood, which would be followed by motherhood. I was wondering if sleeping in a separate room was scary for her.

D: So ammamma, all throughout you were in a separate room, right? [she acknowledges with a nod]. Was there someone with you during that time?

W: Were you allowed to play with other children or eat with others during that time?

G: I could neither play nor eat with others during that time. I was alone in the room.

I was wondering how she felt about it, when the grandmother's daughter began to speak excitedly:

W: [To me] Ask her on what she slept. [Before I could respond, she asks ammamma] Amma, on what did you sleep?

G: I slept on the sheet.

W: [Reminding the grandmother] Amma, you did not sleep on the sheet!

G: It was a hay mat.

W: Amma, don't you remember they put fresh paddy on the floor and then they put the hay mat on top of it?

G: That is correct. They put the fresh paddy along with rice on the floor. Then the hay mat was placed on top of it. A fresh sheet then covered the hay mat. I slept on top of that.

W: [To me] I remember that from my own memory. They did that for me too. Did you have a bath during that time?

I was going back and forth between the grandmother and the women—trying to catch every piece of conversation, excited and amazed, my heart in deep gratitude to these women. Their cross-questioning helped the grandmother share the finer details of the ritual. Paddy (rice in its husk) is the most auspicious grain for the Keralites and is considered to be Bhagawathi (the Goddess) herself. But the paddy husk pricks and irritates the back. I wondered what it must have felt like sleeping on a mixture of paddy and rice! Was it teaching the girl qualities of perseverance and patience? I was surprised that there was no thought of polluting the rice by the menstruant's touch and it felt more like an exchange of auspiciousness from the paddy to the menstruant and from the menstruant to the paddy. I only arrived at this knowing during the transcription process, and somehow I never got around to asking the grandmother or the women about it later.

D: Did anyone sleep with ammamma?

G: Yes. Yes. Someone slept with me on the other side.

W: [Making it clear] Without touching her, someone slept with her in the room.

D: Who slept with you ammamma?

G: My mother slept with me.

> D: Your mother slept with you?
>
> W: No one slept with her. Her mother slept away from her, without touching her by laying a hay mat next to her.

The women were speaking as though they had been present. I appreciated their comments, which came from their personal experience, since this ritual had continued into the present generation with Madhavi Amma's granddaughters and grandnieces also observing the first blood ritual in its entirety. I wanted to understand the feelings of a young girl made to sleep alone for the first time.

> D: Ammamma, when you were made to sleep like that for 4 days, what feelings did you experience?
>
> G: [In a surprised tone] What feelings?
>
> D: Were you scared because of all the rituals, ectera? Did they tell you anything as to what was happening?
>
> G: No one told me, but I was given good food to eat [her eyes sparkled as she spoke about food].
>
> D: Were you happy then?
>
> G: [Nodding her head in agreement] Yes. Yes.
>
> W: That time she was given extra care.
>
> G: [Excitedly] They made nice neyyi-appams for me to eat.

Her eyes lit up as she spoke about the *neyyi-appams*, a deep fried red sweet delicacy made of rice flour, jaggery, coconut and spices, which happen to be one of my favorite Kerala sweetmeats as well. I could imagine how excited I would be about my menarche if I were going to get hotly prepared *neyyi-appams*. The women continued adding details to the ritual:

> W: During that time, there would also be an oil lit nellavillakku burning continuously without extinguishing in her room, next to her head, near the hay mat.

> G: [Acknowledges and then points to the woman speaking and says] She knows that because we did the ceremony for her as well.
>
> D: So was there a lamp burning all the time in the room, ammamma? [Ammamma nods "Yes"]
>
> W: From the day the girl gets her periods to the fourth day morning when she is taken for her ritual bath, the oil lamp is burning continuously in the room. Then she is taken for the bath amidst all the women ululating.

The lighting of a lamp signifies auspiciousness and purity. It marks every major (birth, marriage, death) and minor (daily in the prayer room, birthdays, naming ceremony, honoring a special guest or saint into the house) occasion in the family. A lamp burning continuously by the side of a menstruant signifies the death of one phase of life and the birth of another, and it raises the menstruant to the status of the goddess, protecting her and warding off evil energies. The women were getting animated and could not stop themselves. I had to contain my excitement and continue calmly:

> W: Amma, tell her about that? On the fourth day when they took you to the kullam (or pond), what were the rituals?
>
> G: On the third day night, we had a special ritual ceremony. For every house or taravad there is a Thiyyan (a special caste). He would pluck fresh tender coconut leaves and a whole fresh kola (bunch or groupings) of coconut blossoms from the tree. He would come and give it to the taravad.
>
> W: The kola of coconut should not be open. The flowing coconut kola will be still within its cover. Then these will be kept in the room.
>
> G: And then next day, my ammayi (maternal uncle's wife) will be walking in front with an oil lit nellavillakku in her hand followed by me with a kindi of water in my hand. We will be walking toward the kullam. Any women we meet on the way, we would give them coconut oil. We will pour it for everyone on the way.
>
> D: Who will pour it?
>
> G: The women will pour the oil on their heads.
>
> W: Amma, who does all that?

A: [Turns around look at her seriously] What do you mean who will do that? There will be other women walking with us [everyone starts laughing].

W: There will be 2 to 3 women walking with the girl carrying the oil. One would be the Ammayi (maternal uncle's wife) with the oil lamp in front. Behind her will be the girl and then following the girl will be another woman carrying the hay mat on which she slept. That needs to be washed too. As they are walking they will be making sounds (ululate) announcing to everyone that their daughter has reached her age[as though remembering everyone starts laughing together].

W: It is like announcing to everyone "I have become a mature girl now." I think that was the meaning behind it.

W: Using the fresh tender coconut leaves, they made earrings, bangles, and necklace for the girl to wear. Even something beautiful for her hair.

W: They adorn the girl with all this and then take her to the kullam.

G [agreeing]: Yes. They made all that using the tender coconut leaves (called Kuruthola). Once at the kullam (pond), the jewelry is removed, broken into pieces and thrown into the kullam.

G: [Remembering]And then they also take the closed coconut kola (or blossoms) with them.

As the women described the ritual, I was transported to a different time. Although I wanted to soak in every detail of the ritual and not miss anything, I could not keep up with all the information the grandmother and the women were sharing. It was only later when I transcribed the interview that I realized the depth of their sharing. Many of the nuances shared by the women were unlike anything I had read in writing. I have described them in greater detail in the chapter on female-centered rituals. While the interview was happening, I only wanted to listen without wanting to ask any questions. I let the women continue with their questions to the grandmother. They knew the direction to take and I let them.

W: [Encouraging a response from the grandmother] Why were they taking the coconut kola or the coconut blossoms?

G: Once they reach the kullam (pond), one of the women would hit the kola on the ground several times. Then they open it and see how many young coconuts blossoms are still there inside. If there is nothing inside, they think this girl is going to be barren [some women scream their disapproval at this and some burst out laughing]. If there were some small coconuts still present in the kola, they would count it. That would be the number of children the girl will have in the future. Then everyone would tease the girl about it. After that the women will place a tamarind branch (pulli-kombu) on the ground and ask the girl to identify it. When the girl identifies it correctly, the women teasingly tell her, "Always remember to catch the branch of a tamarind tree and not that of a mango tree."

W: [Seeing my blank look, they explain] The branch of a mango tree breaks easily while the branch of a tamarind tree is very strong and it doesn't break easily.

W: [Continuing to explain] So, it means catch a nice handsome strong able Nayar man for yourself [Women laugh together, there is a lot of excitement in the room].

G: [Continues amidst all the chaos unaffected] And when you return back to the taravad, in the courtyard there would be urulli, rice, water, kindi, and hay mat.

W: [Making it clear for me] They have now come back after the ritual bath.

G: [Continues] You are made to sit there. They put the nellu kadir (paddy with husk) on the girl's head and pour water. Put the kadir on the head and pour water [Grandmother uses her hands to demonstrate the action she was describing]. Then they put water in the rice and put thumba flowers in it. Then they see which side of the urulli the thumba flowers move toward. If it moves toward south, it is not considered good. East, West and North directions are good. Sometimes even north is not good. And then they take that rice inside and cook it.

W: And with that rice filled in the urulli they make chakkarapongal (a sweet dish made with rice and jaggery) with jaggery.

> M: [My mother speaks for the first time] Like payasam (meaning of a watery consistency)?
>
> W: Not payasam. It is made really thick . . . and then it is given to the girl.
>
> G: [Continues] Once it is made, they take some out and keep aside for me [here she means the menstruant]. The remaining is kept aside closed. In the morning it is opened and looked at [Ammamma bursts out laughing reminiscing the past, all the women laugh loudly, I was beginning to wonder about the joke]. If the rice groups to one side, it is said the girl will have a son. If it is in the center, it is said that the girl will have a daughter. Nowadays there is nothing like that.

I was listening deeply to every word as if it was happening to me. I felt elated and uplifted just listening to the entire narration. I wanted to know if grandmother was elated and thrilled about everything at the time when it happened to her.

> D: Ammamma, what were your feelings around all this? What was going on inside you when all these rituals were happening? Were you happy?
>
> G: [Eyes round up] Happy!
>
> W: Yes. Yes. She is very happy.

For a moment, the grandmother seemed surprised that I was interested in her feelings as a young girl in the ritual. The other women were prompting her to say yes. There was chaos in the room, but I wanted to hear the grandmother's truth without the women pushing her. This was a moment to speak out and shush the extra noise in the room.

> D: Please let ammamma speak! No one speak now. I need ammamma to share what was happening to her [all the while ammamma is looking at me with wide open eyes and appreciation].
>
> G: You feel pity and sorry . . . everyone coming to know about all this . . . all the students in the school knows about it . . . it was a matter of shame.

There was sadness in her voice suggesting she was embarrassed and ashamed among her friends because of this ritual. I wanted to understand her response.

> D: Why was it a matter of shame, ammamma?
>
> G: Then with all this . . . it is kind of bad to go to school and everything . . . and because of that…

I could sense that she really felt embarrassed to go back to school because word had spread and everyone knew about it. I sensed the familiar feeling of facing embarrassment and ridicule in the eyes of the boys in my class. I was wondering if it was the school environment and the modern education that introduced *shame* around menstruation. Sensing her discomfort, I did not probe this further. However, I wanted to know what coming of age meant for a girl. In my mother's story, she was pulled out of school. What happened to Madhavi *ammamma*?

> W: Will they stop school because of this? Will they let the girl continue studying?
>
> G: No. After periods in most Nayar homes, the girls would stop going to school. But
> I went [she declares proudly]. Usually they wouldn't send her to school.
>
> W: How did you go then?
>
> G: I went [she declares confidently].

Madhavi *ammamma's* response was so confidant like she was saying; "Who do you think could have stopped me from going to school." I could not stop from smiling and could imagine the young Madhavi Amma coaxing her father to let her go to school. It seemed to me that the women in the room did not know this about Madhavi Amma.

> D: No one told you that you couldn't go to school.
>
> G: [Questioningly] From my house? No! No one told me that.

> W: [Explaining]: See her life was with her father and mother. There was no karnavar or other relatives involved. So there was no one to stop her or tell her otherwise.

This was again interesting piece of information. The women were justifying this by telling me that Madhavi *ammamma* went to school because it was only her father who had to make the decision in her case instead of the *karnavar*. I know in my mother's case her father did not let her pursue education further. My grandfather was also a *karnavar*. Did his role as a *karnavar* influence that decision? Was it too complicated for men to switch between the roles of a *karnavar* and a father? It made me think that there was so much more to the events of the past. At the same time, I also realized that in many other parts of India, a daughter would never have dared to go and speak to her father about this.

> G: When I completed my eighth standard, I went to the municipality school to give the exam. But before my exam results came out, they got me married. All the girls who studied with me became teachers [she sounded disappointed].
>
> W: That day they only needed eighth grade to become teachers.

I could hear the disappointment in Madhavi *ammamma's* voice. It was like she dreamed to have a job and be independent. She did not contemplate marriage and it happened unexpectedly. I wanted to know more about this new phase of her life.

> D: Do you remember about your marriage and everything? Did you see or know the groom before marriage
>
> G: The groom was from our village only.

I did not know if that meant she knew the groom or she did not.

> D: Did you see the groom or did anyone ask you whether you liked the groom?
>
> G: No way! No one ask such things [she looks astonished at the question] . . . It didn't matter . . . father and karnavar decided. I had a friend. All the boys in my class told my friend that the boy I am marrying was a drunkard, and that he would beat me up. My friend

was concerned. She came and told me about it. I told her, "What can I do? I can only listen to whatever my father and uncle's decide." I couldn't say anything.

W: During those days, they wouldn't allow the girl to see the boy. The father or karnavar would see and decide.

I felt sad to know that the grandmother had no say in her own marriage. It was quite unlike my mother's experience. I could not believe that someone as powerful as she was could not have pulled out of a marriage not to her liking. These statements from the grandmother had caught everyone's attention. There was considerable seriousness in the room, as everyone listened intently. One of the women broke the ice by asking the next question, and I am so glad she did.

W: [To grandmother] Where you scared before marriage?

G: Scared? Why should I be scared?

W: Because you were told he was a drunkard.

G: So what! He would only hit me one day. The next day do you think I will be there for him to hit me again?

Madhavi Amma's eyes had gotten big, her voice more pronounced, and her whole body had became animated as she responded. Her outright honesty was so empowering for all of us, I wanted to stand up and start clapping. Everyone in the room was excited and laughing and happy. It made complete sense to everyone why she would agree to the wishes of her father and *karnavar*. If she did not like the groom, she had the complete freedom to show up at her natal house the following day. Her response shifted the seriousness from the room, and everyone burst out laughing. It made me realize that the grandmother was not at all scared or even sad. She was quite amused at our laughter and joy at her response. She sat grinning and looking at all of us while we laughed in sheer wonderment. I wanted to make sure if I got her right.

D: So if you came back home, there would be no problem?

G: No. There would be no problem.

D: So if the groom was not taking care of you, you had the freedom to come back home?

G: Yes. I did.

D: Today, so many girls don't have that freedom.

G: Yes.

D: Today, if a girl goes through a bad marriage, and she wants to come home, her parents ask her to stay back in the marriage and not to cause shame to the family. It wasn't the case with you, was it? You are saying that you had the freedom to come back.

G: Yes. Of course! And as a matter of fact my husband's home was in the same town as my mother's home.

It was empowering not just for me but also for all the women in the room to hear this response. Her confidence in herself was beyond anything I have seen in anyone in the modern generation. She was completely free of the religious dogma of the *husband-loving self-sacrificing wife*. When she said that her husband's home was in the same town, I just started laughing. What she meant was if I needed to leave my marriage, I could have just packed my bags and walked home. Unlike many families who get their daughters married of to another town or city, Madhavi Amma's father had chosen a groom from the same town.

Today, marriages in Kerala are an expensive affair. The dowry system is not visibly evident in North Kerala yet, the way it is in South Kerala. However, parents do lavish weddings for their daughters, because it is an opportunity for the girl's family to display their ability to give gifts to their daughter. Today, a girl's wedding showcases the prestige and economic stability of the girl's father, as opposed to the prosperity of her maternal *taravad*. This puts a lot of burden on the girl's father. From the amount of gold jewelry the girl is wearing to the chosen wedding hall to the car that drives the groom and bride to the bus that transports the guests to wedding hall to the garments worn by the men and women—everything makes it an expensive affair. I wanted to understand more about marriage through Madhavi Amma's days.

D: Was marriage in those days different from today?

G: Marriage was called Podamuri. Poda (Cloth) was what decided or fixed the marriage along with some money like 14 annas or 12 annas [anna is equivalent to 1/16th rupee or less than 1 cent].The men would bring cloth and then cut one piece for a mundu. That would be given to the bride to fix the marriage.

Marriages were simple and the transition to marriage not the grandest celebration, requiring only a piece of cloth for the bride for her *mundu*, and the marriage was considered fixed. This practice disappeared with the falling of *marumakkathayam* social organization.

W: [Teasingly] Did you love and marry!

G: Who knew what love was then? Shouldn't one reach the age to know that [meaning she was too young to know love].

W: How did you know when you saw him that you have seen the boy before that?

G: When I was told the name, wouldn't I know that!

D: Ammamma, did you know the person you were marrying?

A: [Shakes her head] Yes. I knew him.

The women were having fun teasing Madhavi Amma. She was quite perplexed by the questions about love like she could not see the connection between falling in love and marriage, and all the excited noises we were making around this connection. Somehow she was quite amused by our excitement.

D: How many years was he older to you?

G: He must have been 22 or 23 years old. I was 14 years old.

Only 14 years old—that really hit me hard. I was thinking of myself at that age. My mother's oldest sister had been married off at the age of 13. My grandfather regretted doing that and waited longer for all his other daughters.

> D: When you were 14 years old, you went through podamuri ceremony. Did it happen during day or night?
>
> G: In the night . . .

Interestingly, today, marriages happen in broad daylight.

> D: Okay. Then did you leave with the groom the same night to his house or did he stay at your house?
>
> G: He stayed at my house that night.

Although this practice is not common in my family, I became familiar with it when my sister got married. My brother-in-law's family still follows this tradition. It is closely connected to the *marumakkathayam* system where the groom spends the night at the girl's home. This was a practice favoring the daughter. I know from my own marriage it was one of the most difficult things for me to leave my entire family behind as soon as my marriage was done and go to the home of my in laws, where the only known person to me was my husband only because we had dated prior to marriage. I was so conscious of people sleeping in other rooms; I did not have a relaxed and comfortable first night. I missed my family terribly.

> W: That was how it was. If the next day the girl or the boy didn't like each other's company, they had the freedom to call it off. The karnavar would never object to this. It was considered normal in that way [Ammamma nods in acknowledgement].

Now, I could see the reason behind it. If after the first night the girl and boy did not like each other, then they could choose to part amicably. In that way, sexual compatibility was seen to be of great importance. That was the *marumakkathayam* practice. It seemed so open and modern in its thinking.

> W: So the guy who gave you the pudava (the cloth) stayed back with you, right? Were you scared?
>
> G: [With big eyes] My heart was beating.

Her response was so unpredictable and funny in Malayalam, everyone burst out laughing. The women wanted to tease her a little about this. It was fun to hear them ask the questions.

W: Why was your heart beating, Amma!

G: What would you do if you were closed into a room with another man, won't your heart beat?

Her responses were hilarious and the women continued to tease her. Madhavi Amma sighed and leaned back into her chair. The women said to her that every time she started talking about marriage, she got tired, and they asked her what happened inside that room. I realized that Madhavi Amma was just humoring all of us with a calm composure and the look of amusement on her face.

D: Ammamma, what happened then?

G: There was a hay mat in the room. I spread it out on the floor, snuggled and slept in it immediately.

Again it was the way she said it—we could not stop smiling. However it really made me contemplate myself in her situation. It would be so scary. For her more than fear, it was strangeness.

D: What happened to the groom then?

G: He came and slept on the cot. I slept on the floor.

D: Did you go back home next day?

G: Yes. Next day early morning we left to his house.

D: Then what happened? You left to his house . . . that is this house, right? You came to this house. What happened then?

G: He only had one little sister and three brothers.

D: How was the life then?

G: I lived.

W: What do you mean? Was it painful? Was it lot of work? Was it tough?

> G: There was a lady to help Amma (mother in law) in the house. When I came, she went back to her family so there was no one to help Amma.

At this point we were interrupted. The husband of that house where we were conducting the interview had returned. He was drunk and kind of agitated. We were asked to take our interview to another home because he needed to sleep. The women apologized to me for this disruption. I could see their embarrassment and sadness that I had to experience this. When we arrived at the new house, I decided to focus on the female centered rituals. I wanted to ask them about rituals that I had read and heard about.

> G: For thiruvathira, we don't eat any rice item. We would only eat wheat or lentil. We would wake up early morning, have a bath in the kullam and, then go to the temple. Then all the girls would dance the kai-kotti-kalli (meaning hand-clapping dance) in the courtyard.
>
> W: [Explaining] Kummi-Adi dance (another name for kai-kotti-kalli dance)!

Everyone started to ask *ammamma* to sing. Initially she refused beautifully —there is no equivalent language to translate her response in English. When we asked her again, sweetly, she sang a few verses, and then asked me if it was good enough? I responded yes, and she stopped. I wanted to know their understanding of the *thiruvathira* festival.

> D: What was the story behind thiruvathira festival? Did all the women participate in it—married and unmarried?
>
> G: Married not so much. It was mostly the young unmarried girls who celebrated thiruvathira. It was mainly celebrated for the young girls to get a handsome husband.

It was only when my chair pointed out that the girls prayed for a *handsome* husband versus a *wealthy* husband that I realized that I had never paid much attention to it. More than the *wealthy* status of the husband, the women prayed for someone who was handsome, playful, and sexual like Kamadevan. I also remembered that in Kerala parents take extra care to not get their daughters married to a family overly wealthy or poor in comparison to their own. The boy's family is supposed to be only a little prosperous than the girl's family, otherwise it is likely to create conflicts for the daughter in her new home.

> D: I read somewhere that the previous night of thiruvathira women applied oil to their hair and body and swam in the kullam. Did you do it also?
>
> G: Yes. We did it in the morning.

I could imagine women waking up early, applying oil and swimming together in the bathing pond. Then dressed in *mundu veshti* with jasmine flowers adorning their hair, they would dance in the courtyard. It was really beautiful to watch the women—very enticing and sensual. Sadly this festival is no longer celebrated. However, the *thiruvathira* dance has gained a lot of popularity in the last decade, having become the symbol of the Kerala people; it is performed at most public gatherings and in dance competitions. I also wanted to ask about the *pooram* festival, which celebrated Kamadevan, the lord of love and passion.

> D: Did you celebrate pooram for Kamadevan?
>
> G: Yes. We did that also for 9 days [she explained the time and the month as to when it happened].
>
> W: From 6 years onward, girls participated in it. This festival was mainly for girls who didn't have their periods yet. It was mainly for the girls to get a husband who is handsome . . . has a lot of style . . . like Kamadevan. It was done for 9 days.
>
> M: And then on the last day we would sing a song to Kamadevan.
>
> W: Amma, can you sing that song also?

Ammamma began to sing. I have included the verses of this song and its English translation in the literature review section.

> W: [Explaining] Usually we make pooram-ada (a steamed dessert made of rice and Jaggery) for Kamadevan and that is said to be his favorite. So it is like warning Kamadevan to not go to far away from us. The women at the Puthilla taravad will cheat you into

eating pooram-ada made with Palm fruit. So don't go to these women but come back early to us.

I transitioned to the third question:

D: [Next question] Ammamma, did you go to the kullam (pond) with your girl friends to swim and bathe?

G: Yes. I would go.

D: Did you go before and after the marriage?

G: After marriage you needed permission. Before marriage, I would go regularly. I would have a set of girls who would go together. All the girls would go and swim. If I go under on this side of the kullam, I would only come up on the other side.

She was really excited to talk about swimming. She seemed to be an expert. However, I was sad to hear that her swimming days ended with her marriage.

D: After marriage would you still go?

G: No. They won't allow.

W: But Amma weren't you washing clothes in the kullam every day.

It seemed that the women did not agree with Madhavi Amma's response and wanted to probe further.

G: But that was going to ambala (temple) kullam (meaning the temple pond).

This is when I understood what she meant by freedom. Her married home did not have a private bathing pond like Madhavi Amma had in her own home. So after marriage she had to go the temple pond and that was her frustration. The women started teasing her how she could not swim freely to her hearts content after she got married. I was glad for the women because I would never have thought of probing further and just assumed that the grandmother was forbidden from bathing in the pond. The women pursued the swimming further. They wanted to show me that the grandmother had a lot of freedom in her husband's home. So they took it upon themselves to explain to the grandmother what I was asking.

> W: Didn't you and ammayi (Madhavi Amma's sister in law) go to a pond and swim.

Ammamma nodded in agreement.

> W: [Continues explaining to ammamma] That is what she (pointing to me) is asking. She is asking if you went to any pond, not just your family pond. Did you go with women to the temple pond . . . wash your clothes . . . swim and come back?
>
> A: [Nods in agreement] Yes. I did that.

I could not help smiling.

> W: In those days, girls would wear a red konnam (undergarment the equivalent of an underwear). When they went to the kullam, the girls would take it off on the side and go to swim. Sometimes when they came back after swimming, it would be missing. Somebody would have stolen it [everyone laughs].

Konnam is a rectangular piece of cloth, which women and men wore underneath as underwear. It was worn inside the *onnara mundu*. I was fascinated to learn that the color of the women's *konnam* was red. The connections to the goddess, menstrual blood and so many others things immediately popped into my head.

> D: When women went to the kullam, would you take off your clothes and bathe?
>
> G: Yes.
>
> D: That time you wouldn't feel any shyness or shame?
>
> A: [With utter curiosity at my question] Why should I feel shame when I am having a bath?

She looked at me like she could not believe I asked that question. Everyone broke out laughing.

> D: Why should you be ashamed while bathing!

I just repeated her response just so that I heard myself say it and also, was curious to hear her response.

> G: Yes. You put water over your body and bathe. Till your shoulder you are in the water.
>
> W: Would you have a towel underneath?
>
> G: Around the waist . . . [gesturing toward her waist] yes.
>
> D: Not anything on top, right?
>
> G: Yes. We dip deep and then swim.

I could have cried in that moment. What freedom—to swim naked with other women without any feelings of shame or body image. It was something I had never experienced in my life.

> D: Seeing other women naked didn't bring any shame?
>
> G: Why! We were all women swimming together.

I wanted to kiss her for saying this. It was both beautiful and empowering for me to hear that.

> W: They were all the same. With her brother-in-law's wife and sister-in-law, she would go to bathe. The women would wash their clothes, swim a little, play a little and before the men came home, they returned.
>
> D: Is that right, ammamma?

Ammamma raised her eyebrows in excitement, nodded in agreement and acknowledged with a smile.

> D: Did women have freedom then? How did the girls or women respond to the flirtatious advances of boys and men? Was talking to boys and men outside the taravad allowed?

> W: The men of that time were not like men of today. Married women were treated with utmost respect. They wouldn't even look at them.
>
> D: How about women who weren't married?
>
> W: Even with women who weren't married, men wouldn't behave disrespectfully. Men had lot of discipline. There might be very few people who did things like that. The majority of men never bothered or even looked at women. Men won't even go where women were.
>
> G: Men and women had separate areas in the kullam.
>
> W: All women will be having bath with just a towel around their waist with nothing on top. Men won't even be looking at them from the men's side of the kullam. Women had nothing to fear. Nayar women especially were considered high in the caste and treated with utmost respect by everyone. Even if someone looked or said something to them, the men folk in the taravad would go and confront them. So no one dared do that.

The responses of these women deeply touched me, bringing tears to my eyes. I felt a deep respect for the men of earlier years. I could not help but wonder—what happened to our men?

> D: So it was safe for women then?
>
> W: Yes. It was really safe [Ammamma nods in agreement]. Women were treated with respect.
>
> D: Ammamma, in those days were women treated with respect?
>
> G: Yes. They were. But you also had to listen to what elders said.

There was a slight tone of complaint in Madhavi Amma's voice. She seemed to me a free bird who must have had to grow up fast into a woman and in the process, many of her wild playfulness might have been compromised. The women sensing the complaining tone had a few more questions for her.

> W: Amma, you were the eldest in the taravad, right? [Ammamma nodded]. So didn't all the women in the house listen to you?

> G: Yes. They did. Both the brother-in-law's wives were there at home. I couldn't say anything to the younger brother's wife, because my sister-in-law (husband's sister) was married into her house. It was an exchange wedding. With her I had to be careful.

This was a new piece of family gossip for the women, who were excited and started teasing grandmother about it. It seemed to me that the women had never heard Madhavi Amma acknowledge this before.

> W: The brothers loved their sister a lot, so it was important that she had no trouble in her husband's house. The brothers would go every day to see their sister at her house and for ammamma (Madhavi Amma), Ammu was like a daughter. She was born after many years.

> W: When this sister had a child, Ammamma (Madhavi Amma) asked her to leave her child with her and go back to her husband's house, so that she could take care of chores without worrying about her child. That is how close they were.

This reflected the relationship between women in the families, where there was so much closeness and caring for each other.

> W: When this sister, Ammu had her first daughter, ammamma's husband (Ammu's brother) announced the arrival of the baby saying: "It is a daughter. Ammu has given birth." There was so much excitement that the baby born was a daughter, that my uncle said that information first instead of Ammu giving birth.

Ammu *ammamma* was born in the *taravad* after 20 years of prayer and austerities so the birth of her daughter was a moment of delight in the family. Ammu *ammamma's* brother was so overwhelmed with excitement that he announced the gender of his niece prior to the information that his sister gave birth.

> M: Ammu herself was born after a long time. So when she had a daughter, it was exciting for the entire family.

> W: [Explaining] It was not only that. In those days, this entire property belonged to her, the daughter. So the birth of the daughter was most important.

> G: Women had lot of importance. She was given great care by her family and treated special!

The women were re-affirming the matrilineal heritage of Kerala and the status enjoyed by women living in that structure. I wanted to know if the women knew instances of *tali-kettu-kalyanam* (pre-puberty ritual).

> D: Ammamma, did you hear about tali-kettu-kalyanam in your time.
>
> G: No. I did not.
>
> W: It was there. Didn't Kovalan marry Kannagi at 4 years of age through tali-kettu-kalyanam?

Initially, I thought Kannagi was a family member they were talking about. Then I realized they were talking about the legendary Kannagi from the *Tale of an Anklet*. I wanted to know how these women knew about Kannagi, because my mother always thought that the Kannagi story had nothing to do with Kerala. I did not ask, because then it would have taken the conversation in a completely different direction. However, it would be fascinating to understand the foundation of their understanding.

> D: Did you have the freedom to ask or tell your brothers anything?
>
> W: No. Women didn't have that freedom.
>
> G: [Cutting them off] It was there. I had that freedom. I could ask for anything from my brothers and get it [everyone laughed at the confidence with ammamma spoke]. My eldest brother would give me anything I ask for.

Madhavi Amma's confidence spoke everything about the Kerala of an earlier time—the strong ties between brother and sister, and one of the primary responsibilities of the brother was ensuring his sister's happiness.

> D: You have seen so many generations pass by. What difference have you seen in the life of a woman from your time to present?
>
> G: Today girls have more freedom . . . they are happier. In those days we would shiver with fear. We had to listen to karnavar or father or mother. We had so much fear. We could not speak anything or say anything. It was like that. But today it is not like

that! Today you can ask or question anything. You can question the truth. In those days you couldn't ask anything.

That is another reality of yesterday: You never questioned your elders—*karnavar*, father or mother. Your life was in the hands of these elders, and it was sheer luck if you had elders who had your best interest at heart, versus that of the *taravad*. However, I also feel that in spite of the fear she speaks of, the daughter had the right to express herself. I was still wondering how a girl so young could take up so much responsibility.

> D: At such a young age, you had to take up so much responsibility. How could you do all that?
>
> G: You just do it. My husband's brother and sister were there. Whatever I asked they would do it. They would be ready to help me out. When I would be grinding the stone, the younger brother would hold in the center and push it to go faster. When I would pull water from the well, the younger brother will hold the end of the rope and run so that the water comes up faster. There was a lot of love. Everyone loved me a lot. We would finish our work fast and then all of us would go to the kullam to swim.

The devotion and love in these words really brought tears to my eyes. Living in a nuclear family we may have easier lives; however we are far from experiencing love in such a deep way.

> D: You were like a mother to everyone.
>
> G: [Sighs heavily] Yes but God should not give such a situation to anyone.
>
> W: There was so much work. They had so much property and rice cultivation. She had to take care of everything around that.

I could totally see what she meant, that even for a young girl, in spite of all the love, it was back breaking work.

> D: Was there any romantic relationship between husband and wife then? Could they speak freely?
>
> G: No. Nothing like that!

> W: From morning 5 AM you wake up, you are working till 10 PM or midnight and in between that is when you see your husband. In that little time, they created nine children. [everyone starts laughing].
>
> W: In those days, a wife was just a means of creating children. There was no love or freedom like today between husband and wife. Sometimes when the children are crying at night, the husband will ask the wife to take the child and go and sleep elsewhere so he could sleep peacefully.

The women were really vocal about this. I could sense in their voices that they were glad to be in this era. Grandmother shared something immediately after that gave me a different perspective to her life. Her sharing emphasized how much she cherished her life in her mother's home.

> G: There was this one time when all the family members from our taravad and the neighboring taravad arranged a bus and went to watch a movie in the neighboring town. This was before my wedding.
>
> W: [Teasingly] That time the groom was also in that bus.
>
> G: Yes. His family was also in the bus.
>
> W: [Teasingly] Ah! So you both went to see a movie [everyone joins in].
>
> G: I didn't even know him then.
>
> W: We tease her that she had a love marriage. She fell in love with the boy in the bus.
>
> G: They are just joking.
>
> W: Did he ever take you for a movie after the marriage?
>
> G: No. Never.
>
> W: Women in those days never went with their husbands. They would go with other women. At that time, a male escorted them to the theatre and back.

There was a lot of laughing in the room. The women were vocal and excited. I wanted to understand how the grandmother felt speaking about yesteryears.

> D: What are your feelings at the end of this interview with remembering the past and everything?
>
> G: Not a good feeling. Those were really tough times. Makes me sad remembering those days!

There was sadness in her tone. She was not very happy remembering the past. I think maybe Madhavi Amma had many dreams—studying, working, and experiencing the independence of the modern day. However, her life turned into something completely different, and it was hard work. She did not have any time for herself. However, I feel her strength, confidence, and grandeur that come from that experience and give her so much depth. She is healthy, strong and mobile. I am sure her life experience has a lot to do with it. I have so much respect for her. I am in awe for her life, and at the same time I am also grateful for the life I have now and the freedom I enjoy as a woman.

It was well past midnight when I completed the interview. I clicked few pictures of the women together. Then we helped *ammamma* get up and went to the *taravad* house to watch the *theyyam*. I felt more connected and fuller walking toward the *theyyam,* close to all these women whom I did not even know a few hours ago. When I went to bid Madhavi Amma good bye the next day, she looked straight into my eyes and asked with a smile, "If you hear that I have passed away, will you drop everything and come see me off?" With tears in my eyes, I said, "Yes." I hope she is there when I visit Kerala next time.

CHAPTER 16.

MEENAKSHI AMMA
THE FADING GRANDMOTHER

Figure 3: Meenakshi Amma with her great granddaughter (leftmost) and two of her grandchildren

I have known Meenakshi Amma (see Figure Above) all my life, as my father's older brother is married to one of her daughters; she is also my paternal grandfather's niece. All the women in her family are enterprising, open and free and she is the glue that keeps the entire matriliny together. She has hardly left the perimeters of her property during her 75 years and yet; she exudes deep knowing, strength and wisdom. In the last 4 decades, she seems not to have aged at all. When I thought of grandmothers to interview, Meenakshi Amma was a natural choice, and she consented enthusiastically.

My grandfather had five sons and no daughters. His second son, Vijay Kurup, married Meenakshi Amma's second daughter, Thangamani. Through the interview I learned that my father's paternal grandfather and Meenakshi Amma shared the same matriliny. Her daughters were treated like daughters in my father's home. In fact based on the tradition of *marumakkathayam*, the children of a brother-sister pair were encouraged to marry each other, partly to keep the inheritance and wealth within the family. It was my grandfather's wish that one of his son's marry one of Meenakshi Amma's daughters. Children from both the homes grew up playing with each other, swimming together and sharing a deep closeness, which I recalled from stories I had heard my father tell about the closeness of the families. In my childhood, I remember spending a lot of time with Meenakshi Amma's youngest daughter, Leela and her youngest, son, Chandran, both young unmarried students at the time, who visited my grandparents' home almost every day.

Meenakshi Amma was born in the prosperous Kommathu Vennappalan (K. V) *taravad* in the city of Vadagara in the neighboring district of Kozhikode. She lived for a few years with her mother and maternal uncle in Seemancheri (another city in Kozhikode district), treasured as the only daughter. Her first blood ceremony was celebrated elaborately at her uncle's home, immediately after which, at the insistence of my father's paternal grandfather, Dhairu Kurup, the *karnavar* of the Kommathu Vennappalan *taravad*, she moved to Taliparamba (Kannur district) with her mother. This was because he was her grand uncle, meaning she was his sister's daughter's daughter, and on his deathbed, he sent for his sisters and their families, including Meenakshi Amma's mother, grandmother, and all the children and grandchildren, to come to Taliparamba. As they were his matriliny, he gave them property and settled them there. Thus Meenakshi Amma grew up with her mother, grandmother and brothers in Taliparamba, which became their new *taravad*. Meenakshi continued to stay with her mother even after her marriage, and today most of her children continue to live with her on the same property with their families. Meenakshi Amma was also related to me through my paternal grandfather, Gopala Kurup.

My paternal grandfather, Gopala Kurup, was the eldest son of Dhairu Kurup through his first wife in Vadagara. In those days, it was considered a bad omen for the women of Vadagara to cross the river and come to Kannur following marriage. So when Dhairu Kurup left Vadagara to work in the Kannur judicial system and bought land and property in Taliparamba, settling there, his first wife and children stayed in Vadagara. Since his work required him to spend long periods of time in Taliparamba, his wife gave him the customary easy consent to enter into *sambandham* marriage there; eventually he had *sambandhams* with two women there. However, he was very attached to his oldest son, Gopala Kurup (demonstrating the switch in the matrilineal system) and brought him to Taliparamba to look after most of his earned property. Gopala Kurup also worked in the judicial system, and it was he who had sent word for Meenakshi Amma's family to come to Taliparamba, Dhairu Kurup having made him responsible for Meenakshi Amma's family when they moved to Taliparamba. Since then my grandfather and his family have been close to Meenakshi Amma and her children. Every visit to my grandfather's home included a visit to Meenakshi Amma's home, which was within walking distance.

Meenakshi Amma, who is the oldest living female of her matriliny, continues to live in the same home in Taliparamba. Her oldest daughter, Sarojini and her son live in the main house. The property around the main house has been divided among the children and everyone has built homes on their respective properties. Sarojini Chechi's only daughter lives on one side of the property with her only daughter (Meenakshi Amma's great granddaughter). Meenakshi Amma's youngest daughter who is married to my uncle, as well as her youngest son, also lives on the property with their family.

We conducted the interview in Meenakshi Amma's granddaughter—her daughter's daughter's—home in the morning, when the men of the household were at work. Meenakshi Amma's two daughters, one of her granddaughters, her 3-year-old great granddaughter, and her daughter-in-law were all present for the interview. Meenakshi Amma wore a new set-mundu for the interview. She sat royally on the sofa with her family of daughters surrounding her. I requested her youngest daughter and my favorite *chechi*, Leela, to sit with her on the sofa. I wanted both of them in the video. That relaxed Meenakshi Amma and made her feel at ease for the interview. Everyone's love and respect for her was visible throughout the interview, creating a deep sense of love and togetherness in the room. I began the interview with my first question:

> D: How did your relationship with your body and sexuality transform as you blossomed from a young girl into an adult woman?
>
> G: I was a little girl, then I had my coming of age ceremony, I studied in school until we moved from Vadagara.
>
> D: Ammamma, you didn't go grow up here?
>
> G: No. I grew up in Vadagara.
>
> D: In your mother's house?
>
> G: Yes.

I was glad to hear that *ammamma* grew up in her Mother's house. I could not wait to hear more of her story. I wanted to know about her *taravad*. Did families really live together? How was it like?

> D: Were there lot of people in your taravad? Who were there?

> G: Lot of uncles, nieces, nephews, my brother, mother . . . when I was 13 or 14 years old, I went to live with my ammavan (maternal uncle) in Seemancheri (name of a city). That is where I had my coming of age ceremony and everything.

I could almost picture it as she spoke. But it was unheard of in today's Kerala that the sister and her children go to live with the brother. Was the uncle unmarried?

> D: So you went to stay with your ammavan (maternal uncle)?
>
> G: Yes. My ammavan didn't have anyone. There was also a school there.

When Meenakshi Amma said her "*Ammavan* didn't have anyone," I assumed that her uncle must have been a bachelor, struggling and living on his own, but my mother was smart enough to ask the next question.

> M: Was ammavan married?
>
> G: Yes, but ammayi (maternal uncle's wife) wasn't there. She was in her mother's home, and so my mother, brother and I moved with my uncle.
>
> M: [Explaining to me] Since ammayi wasn't there, your uncle brought his own sister and sister's children to come and live with him.
>
> G: [Acknowledging my mother's explanation] Yes.

I would never have guessed that the maternal uncle was married. It must have been still in the *marumakkathayam* system, where the concept of the wife accompanying the husband was not yet prevalent. Relations through birth were still honored over those through marriage or *sambandham* practices. When she said that her uncle did not have anyone, she meant that his closest kin (his sister) was not with him. So the sister hurried to her brother's home to take care of him, since she was living in her maternal *taravad*. I am so grateful to my mother for putting it into perspective for me.

> D: With whom and why did you come here (Taliparamba)?

> G: Your paternal grandfather's father lived here. All this property used to belong to him. He was sick and on his deathbed. So your grandfather sent word to my mother, "If you want to see him, come fast." In those days, it was the marumakkathayam system.

This is where I learned that my great grandfather was somehow related to Meenakshi Amma. I wanted to know more about that.

> D: What was your relationship with achachan (my grandfather)?

> G: My grandmother's brother's son was your grandfather; that is my mother's own uncle's son was your grandfather, and that uncle was the karnavar of the taravad.

That was when it hit me hard that my father and Meenakshi Amma's children are cousins and closely related!

> D: Oh! So you were cousins?

> G: Yes. So my mother's own uncle was on the deathbed. So your grandfather sent word, "Come fast to see him." The karnavar had already divided all the property for his two sisters' and their children—the Vadagara property and also, the Taliparamba property. Your grandfather did all this with instruction from his father.

It was great to hear about the history of my family, as no one had ever spoken to me about these facts. My father shared later on that his father (Gopala Kurup) did not take any property from his father (Dhairu Kurup) for himself. He rightfully divided it among his father's nieces, as was the custom of that time. I had a deep sense of respect for my grandfather, a man of his word.

> W: When karnavar died, some of his own children were very angry that he gave a lot of his property to his sister's children. Ammavan (or karnavar) had three wives. We need to tell you the history a little. In those days, Vadagara women couldn't leave their natal homes after marriage. It was considered inauspicious for women to cross the river to go with their husbands.

> G: Today women are going in planes leaving their homes [everyone laughs].

> W: His first marriage was in Vadagara.
>
> G: In that marriage was born your grandfather. He was the eldest. Your grandfather had two sisters. When your grandfather's father left for Taliparamba on a job, his wife could not leave with him. So she gave him permission that when he goes to Taliparamba, he can keep have another sambandham there.

All this information was so thrilling; it was like out of a storybook. I was fascinated by my great grandmother sticking to the tradition of never leaving her Vadagara and consenting to her husband having relationships in Taliparamba—in fact, encouraging him to do that. These women's lack of possessiveness and jealousy in their relationships of marriage was proof to the matriarchal past of Kerala, and I was thrilled to know it in such a near and intimate way.

> D: since that lady couldn't come here, she allowed him to have a relationship here?
>
> G: Yes. He came here and had two marriages. That time granduncle had lot of property. In fact all the property around here belonged to him.

She gave me names of families and people, clearly explaining how everything fit into this new equation of marriage and matriliny. I had lived nearly 39 years of my life meeting and interacting with relatives on my father's side, without actually understanding their stories and the roles they played in the history of my father's lineage. Their time of life was so different from mine.

> M: How much freedom men had in those days!

It was evident that these women's lives were completely independent of their husbands, and the presence or absence of a husband did not conflict with their social engagements because they lived in their matrilineal home. While my mother was fascinated by how much freedom men had to have multiple relationships, I was wondering if women also had this freedom in their sexual relationships. Grandmother's youngest daughter continued the story by narrating an incident:

W: Once granduncle took his wife from here (meaning Taliparamba) to Vadagara. These women were not allowed to enter the kitchen since they came from across the river. These women were Nairs. We were all Kurups. So, they had to wait outside. That is where they were fed food.

G: [Laughing and mockingly] These Nayar women could become wives, but they couldn't enter the kitchen. That home in Vadagara was huge. So when these wives came back, they demanded a bigger house be build for them here. That maternal taravad was huge. It was given to my grandmother and her sister. Later on my grandaunt's son, Balettan, asked me if I wanted that home or the one in Taliparamba. I said, "I want the one in Taliparamba, and I got this house."

The caste prejudices were predominant in Kerala. Even within the Nayars, there were sub-castes, which ranked higher or lower in the hierarchy. Those considered lower in the hierarchy did not touch or enter the homes of those higher in the class system. The system was extremely complex with different restrictions and separations connected to it.

D: So ammamma came here?

G: A day or two after we came here, my grand uncle passed away.

D: How old were you then?

G: Maybe 13.

D: Did you have siblings?

G: Yes. One brother. He is 6 years older to me. He is still alive, and living in Vadagara.

M: His wife is your grandfather's sister's daughter.

D: Oh! Okay.

I was fascinated to learn about this web of relationships that kept emerging, although it was all very confusing. The first thing I did during the transcription was to sit with a paper and pen, and draw the family tree with the various relationships. It has become clearer to me since then. I have shared the family tree to help with your comprehension (see Appendix E).

> G: When karnavar died, his children and his sister's children, everyone did his final rites together.
>
> W: When did you get married?
>
> G: Maybe around 18 or 19 [she laughs]. I got married here and went to Vadagara. Your grandfather's uncle (father's sister's husband) taravad—the groom was from there.

I was glad that we were moving into *ammamma's* marriage, as I want to get more details.

> D: How did all that happen? Did they come to see you before marriage? Did anyone seek your permission for the marriage?
>
> G: [Laughs] Permission? In those days there was no permission. When uncles ask, you agree.

I recalled Madhavi Amma's similar response. I wanted to know if this grandmother had the freedom to reject a groom if she did not like him before marriage.

> D: But if you didn't like him, did you feel you had the freedom to say so?
>
> G: No. There was no freedom like that. There was no chance of me seeing the groom. In those days I was staying with Balettan. The groom used to come there. The groom was from Balettan's father's taravad.

The grandmother knew the groom and did not feel that she could reject him, as he was someone from within the family. My mother reaffirmed this for me with her next question.

> M: So the groom was someone known within the extended family?
>
> G: Yes. So they liked and asked me to marry him. In those days there wasn't so much freedom. However the boy was, you could only say yes—even if he wasn't good looking!

W: What karnavar said, you did it!

I realized that the *karnavar* had a great deal of responsibility. Most *karnavars* deeply cared for their sisters and their children. However, if a woman was not lucky enough to be born into a family like that, she was deep trouble. Most *karnavars* I have heard about, including my own grandfather, have been honorable men.

D: So the karnavar was taking care of everything?

G: Yes. Everything was the karnavar.

D: So nothing really belonged to his children. Everything belonged to his sister and their children?

G: Yes. It was all marumakkathayam in those days. All the property we got is through that system.

It is clear that in the *marumakkathayam* system, children had no right over their father's property; inheriting property only from their mother. Knowing that *ammamma* experienced the *marumakkathayam* system in her life reaffirmed my own sense that her strength was connected with the salient features of that matrilineal system.

G: I got married at night. In those days marriages were at night. It was called podamuri—a piece of cloth or saree is given. Next day morning, we went to Vadagara.

I could see the similarity with what Madhavi Amma had shared about her marriage and that she had stayed at her mother's house the night of the marriage, leaving the next day for the new place. I wanted to know about the age difference between her and the groom and, going forward, if she lived with her husband.

D: Was there an age different between you two?

G: Yes. Big difference. Around 10 to 15 years. Those days you couldn't say anything. Today you have the freedom to say you don't want to marry if you don't like the boy.

> M: Karnavar did everything for our good and welfare was the trust and feeling we had. Isn't that so?
>
> G: Yes. That is true.
>
> M: There was complete faith in that system.
>
> G: Yes. In those days, they would look at the taravad of the groom.

I could see that the *karnavar* and the family elders spent considerable time making sure that the groom was the best choice for their daughter as well as the *taravad*. The women in the *taravad* had considerable faith in the elder's decision, which was part of their unwavering trust in the men in their lives—their uncles and brothers in the matrilineal system. *Ammamma* continued talking about her marriage.

> G: I went to the groom's house for some days and then I came back to my own house here. In my house I gave birth to four children.

This brought a smile on my face. On one hand she spoke of having no freedom, yet a few days into living in her husband's home, she returned to her mother's house to live.

> D: So you came back to your house?
>
> G: Yes. I stayed there for sometime and then I came back. In between for few days I would go and stay at my husband's house. My husband was in Coimbatore (a city in the neighboring state of Tamil Nadu) those days.
>
> D: that time you had the freedom to come and stay in your house?
>
> G: Yes. In those days, my parents did not want to send me there so far away. They only had two children and I was the only daughter. So we were the prestige of the taravad. My brother was in the army and away. So I was the daughter and so my parents wanted me to be with them.
>
> D: So ammamma spent most of the life in your home?
>
> G: Yes.

I was so happy for her, remembering the time when I had to leave my parents behind. It was and still is one the most painful memories of my life. At that moment in my mind, I bowed down to this earlier system of living, which had believed in never severing a daughter's relationship with her matriliny.

> D: that is so different from most other parts of India.

> G: Really?

Ammamma had no idea that outside of Kerala life was so different for women. I took sometime to share with her about the traditional Hindu Indian marriages, where the woman once married belonged to the husband's house. She seemed ignorant about this, and rightly so. Because in her home, even in the present generation, most of her daughters and granddaughter's live in their mother's home.

> G: I was always here. It wouldn't suit me to stay there. So I was always here.

She said it so easily that I could not help smiling. I loved the way she said it —*It wouldn't suit me to stay there.* That is the best way to put it. Every woman feels this, yet within the modern system, they are not allowed to exercise this choice. I wondered about her husband's family—how did they respond to it.

> D: And your husband's family didn't have any objection.

> G: No. They had no objection.

> M: In those days, it was important for the karnavar to make sure that their nieces had a good life and were happy.

> G: [Agreeing] Yes. That is true.

> M: They had enough food to eat and were comfortable. That is what the karnavar wanted.

> G: [Agreeing] Yes.

> M: They knew that the daughters would be safer in their mother's home.
>
> G: [Agreeing] Yes.
>
> G: All my children were born here. We didn't have much connection with Vadagara. Sometimes we would visit for a wedding or when someone died or something. That's all!

My mother got really engaged in the conversation. I was happy to see her participating fully in the discussions. I could see that she was beginning to appreciate this discussion, and was seeing great value in the traditions of yesterday. I remembered having read that fathers had no responsibility in the *marumakkathayam* system. I wanted to know if it was so.

> D: Did the husband or his family have any commitment in your life? You were fully looked after by your own taravad people.
>
> G: Yes. My husband's family did not have much responsibility. Sometimes I would visit them. My family would never allow me to visit regularly. I was the only daughter [she laughs].

So it was true—the husband and his family did not have much responsibility toward Meenakshi Amma's children. I was deeply touched by the Meenakshi Amma's family's attachment to her.

> D: So all the property everything you received from your family!
>
> G: No. My children received my husband's property. My husband only had a brother.
>
> D: No sisters?
>
> G: No. One share was given to one brother and the other share to my husband.

Because Meenakshi Amma's husband had no sister, he gave his property to his children, which would probably not have been the case if he had a sister. I wanted to know if Meenakshi Amma's was a rare situation or the norm in the culture.

> D: Was the situation like this in most women's lives in those days?

G: [With full affirmation] Yes.

I wanted to jump up and down in joy that she said this with complete ease, like it had always been true.

> D: When ammammas daughters were getting married, that system did not exist, correct?
>
> G: Yes.
>
> W: Yes. It had changed.

I decided to engage in this change in the later part of my questions, moving instead into the next step of the questionnaire.

> D: Do you remember participating in any female-centered rituals? Can you describe what they were like? How did you feel?
>
> G: Yes.

She had mentioned her first blood ceremony in the beginning of her interview. Now I wanted to know more about that.

> D: You spoke about the coming of age ceremony. Did you have a ritual? Do you remember?
>
> G: Yes. In those days it was different—for 3 days you are separate. You stayed indoors. You couldn't step out of the house. You were served food everything inside. Fourth day a huge feast is organized and there are lots of celebrations.
>
> W: Wasn't there something like putting turmeric?
>
> G: Yes. None of these girls went through that ceremony.
>
> M: As soon as they came to know that you were menstruating, did they do something?
>
> G: Only that you had to sit in a corner—not go anywhere. That's all
>
> M: [To me] There rituals are slightly different from Azhikode (my mother's ancestral taravad where Madhavi Amma's interview was conducted).

Just like Madhavi Amma, Meenakshi Amma also did not remember the details of the ceremony on her own. In Madhavi Amma's case, her daughters had asked her specific questions, because each of them had experienced an elaborate ceremony of their own. However, in case of Meenakshi Amma, none of her daughters had had the first blood ceremony performed, although they did keep the 4 days of ritual every time they got their periods after that. Hence, they did not know what questions to ask their mother.

> D: Did they make any special foods for you during those 3 days?
>
> G: Maybe they made some sweets for me. I don't remember now.
>
> D: How about sleeping arrangements? Did they do anything different?
>
> M: Did they put paddy and rice on the floor underneath the floor mat?
>
> G: No. Nothing like that.
>
> W: There was definitely no mattress.
>
> G: It was a hay mat! It was to be washed on the fourth day. Even the space I left was purified with cow dung on the fourth day. For the 3 days, you kept out of the sight of men.

So Meenakshi Amma did not have to lie on the paddy and rice, but just slept separately on a hay mat. There were some differences. It could also be that *ammamma* doesn't remember. I will not know for sure.

> M: On the fourth day was there a procession to the bath led by the Ammayi with a nellavillakku?
>
> G: Yes. There was . . . a pookkula (coconut blossoms) was also brought—I vaguely remember.

The grand procession for the ritual bath along with the *pookkula* seemed to be a common thread between both the ceremonies. I wanted to know if the menstruant was decorated by young coconut leaf jewelry.

> D: Did they make something with the kuruthola (tender coconut leaves)?
>
> G: Yes. There were rituals like that. I don't remember very much. There was something like the pookkula was beaten on the ground and depending upon how many young coconut flowers remained, the women would say that many kids you would have. There were many things like that. Then in the kullam when you dipped and came out, women will ululate loudly.

Meenakshi Amma kept saying that there were many small rituals, but she could not recall them.

> D: And after that . . .
>
> G: And that day at home there will be huge feast.
>
> W: It was called thirandukalyanam in those days.
>
> G: All these women who came and other guests would be invited. Everyone would eat and then it would be over.
>
> W: And then every month for those 3 days you had to stay indoors and away from the kitchen. Then there would be something called mattu.
>
> M: A special caste called Vannan would come and take the menstrual cloth with them, wash and bring it back.

Ammamma and other women nodded their heads in agreement. I still was finding this *Vannan* caste washing the menstrual cloth quite unbelievable based on the social conditioning of how blood is perceived in the culture today. I wanted to know more about *mattu*. What was the purpose of it?

> W: They would bring a washed fresh piece of cloth. It was called mattu. On the fourth day bath, we would take that piece of cloth with us, and then dip and bath to become pure. We all did that growing up.

So *mattu* was directly connected to attaining ritual purity, and came through the energy of the *Vannathi*, the washerwoman. It was the right of the washerwoman to provide the freshly washed piece of cloth holding which the Nayar women took dips into the water and emerged ritually pure. This idea of purity attained following menstruation through a ritually laundered cloth must have given the girls of the past such a powerfully empowered experience of togetherness, community and womanhood.

> G: On the fourth day, you had to apply talli and oil on your hair and then dip completely and bathe.

Every time I go to Taliparamba (my father's home), I apply the *talli*, a gooey mixture made of the hibiscus flowers and leaves, to my own hair. It is a natural conditioner and cools the head from the hot summers of Kerala, and additionally makes the hair extremely soft to touch. The red hibiscus is also a flower offered at every goddess temple, and present in every Nayar home.

> M: Was there a kullam (or pond) in those days?

> G: Because they didn't want women to go outside, they built a deep kullam in our land, the one that you see outside. Women couldn't go outside.

> W: We were from a big taravad and our women couldn't go outside.

> D: Every month you would do that?

> G: Every month on the fourth day they had to go to kullam and dip and bath.

> D: For those 3 days, you didn't have bath.

> G: No. You did not. You could not touch anything. You stayed in a corner.

> M: Your body shouldn't move so much in those days.

I enjoyed hearing the various observances about menstruation, showing how much thought had gone into caring for women during their days of bleeding. They were given rest from 3 days of cooking, cleaning, and running the household and did not even have to care for their children during those times.

> D: What would you do in those 3 days?
>
> G: Nothing. You would eat and sleep—that's all you did [everyone laughs].
>
> W: Did women work at all?
>
> G: What work? No work could be done.
>
> W: Even all the eatables would be brought in covered [everyone laughs].

I could clearly see that women took these 3 days as a break from attending to the never-ending affairs of the taravad. Recently, I have also chosen to engage in rest during the first 3 days of my blood, which has completely changed my relationship with my body, mind and my blood; my pains have also lessened. I am beginning to really appreciate these ancient systems of knowledge and ritual.

> G: On the fourth day after the talli and the oil and the full dip in the kullam, we become pure.
>
> W: [Correcting] Actually, when we touch the mattu (fresh laundered cloth from the washerwoman) we become pure.
>
> D: What is the significance of the mattu brought by the washerwoman?
>
> M: Wasn't the mattu also there for other occasions like at death, etcetera?
>
> G: Yes. It was there. It was kind of like their right.

This was again fascinating—*It was kind of like their right*. I was beginning to recognize that in the earlier days each class of society was associated with a certain job and were considered the ritual experts in it. The washerwoman or *Vannan* caste was considered the ritual expert in reestablishing the purity of the cloth, and the *Thiyyan* caste was the expert in climbing coconut trees and gathering coconuts. However, with class systems getting rigid and influenced by Hindu themes of hierarchy and purity of the body, different classes got ranked in the hierarchy as lower and higher, creating a complicated system with complex prejudices.

> D: Did you do the thirandukalyanam for your daughters?
>
> G: No. They didn't even know it. Everyone was busy going to school. When it came also it was difficult to know. In those days, once you got periods, they no longer sent you to school. You have then become a big girl. Then you don't step outside.

I can begin to see the influence of schools and education in the fading of these systems. The first blood of menstruation was no longer was honored or acknowledged in the modern culture of Kerala—women were expected to go on uninterrupted without paying any attention to their bodies.

> D: After this is when proposals came for girls.
>
> G: Yes. Then kalyanam (or marriage as it is known today) [everyone laughs].
>
> D: Do you remember anything about tali-kettu-kalyanam?
>
> G: Was it there in our caste? I don't remember anything.

I have read about *tali-kettu-kalyanam,* but none of the grandmothers seem to know of it. Maybe it was way before their time. I wanted to know if they did any other rituals.

> D: What other rituals do you remember?
>
> M: Did you have the pooram ritual—putting flowers for Kama?
>
> G: We don't celebrate that in Vadagara. So we never did that when we moved here. People here do it. We never did.
>
> D: Did you participate in thiruvathira?
>
> G: We will go to temple, have a bath in the kullam. That's all!
>
> M: Did you swing in the oonjal (the swing)?
>
> G: No. We didn't have that.

> M: Was dancing the thiruvathira done?
>
> G: No. We didn't have permission to go outside the house. How will we learn thiruvathira?

These women seemed to have lost many of their rituals on account of moving from Vadagara to Taliparamba. Although the cities are quite close to each other, I began to see the difference in the cultures.

> M: In Thrissur, the women were freer in those days. Women my mother's age had gone to college. I think they celebrated these festivals quite differently. I heard from one of my friends. They were quite forward in their thinking.

My mother had always felt that women living in Thrissur (Central Kerala) had more freedom, because they danced, sang and enjoyed their lives as women.

> G: For thiruvathira when we swam in the kullam, wasn't there a game that was played by hitting the water, Vellum-Adichal?

I was excited to hear about this, because I had read about this game and I wanted to know more.

> D: What was that game, *ammamma*?
>
> G: It was a game played in the water by all the women, which involved hitting on top of the water. Women would go the Vaidyanathan temple in Taliparamba. It is the Shiva temple, famous for thiruvathira.

In the female-centered rituals chapter, I included this game in detail. Meenakshi Amma could not recall it. It was a good transition into my next question.

> D: You all grew up bathing in the kullam? Who taught swimming?
>
> W: You just learned swimming. No one really taught [women start laughing]. You go to swim with your mother and then automatically you learn to swim.
>
> G: [Nods in agreement] Yes.

> W: You just held to the sides of the kullam and swim initially and then slowly learn.
>
> G: The women here were all into learning how to swim.

I recalled this from my childhood. Meenakshi *ammamma* had a *kullam* in her house where everyone swam. I sat on the sides and watched them. I only remembered seeing women, so I asked:

> D: That time did everyone swim together—men and women?
>
> G: Yeah. One side the women swam, and the other side the men swam.
>
> W: In those days everything was open. Today you can't do that.
>
> D: There was no problem in those days.
>
> G: There was no problem. Women would finish their baths and then coolly put on their clothes.

There it was again. Women swam bare-chested in the water.

> D: So women would bathe without clothes on?
>
> G: Yes. In my times, women would take off all their clothes.
>
> W: There is a grandmother even now here who has a bath like that. Recently someone told me, "The grandmother has no shame. She removes all her clothes off while bathing."

I felt so sorry for the girl who said that. These grandmothers, to me, were real women living in their bodies without shame. Even a bikini-clad modern woman of today might not be able to display such a deep sense of confidence and presence in her body no matter how her body looked.

> M: If we go back a few more years, women didn't even wear any clothes on top..
>
> G: Yes.
>
> W: Even when the groom is coming to see you, women never wore anything on top. They just stood like that.

I just started laughing trying to imagine of this, it was so out of my comfort zone.

> D: Did you know any women who did that?
>
> W: Of course! Your grandfather's sister never wore any cloth on top.

My grandfather's sister lived with my grandfather in his home all her life. My father often shared fascinating stories of this aunt of his but failed to mention that she never wore anything on top. I could see that she was a woman of her own making.

> D: Even when she was young?
>
> W: Yes. Always.
>
> M: Maybe they casually put a thin muslin cloth on top.
>
> G: Maybe.
>
> W: Not then. All that came much later.

This was a reaffirmation that putting the muslin cloth on the shoulders to cover the breasts came much later. In the earlier days, women and men never wore anything on top. Recently I had a conversation with Savithri de Tourreil (personal communication) in which I learned that the moguls introduced stitched cloth in India. Before that, the act of a needle piercing into cloth was considered an act of violence. People just wrapped themselves in woven cloth. There was no concept of a blouse.

> D: Were most women like that?
>
> G: Yes. I think.

I was thrilled to hear this.

> D: Did you have fear of being with a man after the marriage?
>
> G: Yes. Lot of fear! You didn't know what it would be like . . . what would happen to your life . . . where you would go . . . how you would be treated.

I could feel her words. It is indeed frightening for any girl to be intimate with a complete stranger on her first meeting. What could she do if she did not like the person?

> D: But did you also know that if this new place wasn't good for you, you could always come back to your mother's house?
>
> G: Yes. That was always there and anyway, the mother's family never let you stay for long at the husband's house. They will bring you back.

Her confidence reflected the truth of what she saw and experienced in her own life and in the lives of other women in her time. She assumed that it had been the same everywhere and was surprised to know it was not the same even across Kannur. I wanted to know more about the flirtatious advances of boys and men.

> D: How did the girls or women respond to the flirtatious advances of boys and men?
>
> G: There was no occasion for that. Anytime you go outside the house after your coming of age, there would be people in front and back to protect you and guard you. By the time my daughters came, there was more freedom, I think. They would go to movies, and so on. In my time, it was all the old system.

The daughters were kept safe and closely guarded by the men of the family. I wanted to know if young unmarried girls had the freedom to talk to boys and men outside the *taravad*.

> D: You couldn't even talk to boys and men outside the taravad?
>
> G: No way you could do that. There was an incident I remember. In those days, bangle-vendors used to come home to sell bangles. They would take your measurements and then sell you bangles. In those days my brother was home from military and he was in the neighbor's house chatting. That time he saw a bangle vendor come to our house and return back. Immediately he left the neighbor's house and came rushing home. "Did you allow him to put bangles on your hand?" was his question to me. Luckily I had not brought any bangles, so I said, "no," and only then was he relieved. It was like if the bangle man had touched me and put bangles, it was a

matter of shame for the family. The girls in the family were safe guarded.

W: In those days, the love and bond between brother and sister was very strong.

I was quite intrigued by this story. What made the brother rush back in panic? What was the panic about another man touching his sister? Was this behavior that came from treasuring the daughter like a precious gem, or was it more about the family prestige and the virginity of the daughter? I had so many questions in my head. I did not think it was appropriate to ask the grandmother.

D: So young men don't indulge in any such things because of fear?

G: They wont do any such things and we also will never involve in anything. There was too much fear.

D: How about people from within the taravad like male cousins

G: No. With them we had ample freedom. With men from within the taravad we had enough freedom. Within the taravad, girls had all the freedom.

So it was not that men and women could not interact with each other, but that this interaction and closeness was confined to men within the *taravad*. In those days, the *taravad* was a huge establishment with many people living together, with many extended connections to other *taravads*. Within known parameters, the interactions between men and women seemed to have been allowed. Was a woman's protection and safety the main reason for restricting her freedom with strangers? Meenakshi Amma had left me with many unanswered questions, but I realized I had arrived at my final question.

D: What changes are you seeing good or bad in the culture? Are there any changes that you are seeing that are not supportive of women?

W: I feel these new changes are not good. Like the mobile phone! Since the mobile, so many unnecessary problems are happening.

G: Yes. I agree.

W: There is usefulness to the mobile, but there are also lots of problems.

A lively attack against the mobile phone ensued from all the women present, so I was curious to know what problems they were seeing.

D: What problems are we talking about?

G: So many boys and girls . . . because of love and things like that . . . destroying their life . . . everything is happening because of the mobile phone. Today girls have lot of knowledge of things, but with that there are lot of accidents like this also happening. Falling in love and when the boy says I can't marry, the girl goes and commits suicide. We are hearing many stories like this. Today's generation has less patience. It is all what I want!

I learned that there have been many instances of phone bullying, and increases in romantic interactions between boys and girls on phones, some leading to suicide. The women shared with me later how boys and men were coaxing young girls through texting and phone calls into leaving their families, having sex—all in the name of romance and love. I was quite shocked at some of the recent incidents of teenage suicides in their neighborhood.

D: Was a girl's birth celebrated?

G: Yes. However, when I had three girls in a row, I felt sad and there was a strong desire to have boy and then by God's grace, I had a boy.

D: How did that shift in thinking happen?

G: When you continuously have girls, then you feel bad, right?

I could not see why having girls continuously, was a sad thing—was this a natural feeling or the result of a patriarchal transition—I could not help wonder!

D: Why? In the past it wasn't like that, right?

> G: One and two girls then you feel bad.

I was still trying to understand the sentiments behind this sharing when my mother jumped in to bring more clarity into my thought.

> M: Maybe because you need sons to protect the family also.
>
> G: Yes. That is needed. When you have a son, it is like the family has some strength.

That is when I got it—sons were needed as much as daughters. It was a natural desire to have both sons and daughters. Meenakshi Amma was living on her own in her mother's house. Her brother lived in Vadagara. So she deeply desired to have a son to protect and care for her daughters. It made sense to me. I really wanted to know what had kept her entire family together even during the present time.

> D: Ammamma's entire family—children, grandchildren and great children are all living together. How did you make it happen?
>
> G: Together means land is the same, but everyone lives in their own houses. If there is any sadness or problem, everyone comes together and helps one another. For any function or festival in the family, we are all together.
>
> W: It is all because of Amma (meaning the grandmother).
>
> G: That is truly a matter of happiness and peace of mind.
>
> W: That love and belongingness we share has not yet left us. It is very much holding us together today. I can't talk about tomorrow, but today it is the foundation of our lives.

I was deeply touched by the responses of the women. I congratulated Meenakshi Amma for having the ability to keep her entire family together. I pray that the next generation will learn from her perseverance and patience to carry on the tradition. At the end of the interview, she insisted that my mother, sister, and I stay for lunch. Her older daughter, Sarojini Chechi, also arrived from the main house to invite us to stay for lunch, which we did, having the loveliest meal with *ammamma*'s family. My father arrived just in time for lunch and joined us. By then the men had also returned from work and everyone excitedly inquired about the interview.

CHAPTER 17.

YASHODA AMMA
THE FADING GRANDMOTHER

Figure 4: Yashoda Amma (left) and her daughter, Anita

Yashoda Amma (see Figure Above) is my father's younger brother's mother in law. She is physically strong and very tall in height. Her sweet, soft and gentle tone of voice makes me feel loved unconditionally by her and at the same time; I know that she can be fierce and stern when necessary.

She has two children—a son and a daughter. The daughter, Anita is married to my paternal uncle (father's younger brother, Ramachandran). Anita *Ellemma* (*Ellemma* meaning little mother) has an impeccable sense of humor and she is an adept storyteller. I recall as a teenager I would follow her around—constantly talking to her, hearing her stories and laughing the whole time at her amusing responses. She is never afraid to speak her mind. I always wondered how Anita Ellemma's life would have been, if she had been born in another country like the United States! Just like her mother, she is open, exuding confidence and fearlessness. This interview gave me an opportunity to look into her upbringing and understand her through Yashoda Amma, her mother's life.

Yashoda Amma belonged to a maternal family of many daughters. Yashoda Amma's maternal grandmother had two sisters and no brother. She herself had only one daughter (Yashoda Amma's mother), her older sister had four daughters, and the younger sister had one son. That son was the only male in the family and hence took on the role of the maternal uncle. All these people lived together in Yashoda Amma's maternal *taravad*. The first few years of her childhood, she grew up with all these people. Then her father built a home close to her maternal *taravad* and moved his wife and children into that home. Yashoda Amma's parents were deeply in love with each other and that love transferred to the entire family eight children—strongly binding the siblings together. Yashoda Amma was the eldest daughter of the family, deeply valued and loved by everyone. In the last few decades she has become an expert in the know how of the game of cricket. She sits in the living room with all the men watching and discussing cricket. She knows the history of the games, the current players, and their game strategy, and just about everything connected to cricket. Her memory is sharp as a laser and often I hear recount past scores and events from the game effortlessly. During the interview, I learned that Yashoda *ammamma* was also related to my paternal grandfather, Gopala Kurup, through marriage. Her husband was his stepsister's son; meaning Yashoda *ammamma*'s husband was born to the daughter of one of Dhairu Kurup's wives in Taliparamba. I saw numerous of these emerging webs of relationships between families in my interviews.

I interviewed Yashoda *ammamma* next to the prayer altar at my grandfather's home in Taliparamba. My mother invited Anita *ellemma* to sit with her mother in the interview. Yashoda *ammamma* changed into a freshly starched set-mundu and sat down for the interview with her daughter. My mother and I sat facing them. My sister was not present for this interview, as she had to leave for Bangalore, so I setup my video camera and focused it. We lit the *nellavillakku* (the traditional lamp) and began the interview in the early evening.

> D: How did your relationship with your body and sexuality transform as you blossomed from a young girl into an adult woman?
>
> G: My earliest memory is when I was 5 years old. That time I had to learn letters. My father would do all that on time. You learned to write on sand. I learned to write all the 51 letters of Malayalam on sand. Then for first grade, I went to school.

My mother acknowledged that she too learned letters like that.

> D: That time where were you living, ammamma?
>
> G: I was at my home with my father, and my mother. We were eight children—four girls and four boys. My father had his land and property and everything. We lived there with him.
>
> D: Did you have relationship with your maternal family?
>
> G: Yes. We just had a theyyam in that taravad. I was gone for that. I was born there, and also grew up there for sometime. Then I came to live with my father.

Ammamma had just returned just for this interview a day earlier from her maternal *taravad*, where she had been taking care of the guests, and overseeing the *theyyam* preparation. I was grateful that she chose to return immediately for this interview.

> D: Were you the eldest?
>
> G: I had an older brother and then me, and then everyone!
>
> M: What about on your father's side? There weren't any females?

> G: My father had three brothers. There were no daughters in his family. Everyone grew up together. Slowly the brothers also died and then it was only my father. That is how it was! My father didn't have any sisters to take care of.

In that moment I realized why *ammamma*'s father built the home close to his wife's maternal *taravad*. The families had been close growing up. *Ammamma* continued her story.

> G: I only went to school till the sixth grade. My mother didn't have anyone. She kept having babies and since I was the oldest one, I stayed back to help her. My education ended like that. My sisters studied till like 8th or 10th grade. For all these people food had to be prepared every day—it was a lot of work. That was how the life was then.

I would never have imagined that *ammamma* only studied till sixth grade. She is so capable and worldly literate. But just like my mother, she had also quit her education to take care of her siblings and help her mother.

> G: Then when I was 16 years old, my Vayasu-ariyikucha ceremony happened. Vayasu-ariyikucha in those days if you didn't inform your father's side and mother's side of the family, people would get really mad. Once they come to know, the women from that home would come. Only then would I be made to sit inside in a separate room by them. Then I cannot come outside. Everything would be brought to where I was.

This added a few more nuances to my knowledge of the Menarche ritual—women from the girls maternal and paternal *taravad* had to be invited immediately. These women would guide the girl into seclusion. I wanted to confirm if I had heard it correctly.

> D: So moving you into another room would only happen when the women from these homes would arrive?

> G: Yes. One woman from my father's side and then my ammayi (maternal uncle's wife) came and made me sit in the separate room and then they went back to their home.

So it was a right reserved by these women, mainly the father's sister and the mother's brother's wife. Interestingly both are women from different *taravads* (outside the matriliny of the menstruant). They would come just to guide the girl into seclusion and then go back to their respective homes. I was curious if these women returned again on the fourth day?

> D: Would you be alone then?
>
> G: Yes. Yes. Everything would be brought to me. Then on the fourth day, invitations would go to all the homes to come. That was called thirandukulli. People had to be invited and a huge feast had to be prepared. Payasam was jaggery rice in those days. I am telling you about my ceremony. On the fourth day, when I go to the kullam (or the pond) I have to hold a vallukannadi in my hand.

Yashoda Amma differentiated between the first day marking the onset of seclusion and the fourth day of ritual bath as *vayasuariyikucha* and *thirandukulli* respectively. The grandness of the *thirandukulli* ritual was evident in the narration of all my co-researchers. *Vallukannadi* is a handheld mirror made of bell metal. The original *vallukannadi* did not have any mercury in it. The surfaced of the mirror was polished to such an extent that it acted like a mirror. Today, it is hardly possible to buy this *vallukannadi* in a store. The one used now is more like a modern mirror fixed to a bell metal frame. The *vallukannadi* is considered very sacred and used for ritual purposes. It is most commonly found in the puja (or prayer) room next to all the ritual objects. The menstruant walked the length of the pool holding this mirror.

> D: Did you have to hold the vallukannadi when you were in the room also?
>
> G: Yes. I had to keep it with me when in the room for the 3 days.

I wanted to know if the sleeping arrangements were same or different from the previous narrations.

> D: On what did you sleep? Do you remember?
>
> G: Hay mat to sleep. On one side of the mat was spread paddy and on another side was spread raw rice. In the middle the girl had to sleep with the vallukannadi in her hand. After sleeping like that for 3 days, on the fourth day you go to the kullam for the ritual bath. On the way to the bath, you are walking with the vallukannadi in

your hand. Then there are people holding mundu over my head—two people in front and two people in the back (she makes action with her hands to demonstrate). Only mine was done this way. No one else it was done this elaborately. On my father's side there were no girls. Same was the case on my mother's side. Since I was the first daughter in the house, my ceremony was done very elaborately. In the front of me is my ammayi (maternal uncle's wife) holding a nellavillakku in her hand, and then there are women from my father's home. When coming back after the elaborate ritual bath in the kullam, the cloth is put over the head.

So in her ritual, the hay mat was not placed on the rice and paddy, instead paddy and rice heaps were placed on either side of the hay mat. The girl slept on the hay mat surrounded by the rice and paddy. I was interested in her description of the *mundu* held over the girl's head by the women—two women in the front and two in the back holding the edges of the *mundu*. I have known this to be done in Goddess procession and often for members of the royal family as a sign of honor and respect. Doing the same to the menstruant honored and lifted her status in comparison to everyone else present. It was a beautiful sight to behold in my mind!

G: Yes and then the girl is taught how to wear the onnara mundu.

D: When does the girl wear the onnara?

G: Only after wearing the onnara can the girl come back.

She was the first grandmother to speak about the *onnara mundu* so directly. In fact, she had mentioned it to me earlier when I spoke to her about my topic of study, saying that I needed to know about the *onnara mundu* because it was closely connected to a woman's femininity. I was really excited that we were finally talking about it.

D: So is the girl taught for the first time how to wear the onnara after the ritual bath?

G: Yes. That day she wears the onnara and then with the cloth over her head she is brought back home. In the courtyard a palaka (a wooden plank used to sit on) is kept on which the girl is made to sit facing east. An urulli with some thumba flowers, and some raw rice is kept on the side. Also is kept a thallika (brass plate), and kindi filled water. Then the women from my father's side bless me by putting rice on my head following which they sprinkle water on me as an act of purification. At that time, they will also put some money aside for me.

D: Do all the women do that?

G: Yes. Every woman does that to the girl and then it is over.

D: What about the thumba flower?

G: It is kept there in the urulli with water. It remains there. Later my father would examine it to see which side the thumba flowers have moved or floated.

M: Based on which side, they determine the direction from where the groom is coming.

G: Yes. That is correct.

D: When you went to the kullam, did the women use kuruthola to adorn you?

G: No.

D: How about coconut pookkula (or blossoms)?

G: Yes. The pookkula is carried in the hand. After bath, it is hit on the ground and then seen. All this was only done for me. None of my sisters had a ritual done this way. On the fourth day they had to go to the kullam themselves, have a bath, and come back. In those days, I used to be nicely fat and healthy. I had lots of style. Even today people remind me how good I looked in those days.

I listened patiently to everything she was saying, finding it quite similar to what the other grandmothers had said. My mind was still thinking about the *onnara mundu*.

D: You said you were taught to wear the onnara mundu. Did you have to wear it after that?

G: Yes. I wore it.

D: Was it compulsory?

> G: It was not compulsory. It was based on people's convenience. Everyone wore it. I wear it to this day.
>
> M: [Encouraging me] You can learn to wear it from ammamma.
>
> G: In those days, it was only onnara. It would give a lot of strength to the women. My mother wore it till her last breath. Whenever she would go to take bath, the onnara would be kept next to her.

Women wore the *onnara mundu* their whole life and never parted with it. It was like her companion into womanhood. I needed to know why the women wore it in the first place.

> D: Why did women wear onnara?
>
> G: It provided a huge strength for the waist and also, for the backbone and hip. Even at this age because I wear the onnara I have the strength to walk some distance. Without tying that, my mother wouldn't do anything. Today in my house, I am the only one wearing it. Everybody else is wearing chaddi (or underwear) [I could sense her disapproval].

It was like a light bulb going off in my head. Could the *onnara* be the secret to the groundedness and earthiness of the Kerala women? Most women wear it during their childbirth and afterwards for months, as it is known to strengthen the back and the hip. My mother did not do that, because no on instructed her in it. Both Anita *ellemma* and her mother wear the *onnara* to this day. Yashoda Amma even connected it to her strength and ability to walk and move about at her age. After the interview Anita Ellemma taught me how to wear the *onnara,* reaffirming the experience of strength and womanhood for me. I have shared the experience in the Methodology chapter.

> G: And then slowly with time I got married.
>
> D: When did you get married?
>
> G: Marriage was late. It happened in my house.
>
> D: Was your wedding in the evening?

> G: Yes. It happened at night and next day you go to the groom's home.
>
> D: Did you stay at his house or come back to your home?
>
> G: No. I went to stay in his house.

So this was different from Meenakshi Amma, but similar to Madhavi Amma, who had also left her home to stay at her husband's place. I wanted to know if *ammamma* knew her husband before marrying him.

> D: Did you know the man?
>
> G: [Laughs] The man I married?

She laughed at my question. I could see that my question was amusing to her.

> D: So, you didn't know him?
>
> G: Not really.
>
> M: In a way, through some relationship or the other the family always knew the man.
>
> G: He was actually your grandfather's nephew.
>
> D: You mean his sister's son?
>
> G: Stepsister's son! He was the son of your great grandfather's daughter born through one of his wives from Taliparamba. That way he was Gopala Kurup's stepsister's son! He was living with his mother. So after marriage I came to his house.

This was when I learned that Yashoda Amma was related to me apart from her daughter, Anita *ellemma*'s marriage to my paternal uncle.

> G: And then I had children. When you have children, you have to inform everyone. In those days the dried end stem of the coconut leaf, mattal, is hit on the earth three times along with ululation, to announce the arrival of the boy in the family. When it is the girl, the sound is made using the kinnam (it is a bell metal vessel like kindi without the snout).

This was another interesting differentiation in the way the birth of a child was announced. The dried end of the coconut leaf made a thud on the ground—a very flat and unpleasant sound. While the *kinnam* is a bell metal vessel just like kindi without the snout and when struck it makes a loud clinking or bell-like sound. The stark distinction in the sounds associated with the birth of a boy and girl respectively made it obvious that the birth of a girl child was considered more joyous and exciting.

> D: Kinnam would make a louder pleasant sound, right?
>
> G: Yes. It would make a loud and heavy sound. That was how it was in the olden days.
>
> M: In those days the birth happened at home through the help of the women from the lower caste.
>
> G: Yes. There was no problem in those days with home birth. Then slowly my sister's got married one by one.

In the modern culture of Kerala health is heavily influenced by western medicine, and home birth is considered scary and unhygienic, and a majority of the women prefer C-sections.

> D: Was the thirandukulli ritual done for your daughter?
>
> G: No. It was not done.

I was sad to know that.

> D: How about observing the 3 days of segregation?
>
> G: Definitely. That was done. Relatives came with sweets and gave it to the girl. That was very important for my mother. In those days, you can't go to the puja room. You can't cook or go into the kitchen. All that was strictly followed. There was separate plate and glass to eat and then on the fourth day all these items were also washed, and the place where the girl slept was cleaned with cow dung. The hay mat was also washed in the kullam and then using the mattu the girl had to dip in the kullam and have her ritual bath. The menstrual cloth was given to the Vannathi (the washerwoman). She would wash and bring it back.

Although Yashoda *ammamma*'s daughters did the menstrual seclusion and ritual bath every month, the first blood ritual was no longer performed in a grand celebratory way. I reconfirmed it just to be sure.

> D: Was it done every month?
>
> G: Yes. Three days every month—it had to be followed. As long as there were older generations living in the house, the women had to do it and then slowly it disappeared as the household became bigger. There were four sisters and their children. Their husbands didn't stay with them. The four brothers married and brought their wives home. Till my father and mother passed away, we all lived together in the same house. We had lot of land and cultivation.
>
> M: So there was no shortage of food.
>
> G: Food was ample. My father would send the necessary items home. Whenever he came home, there would always be a few people with him for food. Sometimes after feeding the guests, there wouldn't be so much food left for us. That is how life was in those days.
>
> D: Did you celebrate thiruvathira?
>
> G: Yes. We did.
>
> D: How did you celebrate it?
>
> G: My eldest brother's wife fasted on thiruvathira till 1:00 AM in the morning. Then she would go to the kullam, dip and have a bath. I would also go with her and then we would come back and eat.
>
> D: Was there any fun activity like singing that women engaged in?
>
> G: Yes. For 7 days women would go to the kullam sing and play water games.

Then *ammamma* started singing the *thiruvathira* song, transporting me back to another time when women cherished each other, played games in water, teased each other, and swam to their hearts' content. *Ammamma* continued.

> G: They would sing and play in the kullam. It was fun. Men were not involved in any of this. Only women! It was lot of festivities that time—lot of women in the kullam.

Today most Kerala families are nuclear, and in most homes women are working and have no time to engage in any swimming. The modern generation is getting even busier and focused on acquiring more materials things. The simple joys of togetherness are fast getting lost.

> D: Did you celebrate pooram?

> G: Yes. We definitely celebrated pooram. Only girls who were yet to have their periods offered the pooram flowers. They were called the pooram kunjingal (or the Pooram Kids). After my children grew up, it was my sister's daughter who did that in our house. She was then the only pooram girl in the family. For her pooram I walked miles to get different kinds of flowers. In those days, we had a huge courtyard. Once I drew a huge horse with paddy and on top of that we put the flowers for Kamadevan.

Her descriptions of the *pooram* were very different from the celebrations in my mother's home. In my mother's village, the unmarried menstruating women celebrated *pooram*, whereas, in *ammamma's* village, it was only girls who were yet to have their periods. It was difficult to really know which one was the original.

> D: Did you make the Kaman with cow dung?

> G: No. We did not make Kaman with cow dung. We made Kaman with flowers.

> D: Didn't you make it with mud?

> G: In our side, we didn't make Kaman with mud either.

This was another very different expression in the practice of the ritual.

> G: For 3 days, these kids after having the ritual bath, made Kaman with flowers next to the well. Three times they offered water and rice to the Kaman and then the Kaman was made inside the house.

> M: Then did you make with it mud?

> G: No. In our side we never made Kaman with mud. At least I never saw one like that.

Both my mother and I were thinking that they would make the Kaman with mud or cow dung at some point in the ritual. I could not visualize how a Kaman could be made with flowers or to what the offering was being made.

> D: But then what were you offering the flowers to?
>
> G: There is a palaka (small table made of wood used to sit on) to which the flowers are offered. The nellavillakku was lit next to it. In the evening, we would give water to Kamadevan and then in coconut shell we would put amber and then offer smoke to Kamadevan, and then the women would ululate.

My mother said that in her village, they used the *palaka* too, but then it was used to sit the Kaman dolls made of clay and cow dung. In the *ammamma*'s village they used the flowers to symbolically represent the Kamadevan or in other words the flowers were Kamadevan.

> G: Then we would make poora-kanji for Kaman without adding any salt in it. We would also offer coconut and jaggery. The kids would make these offerings three times to Kaman, and then in the temple there would be poora-kalli.

These rituals were similar to those in my mother's village.

> G: On the last day, sending off the Kaman was also an elaborate ritual. A Vellichapadu (or oracle) would come to send off the Kamadevan. All the pooram children would be taken to the river that day and given a ritual bath. The Vellichapadu would accompany them to the river. These kids are expected to fast the entire day and then the Vellichapadu along with the dressed up children would visit all the neighboring homes, and it was only after their visit could any house send off the Kamadevan. The Vellichapadu would give turmeric and rice powder as blessing to every home. Only after receiving that could the Kamadevan be send off.

My mother looked at me as Yashoda Amma was speaking and said that she had never heard of this version of the *pooram festival*. The *Vellichapadu* is a shaman or oracle that channels the energy between the two worlds: the world of matter and the world of spirits. So the *Vellichapadu* accompanying young girls to the river and then these dressed up girls walking from home to home blessing the Kaman altars was new information. It reminded me of the Kumari practice of Nepal and West Bengal.

> G: That day pooram ada is made for Kaman. Rice wrapped in a cloth, two bananas, coconut flowers, along with this Ada are all offered to Kaman. After the women ululate, everything is swept and collected into a vessel. Then with a nellavillakku, plate, kindi, water and everything around four to five women along with the little kids go under a Jackfruit tree, make three circles around it, and then facing east (Kizhakku) they let Kaman go. At that time the women sing a song to Kaman asking him to come early and faster in the next year.

Just as Madhavi Amma had done, Yashoda Amma started singing the song to Kaman.

> D: What is the significance of this festival?
>
> G: It is mainly done to satisfy and appease Kamadevan, and only performed by very small girls usually below the ages of ten.

I was happy to learn that the connection to Kamadevan was still maintained.

> D: Did you bathe in the kullam?
>
> G: Going to the kullam and bathing was the main pass time for women. By the time it was evening, all the women would come to bathe—swimming, washing our clothes, bathing—all these activities were completed at leisure and then women returned home.

Kerala is very tropical, so swimming in the pond is a much-deserved break for women after a long day of sweating hard work.

> D: Was it for long duration?
>
> G: Yes. Women would be together for a long time—swimming, talking . . .

It was wonderful to know that women had the time to just relax and talk with other women folks.

> D: Women took off their clothes and washed themselves?
>
> G: Yes. All the women took off their clothes . . . in those days no one came in that direction when women were bathing. Before leaving, everyone would promise to come back at the same time next day . . . to swim . . . everyone was always excited about that.

The poetry in her sharing was so beautiful. My mind was imagining women making promises to come back the next day. They must have looked forward to each other's company.

> D: Did you continue to go after your marriage?
>
> G: No. After marriage I didn't go. With my marriage, the bathing in the kullam ended. Then you can't go.

The memory that grandmother was talking about so fondly was from before she was married. The strength of the memory made me think that she had been swimming with the women folk most of her life.

> D: What were women wearing in those days?
>
> G: There was no saree in those days. I never saw any saree. Skirt and blouse or mundu. Women wore a bodice inside their blouses. They made it themselves.

In the last few decades, most women in Kerala are wearing something called the *Nightie* (a full-length free flowing gown). Initially the trend of *Nightie* began as a nightgown, and slowly women started wearing it all the time perhaps because of its ease of use. Literally *Nightie* is taking over as the traditional dress of the present day Malayali women. However, in comparison to the auspicious set-mundu, the *Nightie* has no beauty and completely destroys the erotic sensuousness of the Malayali women. I feel this is a research topic in itself.

> D: Were there women who never wore anything on top?

G: Yes. There were women. My ammayi never wore anything on top. My mother also stopped wearing anything.

D: Even when she was young?

G: Yes. Till the day of her death, ammayi never wore anything on top. Her entire life she never wore anything on top.

It was so freeing to hear this reinforced by every one of the grandmothers.

G: She might sometimes put a muslin cloth over her shoulder. That's all. They would wear a black thread with a small gold amulet in their neck.

The minute I heard about the amulet, my curiosity was sparked. Was this amulet connected to the *talli-kettu-kalyanam*?

D: Was it worn after marriage?

G: No. It had no connection to marriage. I don't think so. In those days most women wore that. Marriages only had the custom of giving the cloth. There was no tying of anything in those days.

D: Where do you think the thread came from? Do you think someone from their family would have tied it for them?

G: I think so.

The more the grandmother spoke the more I was beginning to think the amulet came from a practice of a family member, such as the mother, tying a *talli* around the young girl's neck years before she began menstruating.

D: Was it tali-kettu-kalyanam?

G: Maybe. I don't know. The gold amulet had a small hook through which the thread was taken.

Grandmother did not know anything more about the amulet. I forgot to ask her if she still had it with her. However, it stayed in my mind that most women of that time wore that amulet. The grandmother continued talking about her mother.

G: Once my mother went to Madras.

> D: Naked on top?
>
> G: No. That time a bodice was stitched for her so she could wear a blouse. But within a month she came back saying that she got suffocated inside the blouse. She asked her brother to take her back home.

Everyone broke out laughing. Madras was a modern city in those days, so I could understand that the grandmother could not visit without a blouse. But the reason she gave for her hurried return from the modern city was hilarious—she got suffocated inside the blouse. We were all laughing hard at the irony in the story. To my surprise, my mother shared a story too.

> M: My female cousin's mother-in-law also never wore a blouse. Whenever she had to visit her son in Coimbatore, she would take the blouse with her to the railway station and then wear it before boarding the train and as soon as she came back from Coimbatore and got off the train, she took off her blouse and went home.
>
> G: What to do? They felt suffocated inside the blouse.

We burst out laughing again. I continued with my next question.

> D: How did the girls or women respond to the flirtatious advances of boys and men? Was talking to boys and men outside the taravad allowed?
>
> G: When you are very young, boys and girls everyone played together. There was no difference. But once you have your periods, you don't step outside the house. There was no occasion to talk to boys outside the taravad. Even if you had to go to the temple, either your mother or your ammayi accompanied you.

This was the same for all the grandmothers. There was freedom of movement before the girls began bleeding, but following the bleeding, it was *lock down* for the women as far as any contact with men outside the *taravad*.

> D: How about brothers or men in the taravad?
>
> G: We were extremely close then and even now. There has been no change in that relationship . . . all of us . . . very close. I had

> complete freedom to say or ask anything of my brothers—little brother and also, my elder brother. My elder brother would come and sit in the middle of all of us and inquire about our life and problems. There was laughter and talking and all that. We never went to any houses. My mother would come with a chalk and then we would all play the game of dice. My mother and all of us would spend our evenings playing games. By the time we finished it, it would be time for dinner.

Yashoda Amma experienced real depth in her relationships with her brothers and sisters. I could sense from all the grandmother's lives that the relationships within a *taravad* were free and open. In earlier days, the *taravad* was like a whole enterprise; sometimes more than 100 family members living together. As it disintegrated, as families moved out and nuclear families emerged, this freedom of interaction between men and women became more restricted and closed, perhaps emerging out of the need to protect the daughters from the influence of strange men and unknown relationships.

> D: What about your father?

> G: Father would go early morning for work and then he would send all the vegetables and fish and everything for the evening food. In the evening he would come home with two laddus. By evening 6 PM we would all start chanting "Rama, Rama" loudly for father to hear. He would come home, take off his shirt and he would lie on the easy chair. Then he would call each kid one by one and give each person a small piece of the laddu and the final few bits remaining he will fold in the paper and give it to one of us and ask us to give it to our mother. We lived so happily in those days.

I loved hearing of this beautiful exchange of love between Yashoda Amma's parents. I had not seen it in the lives of my own grandparents.

> D: So there was lot of love between your father and mother?

> G: Yes. Immense love between them! My father would only eat a little from his plate and the remaining he would keep aside for my mother, and my mother would only eat that.

> G: My parents would also fast together for Ekadashi (11th day of the waxing moon), and before he ate, he would first ask if my mother ate. There was a lot of love between them.
>
> D: Ammamma, how about between you and your husband?
>
> G: It was fine. There was no trouble. Anyway trouble would only be if I went in that direction. I never did. So it was fine! There was neither good things nor bad things.

Although Yashoda Amma did not share further I could feel that her relationship with her husband was not like the one shared by her parents.

> G: By the time my daughter grew up, movies had come! Sometimes before my husband returned home, one of my women friends and I would go watch a matinee movie. My husband didn't mind that. Children were in school.

We all had a hearty laugh about it. It was getting darker and my mother nudged me to ask the next question, because we still had to cook dinner for the night. I asked my final question.

> D: Have you noticed a change in the images of female sexuality over the years?
>
> G: Life was simpler then. Like weddings were simpler.
>
> D: Was there dowry then?
>
> G: There was nothing like that. Girls were married off with maybe one bangle and a small chain.

I realized that this was the key—life was simpler then. Everything today in Kerala is about material things—more and more stuff and objects.

> D: Did women have freedom then?
>
> G: No. Women have freedom today. You can go anywhere or do anything. In those days, you had to listen to your father or your uncle for everything.

We both had different experiences of freedom. I had the freedom to think and act as I please. My father could object, but I could still go ahead and do it if I wish. That was unthinkable in the past.

> D: Were women safer then or now?
>
> G: Women are not as safe as they were in the past.

I was fascinated by this realization that with more freedom and women stepping out into the world, their lives have become less safe. The number of men who can stand up for them is reduced.

> D: With increase in freedom, safety has reduced!
>
> G: Definitely! Today you hear all these things happening to women and you wonder!
>
> D: Did men in those days stand on the sidewalk and pass comments at girls?
>
> G: I never saw or met anyone like that.
>
> M: It was very much less in those days.
>
> G: Today it is too much. But there was also a time when that was hardly there.

In one way I was relieved to hear that in the past women were safe and could move about without worrying about abuse from men. In today's India, that is almost impossible. Women have to be on their guard most of the time.

> D: Was a daughter's birth seen as a joyous occasion during ammamma's time?
>
> G: Definitely! It was the most auspicious and happy occasion—the birth of a girl in the house. People used to pray in those days, "Please let it be a girl!"

I wanted to stand up and scream loudly, "YES." It was so beautiful! I continued asking.

> D: Were the girl and Bhagawathi seen as one?
>
> G: It was said in those days to see both as one. The girl was seen as a Devi or goddess. Even today that hasn't changed! But it was always said that the girl is the Devi. She is auspicious! If the taravad had to exist without getting destroyed it needed a daughter. She sustained the life of the taravad. Now in our taravad, every child born is a boy! Recently my sister has had a granddaughter. She is the only baby girl in our taravad. Now through her, our taravad needs to continue and she has to give us a daughter. I prayed so hard for this child to be a girl. God fulfilled my wish.

I had tears in my eyes hearing this story.

> D: How about your son's daughter?
>
> G: A son's daughter doesn't matter for the life of our taravad. It has to be a daughter born of a daughter. A girl is needed in the family! At last now there is a small baby girl in our taravad. Now our taravad will exist further!

I took a deep breath in to completely soak in every word—"There is a small baby girl in our *taravad*. Now our *taravad* will exist further!" It was the most powerful statement and beautifully concluded my final interview. I gifted Yashoda *ammamma* with a new set-mundu and touched her feet. She was thrilled at what I was doing. I could see the pride in her eyes. Then my mother and Anita Ellemma hurried to the kitchen to prepare the dinner. I took a deep breath and turned off my video camera. I could not believe that I had completed all three interviews, and we were heading back to Bangalore the following day. The universe had walked with me hand in hand. Everything worked out and ended on time. It was time for me to head back to Bangalore, transcribe the interviews and harvest the fruits.

Transformative: Harvesting the Fruits

> Every spring, masses of tiny blossoms cover the tree. The pollinated flowers turn to fruit, which is harvested for pleasure and for food. Seeds from the fruit may be planted back in the earth to grow new trees. . . . The fruits of organic inquiry lie not so much in the information gathered as in the transformation of the researcher and thereby the readers. The

flowers may be seen as copies of the finished study in the hands of the readers. . . . Both researchers and readers grow by participation in the study so far as they are willing to engage in both the conscious and unconscious aspects of the work and so far as each is willing to be changed by their involvement. To truly experience another's story requires the willingness to be altered by it. (Clements et al., 1999, p. 50)

Once I was back in Bangalore, I was dissolved in transcribing the interviews of my co-researchers. As I transcribed the stories I spent hours listening to my co-researchers recorded voices as well reading the transcribed interviews. The compassion in their voices, the comfort in their bodies, the surrender in their being, the confidence in their feminine existence—everything impacted me in more ways than I can truly express. I have returned back with many gifts in the form of rituals, clothing, songs, dances, embodied transformation and expanded knowing. I will share them in the next section.

PART VI

HARVESTING THE FRUITS

"I realized that the disappearance of the menarche ritual and the emergence of patriarchal marriage as the most defining ritual in the life of a woman was one of the most significant shifts that happened across the three generations of grandmother, mother, and granddaughter."

CHAPTER 18.

ONNARA : FEMININE WEAR OF YESTERYEARS

I learned the tying of the traditional o*nnara mundu*, a 2.5 meter-long muslin cloth worn tightly wrapped around the butt. It extends tightly through the loin in a way that provides grip and strength to the hip as well to the pelvic region. All the three grandmothers wore it underneath their set-mundu. The grandmothers used the Malayalam word *urrapu* to describe the benefits of *onnara* with respect to a woman's sexuality, meaning grip, strength, to secure, to lock, and to control. The grandmother expressed their grief over the women of today abandoning this tradition.

Anita *ellemma* (Yashoda *ammamma*'s daughter), taught me to wrap the *onnara*. As I stood wrapped in the *onnara*, I understood the meaning of *urrapu*—a deep sense of grounding from within filled my body unlike anything I had experienced before. Out of curiosity I asked my aunt the reason she wore the *onnara* and she responded that it gave her control over her sexuality and she felt *urrapu*, that nothing could shake her. When she walked into a crowd of men, she felt confidant and protected because her sexuality was rock solid. It was the most revolutionary thing I had heard., and as I tuned into my experience of wearing the *onnara*, I felt exactly like that—unshakable and protected like a warrior. Also, I learned that women accustomed to wearing the *onnara mundu* rarely experienced pain in their backs or hips or spine during and after menopause. I have promised the grandmothers to spread the wisdom of the *onnara* with the women of the world.

CHAPTER 19.

EMBODIED SEXUALITY AND SPIRITUALITY

The interviews with my mother and grandmothers have deepened my relationship with my body and sexuality. For the first time, I feel I am in the body in an intimate profound sacred sort of way. My shame surrounding the body has mostly disappeared, which became evident during my recent trip to Montana to attend the 11th Council of the 13 Indigenous Grandmothers. The bathroom was a temporary setup with flying shower curtains for walls and doors. I showered naked without any hesitation and dried myself off in the passageway while other women bathed naked. I was not afraid of being seen. It was one of the most liberating experiences of my life. The hunch in my shoulders has literally disappeared, and it is clearly visible in my recent photographs. My comfort in talking about body and sexuality with women and men has increased. I have a sense of ease in my body, as if I am living in her for the first time. This ease, irrespective of the material enclosing my body, flows uninterrupted whether I am in my bed or at a café or the airport or the park.

My spiritual practices have increased in number, no longer restricted to breathing and eyes-closed meditation. Embodied moving is a practice that has naturally happened to me. I have realized that women need to move, and so I move now with or without music. I draw and paint as a spiritual practice. I have no fear around expressing myself because I am no longer seeking validation from someone else. My inner critique has matured. I am my biggest fan. I am amazed at what comes out through me in art, and I am realizing that I never created it in the first place—it happened through me, and I am in awe.

Admiring the earth and the natural elements consciously is another spiritual practice I have adopted. I feel a deep kinship with the earth, like she is my maternal family. I feel the pain in my body when I watch images of animals being killed or trees being cut or the earth being drilled—the pain is intimate and strong. I feel Her presence, Her guidance and Her whispers. She speaks to me through the wind, the water, the fire, and the infinite space. She is everywhere, and spending time with Her is an intimate spiritual practice. Most importantly, I have realized that being myself without the *shoulds* and *shouldnots* based on religious dogmas, conditioning, and the opinion of others, is my greatest spiritual practice.

CHAPTER 20.

MY MATRILINEAL AWAKENING

The stories of the grandmothers and my mother have helped me place my own story in context and reflect back on the shifts that happened across three generations of women. In this section, I will share some realizations (and how I arrived at them) that changed my understanding of my own story and gave it new meaning.

Menarche versus marriage. I realized that the disappearance of the menarche ritual and the emergence of patriarchal marriage as the *most defining ritual in the life of a woman* was one of the most significant shifts that happened across the three generations of grandmother, mother, and granddaughter. Every grandmother remembered her menarche celebration clearly and vividly. Their eyes lit up; there was excitement in their voices as they described the event. The menarche ritual itself involved the entire maternal lineage and in some cases the paternal family. Through this ceremony, the girl was protected and safe guarded, her sensuality was accentuated, and her coming of age was publicly acknowledged, celebrated, and announced to the entire neighborhood. From seclusion, to emergence, to the grand feasting at the end—everything was focused on the girl. Most importantly, the menarche ritual initiated the girl into the next phase of her life, as she consciously entered into sexual activity with a man followed by experiencing motherhood. The sexual teasing and the different games in menarche made the journey easy and natural for a girl. It was now okay for her to be drawn to a man or for a man to be drawn to her. She was consciously made aware of this shift in her body and sexuality. In contrast, the grandmothers did not have much to say about the marriage ritual, as it lacked the grandness of the menarche ritual. In fact, marriage was a private ceremony and happened in the evening after dark with few family members present.

In my mother's time, both the menarche and marriage ceremonies were taking new shape and form. From my mother I learned that my grandmother hesitantly performed the menarche ritual in a subdued way, because my grandfather did not approve of any of these rituals. So it can be seen that the most important man in a woman's life had shifted from her uncle to her husband. Even though this ritual was performed in my mother's life, it somehow lacked the fullness of the previous generation. It did not have the approval of the men in the family. There was a sense of shame around publicly celebrating the ritual, so it was much quieter. By contrast, marriage in my mother's time was a public ceremony held during the day based on a good astrological time involving near and extended family members from both parents' side.

In my life, I did not even know there was a menarche ceremony. Other than my mother, no other female kin acknowledged or congratulated me on this development. In fact, I was living with my grandmother in Kerala. She never said a word to me. My mother did not instruct me to rest or be in seclusion. I formed the relationship with my blood on my own. I did not think of myself as a sexually active person following menstruation. These two events had no correlation in my mind. I was not aware that my body and sexuality would shift in a way that was beyond my control. I did not know that from now on it was natural for me to be drawn to a man or for a man to be drawn to me. On the contrary, my marriage ceremony was the grandest celebration of my life. I did not have a Nayar wedding but a Hindu Vedic wedding based on my husband's tradition lasting three hours, with fire, mantras, and numerous ceremonies.

Although, a traditional Nayar wedding only lasts 20 minutes and does not have any religious elements attached to it, except maybe the venue might be a temple, the matriarchal elements are still visible. The girl's father gives her away and the maternal uncle has to be present. The most beautiful part of the North Malabar Nayar wedding ceremony is the bride's procession into the wedding hall—the girl's maternal aunt (maternal uncle's wife) leads the way with a lit *nellavillakku* followed by the fully dressed bride and a whole entourage of her maternal and paternal females, from her mother to her sister to all her female cousins and aunts holding the *ashtamangalyam* or the eight auspicious objects (consisting of rice, spike of coconut flowers, lit lamp, an arrow representing Kamadevan, sandalwood, small ornamental box containing vermilion, *Valkannadi* or bell metal mirror, and a new *mundu* or cloth) on a brass plate (or *thallika*). Although I had a Vedic wedding, I entered the wedding hall in the traditional Nayar way and it was a powerful experience in the company of my maternal kin, which took away the discomfort of marriage. After learning about the menarche ritual, I strongly feel that the bride procession mimics the menarche ritual. Usually following the marriage, the girl's mother, sister and a few of the female cousins stay by her side to accompany her to the groom's home. I did not experience this because I had a patriarchal Vedic wedding in which the daughter usually leaves alone with the groom's family.

Today in Kerala, a girl's maternal kin no longer acknowledges her first blood as they had done in the time of the grandmothers. In the absence of this, a girl's sexuality and femaleness is informed by external factors like the dominant Hindu norms, mythology, television, movies, and romantic novels. These influences are overly patriarchal and condition women to see their life existence in relationship to a masculine ideology as opposed to matrilineal knowing.

Experience of body and nudity. Another major shift I witnessed across the three generations of women is in their relationships with the body and nudity—this relationship shifted from a natural experience to an unnatural objectified experience of the body. In my generation, nudity was the most unnatural state of the human body in the public domain. In fact, growing up I never imagined or saw any women or men naked. Even if it was visually present, I did not let myself look. Admiring the nude adult body of a man or woman brought immense guilt. Even when I experienced shyness in my nudity, I did not know how to embody it. It was extremely uncomfortable to be *okay* with it, as if I had done something wrong. This was not just in the presence of the other; I could not be nude in my own presence. Most of my adult years I locked the door to change my clothes and refused to look in a mirror. My mother and most women of her generation were comfortable in their bodies. In fact, my mother associated the word *natural* with nudity. She had grown up seeing women naked in a public pond, bathing together, engaging in normal conversations. She saw bare-breasted grandmothers who went about their normal chores without wearing clothes on top.

The grandmothers could not even understand my question of shame and its associations with nudity. They did not experience shame—nudity was natural to them. In fact it was not just when they swam that women were naked, there was a time when women in Kerala wore nothing on top. The grandmothers recalled many women in their generation and those from their mother's generation who wore nothing on top—their breasts were fully exposed to public view as they went about their normal lives. In fact, many of these women felt suffocated inside a blouse, which they were forced to wear when visiting a more *civilized* setting, but immediately afterwards, they took it off.

I realized that in the name of freedom we have objectified our bodies and associated empowerment with wearing fewer and fewer garments on our bodies. Now women wear sexually provocative attire to attract the attention of the opposite sex or to be seen as sexy or sexually attractive. The grandmothers were not naked for men or to attract men. They were naked for themselves. In fact there was no thought or judgment or objective to the nudeness of the grandmothers. These women were natural in their expression, and we have lost that ability of naturalness in the body.

As I stand tall in my knowing of body and sexuality, I realize that the shift from matrilineal to patrilineal Kerala is extremely complicated and vast, and the impacts are still surfacing in the culture. It requires a more in-depth study.

CHAPTER 21.

INTEGRATING TRANSFORMATIVE CHANGE

> In organic studies, the integration of transformative change has been seen to show up in three ways. One may become more self-aware; one may develop a greater facility in connecting to the changes of heart and mind available from the liminal and spiritual realm; and one may come to feel a greater desire to be of service in the world—self, Spirit, and service. (Clements, 2004, p. 38)

I embarked on the methodology of organic inquiry in search of a deeply personal and transformative journey and in the process I have changed—physically, emotionally, mentally, and spiritually. This journey has gone beyond the perimeters of my defined material body to include the cosmic body and the life in it. I have arrived at the realization that my transformation is connected to the transformation of the other. I knew it intellectually but now it is an embodied realization and this drives my commitment to service as an expression of personal joy and way of transformation.

Integration toward self. I walked into the women's spirituality master's program with a burdened body, abused sexuality, and pained self-awareness. Today I am filled with an overwhelming sense of gratitude for every event, person and moment that has passed in my life as if they were gifts given to me, and this knowing has affected every aspect of my life—the past, present and future. It is accompanied by a heightened self-awareness that feels effortless, easy and relaxed. There are fewer strangers, and coincidences—whoever I meet on the road, in stores, in coffee shops and just everywhere seem to me to be alive beings with treasure chests of life wisdom unique to them. Sometimes a simple gesture (a smile, a nod or a conversation) closes the gap of our bodily distance, and in that moment I feel that our spirits come together in a celebration of life in which stories are exchanged and transformation happens. My relationships with my father, mother, and sister have become more intimate, open and deep. I have not journeyed alone in this research study; my matrilineal ancestral consciousness has walked with me every step of the way.

Integration toward spirit. My spirit and body are in contact with each other and I am realizing that a greater intelligence permeates my body and spirit; I am both and neither at the same time—like being full and empty. When I attune to this intelligence, I am able to act in the world more selflessly. My ability to perceive, observe and express thoughts, intentions, ideas, and even images has increased exponentially. I am deepening my spiritual practices to increase my capacity for holding and housing the *Spirit* in the body. I was initiated into my life's purpose through my spiritual path and now it has acquired a focused direction of women's work.

Integration toward service. "One helps not only because there is a need, but also because it is an offering to Spirit, an act of gratitude and reverence, and a natural result of one's own ongoing transformation" (Clements, 2004, p. 39). This sentence captures the essence of my feeling about life right now. I am committed to raising the matriarchal consciousness of the planet through interviews with daughters, mothers, and grandmothers around the world and creating communities of women. I have no choice. I am drawn in, led, guided, and moved by Spirit at every step of the way through everything—dreams, tarot cards, Facebook, nature, people, and events. I am learning to let go and trust the intelligence of this force.

CHAPTER 22.

ANSWERING HER CALL

I am the Rising Daughter.
Rising Tall and Strong.
Voicing the Unsaid
Silent Whispers of the Mother
Giving Her Name.

I am the Rising Daughter.
Rising for All.
Gathering the Fading
Memories of the Grandmother
Giving Her Form.

I am the Rising Daughter.
Between the past and future.
Re-Awakening the Sacred
Blood Line of the Ancestral Mother
Willing Her born.

I am the Rising Daughter.
Answering Her Call.
(Rekha Kodialbail, 2011)

Twelve months of my life spent on this study has been an immersion—preparation, self-reflection, looking for the co-researchers, meeting them, hearing their stories, and later writing their stories—and through this entire journey, I have constantly redefined, reclaimed, and revisited my own story. This has been the one of the most transformational journeys I have undertaken in my life so far.

Today I stand at the doorstep of my matriliny bearing fruits of wisdom from my mother and grandmothers. Although it might be difficult to draw conclusions based on such a small set of interviews, and because this is a journey I will likely be on for the rest of my life; conclusions will surely keep evolving. However, it is clearly evident through the stories of three generations of women—the grandmothers, my mother, and I—that in the last century Kerala made a dramatic shift from a *sexually-open socially-safe mother-centered matrilineal joint family structure* to a *sexually-uptight socially-unsafe father-centered patrilineal nuclear family life*. This shift has affected the psyches of men and women alike and plagued the society with innumerable problems of sexual abuse, domestic violence, suicide, depression, alcoholism, and more. Surprisingly, discussions in media, newspapers, and literature on solutions to these issues lack any mention of this shift in the matrilineal past of Kerala, and in this section I am daring to consciously investigate it.

In my grandmother's Kerala, obligatory menarche rituals grandly celebrated the daughter's auspiciousness and consciously prepared her in her relationship with her own body and sexuality, as well as with a man, as she blossomed from a young girl into a sexually mature woman. Today, menarche (*thirandukulli*) ritual has disappeared, and marriage has emerged as the most defining ritual in a woman's life. In the absence of these earlier Nayar female-centered rituals, female (and male) gender construction is informed by orthodox religious (Christian, Islam, and Hindu) doctrines, media, movies, and popular literature obsessed with the annihilation of sexual desires, disregard for body and sexuality, and the objectification of the female body. These values have affected men and women's relationships with the body and sexuality, moving from a naturally shy embodied experience to an unnaturally shameful objectified experience. Furthermore the concepts of eternalized romance, God-like husbands, and subservient chaste wives have given rise to unrealistic expectations in a marriage that were completely absent in my mother and grandmothers' generations. I projected many romantic expectations on my husband, which he was not prepared to fulfill. Looking back, I feel if I had been guided by my matriliny in the awareness of my body and sexuality, and had the opportunity to openly discuss with women from my *taravad* sexual fantasies, men, and marriage, I would have faced the challenges in my marriage sooner than I did.

I also observed that in matrilineal Kerala, all the three grandmothers had the confidence to return to their mother's homes anytime without shame or guilt in the event of the slightest abuse or violence from the husband or his family, mainly because the daughter was openly valued in the culture, and her happiness was connected to the auspiciousness and prosperity of the *taravad* and its lineage. In fact, matrilineal values were the lived experience of my grandmothers and my parents. On the contrary, matrilineal knowing had no reference in my memory and thus, for a long time, I did not voice the challenges in my marriage to my family, fearing it would bring them shame. Once I revealed my unhappiness, my parents were shocked and immediately assured me that I could walk out of this marriage without feeling guilt, and that they would support me in my decision. Many women in Kerala may not have that choice, or like me, they do not know that they have that choice, continuing to stay in abusive marriages to avoid shaming their parents. Less than a century ago, the daughter did not leave her matriliny after marriage; leaving the *taravad* was not considered in her interest or that of the matriliny. Sadly, women of my generation have not inherited this experience.

Today the younger generation of Kerala are on a fast track to ape the moralities and values of western civilization in clothing, gestures, language, food, behavior, and attitude; this is deeply concerning. In my 14 years of living in the United States and teaching leadership programs in schools and colleges, I have seen the wrath inflicted on young minds by the objectification of the female body in media and movies, with shockingly high numbers of acts of violence toward women in the United States.

According to the *National Intimate Partner and Sexual Violence Survey* (Black et al., 2011), nearly 1 in 5 women in the United States have been raped in their lives; more than 1 in 3 women have experienced rape, physical violence, and/or stalking by an intimate partner (current or former husband, cohabiting partner, boyfriend, or date) in their lifetime, and about 1 in 4 women have experienced severe physical violence by an intimate partner (e.g., hit with a fist or something hard, beaten, slammed against something) at some point in their lifetime. The documentary, *Miss Representation* (released in October 2011) reveals startling statistics on the misrepresentation of women in the media, and media's consistent effort to portray women as sex objects and subordinate to men. These images are affecting the minds of young boys and girls further perpetuating the cycle of sexual violence in the society.

In recent years, I have observed this trend of *misrepresentation* of women penetrate Malayalam cinema and Television culture, portraying women's liberation to mean drinking alcohol, smoking, gossiping, using foul language, having sex anywhere with any man, having fewer clothes on the body, and using sexually provocative gestures with the sole purpose of drawing attention to the female body for sexual fulfillment; men are stereotyped to express overly masculine traits of power, aggression, and lack of sensitivity. These objectifying stereotypes are influencing the quality of relationship between men and women in the culture of Kerala (and also India), changing them from intimate friendships to interactions based on fear and abuse. Are we trying to match our numbers with the west in terms of violence toward women?

With modernization there is an urgent need to understand and redefine freedom in the social organization of Kerala. The Nayar grandmothers living within *marumakkathayam* system might not have had the freedom to do as they pleased (to pursue further education or work to earn a livelihood—all of which I had); however, they had a community of women and men who cherished and honored them. They enjoyed natural freedom in their nude feminine bodies without fear of objectification and judgment, a true freedom that lays the foundation for the blossoming of a complete embodied woman as opposed to a "woman who has been stripped of Goddess recognition and diminished to a big ass and full breast for physical comfort only" (Pinkett-Smith, 2012, para. 1).

I wish every daughter of Kerala could be empowered by her maternal family to stand tall in her body and sexuality, confidently choosing the life she wants to lead (whether single or married), the career she wants to engage in (engineer, doctor, artist, musician, social worker, teacher, and more) and being supported in that journey. In addition, every son also needs to be guided to see a woman as his *partner of balance* in relationships of marriage. In the matrilineal past, women owned property, which gave them immense strength and independence. How can we revive that tradition and make our daughter's financially self-reliant, so that they may be equal partners in marriage and not a dependency on the husband? Furthermore, as a culture we need to honor matrilineal relationships and keep them alive and active even after marriage (especially in the case of our daughters). I understand that Kerala cannot go back to the *marumakkathayam* (matrilineal) social organization, but we can engage in open dialogues on the shift from matrilineal to patrilineal social organization, making efforts to adopt matrilineal values for defining egalitarian gender roles for men and women as husbands and wives, fathers and mothers, and daughters and sons.

I have made a commitment to support women's journeys into spirituality, and to empower the younger generation of women in Kerala to create space in their lives for honoring their bodies and sexuality as sacred and auspicious, in order for them to become powerful social change agents in their communities. Furthermore, I would like to expand my scope of interviews to include more grandmothers, mothers, and daughters across the depth and breadth of Kerala in the next couple of years, and create socially active matriarchal platforms (or centers) in the state to pass on the lived memories of the matrilineal generation to the sons and daughters of patrilineal Kerala.

Before Bhagawathi unleashes Her wrath upon us for our continued negligence and ignorance, I call upon the daughters (and sons) of Kerala to join me in this journey to re-define, re-claim and re-inform our bodies and sexuality through the matrilineal wisdom of our mothers and grandmothers, so that we may consciously dye the cultural fabric of our next generation through our acquired matrilineal wisdom.

A New Beginning

ACKNOWLEDGEMENTS

This book would not have been possible without the infinite blessings of so many people:

The Great Cosmic Mother for Her continuous guidance and company;

His Holiness Sri Sri Ravi Shankar, my Guru, for making every struggle a breeze, every challenge an opportunity, and every moment of this journey a celebration.

My Ancestors for staying by my side and watching over me.

My Mother, K. P. Balamani, for her infinite patience, guidance and friendship.

My Three Grandmothers, Madhavi Amma, Yashoda Amma, and Meenakshi Amma, and their families for sharing their life with me.

My Sister, Reshma Kurup, for being my accomplice in this journey and patiently listening to every single milestone.

My Father, Govindan Kutty, for loving me, as a daughter and encouraging me to go on no matter what the situation.

My Husband, Ram Kodialbail, for being the catalyst in my initiation into this journey.

My Dearest Friend, Arielle Warner, for introducing me to Sofia University and standing by me through the ups and downs of my life.

My Thesis Chair, Dianne Jenett, for mirroring my Nayar home in the United States and supporting me in the completion of my extraordinarily long thesis.

My Thesis Committee Member, Vicki Noble, for patiently guiding me through the entire journey of thesis editing, and improvisation.

My Women's Spirituality faculty at the Sofia University, including Dianne Jenett, Vicki Noble, Dvorah Grenn, Judy Grahn, Luisa Teish, Marguerite Rigoglioso, Mandisa Amber, and Leilani Birely for mirroring the sacred feminine, and embodying the matriarchal wisdom.

My Cohort Sisters for their constant support and words of encouragement: Andrea Fitzgerald, Antonia Hall, Charlie Brown, Hayley Arrington, Heather Yates, Jude Schneiter, Lissa Callirhoe, Liz Turkel, Pamela Almeida, Sarah Scott, and Sharon Rigby Osborn.

My friends for patiently listening, supporting and encouraging me through this thesis journey: Aparna Atmaram, Bill Herman, Brittney Pottier, Emily Lifton, Holly Neubuerger, Irene Yamane, Karen Roth, Kim Buller, Melissa Kevan, Nancy Zalazar, Rekha Allur, Seema Batawia, Steven McDaniels, Supriya Makineni, Tim Lechuga, Wendy Phillip, and Wendy Sanchez.

Special thanks to Robin Ruth, my Sofia sister, for deepening my relationship with my body through eco-femography; Lin Daniels (the director) and Kendra Ford (the coordinator) for Vagina Monologues at Sofia University; Anne Bleuthenthal (Guest Faculty) for inspiring me through movement; Shiloh McCloud (Guest Faculty) for introducing me to Art as a Sacred Practice; and Carolyn Brandy (Guest Faculty) for introducing me to Drumming as a Sacred Practice.

My Art of Living Family and many others (namable and unnamable, known and unknown) who have contributed to my journey.

Lastly, Crema Coffee (San Jose, CA) for providing me the perfect setting to write and engage in my work.

REFERENCES

Altekar, Anant Sadashiv. (1959). *The position of women in Hindu civilization.* Delhi, India: Motilal Banarasidas.

Amazzone, Laura. (2010). *Goddess Durga and sacred female power.* Lanham, MD: Hamilton Books.

Anderson, Rosemarie, & Braud, William. (1998). A preview of new methods. In *Transpersonal Research Methods for the Social Sciences* (pp. 27-32). Thousand Oaks, CA: Sage.

Apffel-Marglin, Frederique. (2008). *Rhythms of life: Enacting the world with the Goddesses of Orissa.* New Delhi, India: Oxford Univsersity Press.

Bahn, Paul, & Vertut, Jean. (1997). *Journey through the ice age.* Berkeley: University of Califorinia Press. (Original work publishesd 1988)

Baring, Anne, & Cashford, Jules. (1991). *The myth of the Goddess: Evolution of an image.* London, England: Penguin Books.

Black, Michele C., Basile, Kathleen C. , Breiding, Matthew J. , Smith, Sharon G., Walters, Mikel L. , Merrick, Melissa T., . . . Stevens, Mark R. (2011, November). *The national intimate partner and sexual violence survey: 2010 summary report.* Retrieved from http://www.vawnet.org/summary.php?doc_id=3072&find_type=web_sum_GC

Chandramouli, K. (2011). *Family welfare satistics in India.* Retrieved from http://mohfw.nic.in/WriteReadData/l892s/972971120FW%20Statistics%202011%20Revised%2031%2010%2011.pdf

Clements, Jennifer. (2004). Organic inquiry: Toward research in partnership with spirit. *Journal of Transpersonal Psychology, 36*(1), 26-49.

Clements, Jennifer, Ettling, Dorothy, Jenett, Dianne, & Shields, Lisa. (1999). *If research were sacred: Organic inquiry* (Rev. ed.). Unpublished manuscript.

Corrine, Tee. (1975). *Cunt coloring book.* San Francisco, CA: Pearlchild.

Danshilacuo, Hengde, & Mei, He. (2009). Mosuo family structures. In Heide Goettner- Abendroth (Ed.), *Societies of peace* (pp. 241-248). Toronto, Ontario, Canada: Innana.

den Uyl, Marion. (1995). *Invisible barriers: Gender, caste, and kinship in a southern Indian village.* Utrecht, The Netherlands: International Books.

den Uyl, Marion. (2000). Kinship and gender identity: Some notes on Marumakkathayam in Kerala. In Monica Boch and Aparna Rao (Eds.), *Culture, creation, and procreation: concepts of kinship in South Asian practice* (pp. 177 - 198). New York, NY: Berghahn Books.

de Tourreil, Savithri Shankar (1995). *Nayars in a south Indian matrix: A study based on female-centered ritual* (Unpublished doctoral dissertation), Concordia University, Quebec, Canada.

de Tourreil, Savithri Shankar (2009). Nayars of Kerala and matriliny revisited. In Heide Goettner-Abendroth (Ed.), *Societies of peace: Matriarchies past, present, and future* (pp. 205-215). Toronto, Canada: Inanna.

devika, J. (2008). *Individuals, householders, citizens.* New Delhi, India: Zubaan.

de Waal, Frans Bernardus Maria, & Lanting, Frans. (1997). *Bonobo: The forgotten ape.* Berkeley: University of California Press.

Dexter, Miriam Robbins. (1990). *Whence the goddesses: A source book.* New York, NY: Teachers College Press.

Dowson, Thomas A., & Lewis-Williams, David. (1994). *Contested images: A diversity in south African rock art research.* Johannesburg, South Africa: Witwatersrand University Press.

Dube, Leela. (1988). On the construction of gender: Hindu girls in patrilineal India. *Economic and Political Weekly, 23*(18), 11-19.

Fane, Hannah. (1975). The female element in Indian culture. *Asian Folklore Studies, 34*(1), 51-112.

Fawcett, F. (1901). *Nayars of Malabar* (Vol. 3). Madras, India: Asian Educational Services.

Flood, Gavin. (1996). *An introduction to Hinduism.* Cambridge, England: Cambridge University Press.

Fuller, Christopher J. (1976). *The Nayars today.* Cambridge, England: Cambridge University Press.

Gatusa, Lama. (2009). Matriarchal marriage patterns of the Mosuo people of China. In Heide Goettner Abendroth (Ed.), *Matriarchal societies of peace: Matriarchies past, present, and future* (pp. 240-247). Toronto, Ontario, Canada: Inanna.

Gimbutas, Marija. (2001). *The living goddesses.* Berkeley: University of California Press.

Goettner-Abendroth, Heide. (2005). Notes on the rise and development of patriarchy. In Christina Biaggi (Ed.), *The rule of Mars: Readings on the origins, history, and impact of patriarchy* (pp. 27-41). Manchester, CT: Knowledge, Ideas, and Trents (KIT).

Goettner-Abendroth, Heide. (2007). The deep structure of Matriarchal society. In Karen Smith (Ed.), *Societies of Peace* (pp. 17-27). Toronto, Ontario, Canada: Innana.

Goettner-Abendroth, Heide. (2009). *Societies of peace*. Toronto, Ontario, Canada: Inanna.

Panikkar, T. K. Gopal. (1900). *Malabar and its folk*. Retrieved from University of California Library database.

Gough, Kathleen. (1952). Changing kinship usages in the setting of political and economic change amond the Nayars of Malabar. *Journal of the Royal Anthropological Institute of Great Britain and Ireland, 82*(1), 71-88.

Gough, Kathleen. (1955). Female initiation rites on the Malabar coast. *Journal of the Royal Anthropological Institute of Great Britain and Ireland, 85*(1-2), 45-80.

Gough, Kathleen. (1961). *Matrilineal kinship*. Berkeley: University of California Press.

Gough, Kathleen. (1965). A note of Nayar marriage. *Journal of the Royal Anthropological Institute of Great Britain and Ireland, 65*, 8-11.

Grahn, Judy. (1993). *Blood, bread, and roses: How menstruation created the world*. Retrieved from http://bailiwick.lib.uiowa.edu/wstudies/grahn/index.htm

Grahn, Judy. (1999). *Are goddesses metaformic constructs? An application of metaformic theory to menarche celebrations and goddess rituals of Kerala and contiguous states in South India* (Unpublished doctoral dissertation), California Institute of Integral Studies, San Francisco, CA.

Gupta, Lina. (1997). Hindu women and ritual empowerment. In Karen L. King (Ed.), *Women and goddess traditions: In antiquity and today* (pp. 85-107). Minneapolis, MN: Fortress Press.

Holdrege, Barbara A. (1998). Body connections: Hindu discourses of the body and study of religion. *International Journal of Hindu Studies, 2*(3), 341-386.

Hua, Cai. (2001). *A society without fathers or husbands: The Na of China* (Asti Hustvedt, Trans.). Brooklyn, NY: Zone books.

Jacob, Sreedevi. (2004). How Kerala behaves with women, *CounterCurrents*. Retrieved from http://www.countercurrents.org/gender-jacob230604.htm

Jayakar, Pupul. (1990). *The earth mother: Legends, goddesses, and ritual art of India*. San Francisco, CA: Harper & Row.

Jeffrey, Robin. (2005). Legacies of matriliny: The place of women and the "Kerala Model." *Pacific Affairs, 77*(4), 647-664.

Jenett, Dianne Elkins. (1999). *Red rice for Bhagawathi/cooking for Kannaki: An ethnographic/organic inquiry of the Pongala ritual at Attukal Temple, Kerala, South India* (Unpublished doctoral dissertation), California Institute of Integral Studies, San Francisco, CA.

Johnsen, Linda. (1994). *Daughters of the goddess: The women saints of India.* St. Paul, MN: Yes International Publishers.

Khandekar, Nivedita. (2012, November 4). *Indus Valley 2,000 years older than thought.* Retrieved from http://www.hindustantimes.com/India-news/NewDelhi/indus-valley-2-000-years-older-than-thought/Article1-954601.aspx

Kinsley, David R. (1988). *Hindu goddesses: Visions of the divine feminine in the Hindu relgiious traditions.* Berkeley: Univeristy of California Press.

Kishwar, Madhu. (1994). Codified Hindu law: Myth and reality. *Economic and Political Weekly, 29*(33), 2145-2161.

Kumari, Anitha. (2009). Crimes against women in Kerala: What do the trends reveal? *Journal of Family Welfare, 55*(1), 18-30.

Kurup, Rekha. (2011). *In conversation: Indian Woman's connection to her Yoni.* Unpublished manuscript.

Leslie, Julie. (1992). *The roles and rituals for Hindu women.* Delhi, India: Motilal Banarasidas Publishers.

Mann, Kamlesh. (1996). Girls' dormitory and freedom of women. In Kamlesh Mann (Ed.), *Tribal women* (pp. 113-122). New Delhi, India: M. D. Publications.

Marler, Joan. (n.d.). *About the Institute of Archaeomythology.* Retrieved November 24, 2012, from http://www.archaeomythology.org/about-the-institute-of-archaeomythology

Menon, Alappat Sreedhara. (1978). *Cultural heritage of Kerala.* Kottayam, Kerala, India: D. C. Books.

Menon, Alappat Sreedhara. (2008). *Kerala history and its makers.* Kottayam, Kerala, India: D. C. Books.

Menon, Leela. (2011, November 15). *Moral police syndrome.* Retrieved from the the EnMalayalam website: http://www.enmalayalam.com/site/english/topic/general/category/column/2011/11/4051-article

Moore, Melinda. (1988). Symbol and meaning in Nayar marriage ritual. *American Ethnologist, American Anthropological Association, 15*(2), 254-273.

Nambiar, A. K. (2007). Malabar's spring festival: Poorakkali of North Malabar. *Kerala Calling, 27*. Retrieved from http://www.old.kerala.gov.in/kercalapr07/pg37.pdf

Namu, Yang Erche, & Christine, Mathieu. (2003). *Leaving mother lake*. New York, NY: Hachette Book Group.

Neff, Deborah Lyn. (1995). *Fertility and power in Kerala serpent ritual* (Unpublished doctoral dissertation). University of Wisconsin, Madison, WI.

Noble, Vicki. (1983). *Motherpeace: A way to the goddess through myth, art, and tarot*. San Francisco, CA: Harper Collins.

Noble, Vicki. (1991). *Shakti woman: Feeling our fire, healing our world*. San Francisco, CA: Harper Collins.

Noble, Vicki. (2003). *The double goddess: Woman sharing power*. Rochester, VT: Bear & Company.

Noble, Vicki, & Vogel, Karen. (1988). Motherpeace tarot deck. Stamford, CT: U.S. Games Systems.

Panikkar, Kavalam Madhava. (1918). Some aspects of Nayar life. *Journal of Royal Anthropological Institute of Great Britain and Ireland, 48*, 254-293.

Renjini, D. (2000). *Nayar women today: Disintegration of matrilineal system and the status of Nayar women in Kerala*. New Delhi, India: Classical Publishing.

Ruxian, Yan. (2009). The kinship system of Mosuo in China. In Heide Goettner-Abendroth (Ed.), *Societies of peace* (pp. 230-239). Toronto, Ontario, Canada: Inanna.

Sanday, Peggy Reeves. (2009). Matriarchal values and world peace. In Heide Goettner Abendroth (Ed.), *Societies of peace* (pp. 217-227). Toronto, Ontario, Canada: Innana.

Saradamoni, Kunjulekshmi. (1982). Women's status in changing agrarian relations: A Kerala experience. *Economic and Political Weekly, 17*(5), 155-157,159-162.

Saradamoni, Kunjulekshmi. (1994). Women, Kerala, and some development issues. *Economic and Political Weekly, 29*(9), 501-509.Saradamoni, Kunjulekshmi. (1999). *Matriliny transformed: Family, law, and idealogy in twentieth century Travancore*. New Delhi, India: Sage.

Saraswati, Swami Sivananda, & Saraswati, Swami Satyananda. (2007). *Devi: Honoring Shakti*. Bihar, India: Yoga Publication Trust.

Sjöö, Monica, & Mor, Barbara. (1987). *The great cosmic mother*. San Francisco, CA: Harper & Row.

Smith, David. (2003). *Hinduism and modernity.* Malden, MA: Blackwell.

Stone, Merlin. (1976). *When god was a woman.* San Diego, CA: The Dial Press.

Suicide in Kerala 2010. (n.d.). Retrieved December 1, 2012, from http://www.ksmha.org

Taylor, Shelley E. (2002). *The tending instinct: Women, men, and the biology of our relationships.* New York, NY: Henry Hold.

Warrier, Shobha. (2010). *There is a lot of sex starvation in Kerala.* Retrieved from http://news.rediff.com/interview/2010/jan/20/there-is-a-lot-of-sex-starvation-in-kerala.htm

Wilson, Shawn. (2008). *Research is cermony: Indigenous research methods.* Halifax, Canada: Fernwood.

Young, Katherine K. (2002). Women and Hinduism. In Aravind Sharma (Ed.), *Women in Indian religions* (pp. 3-37). New Delhi, India: Oxford University Press.

Zak, Paul J. (2012). *The moral molecule: The source of love and prosperity.* New York, NY: Penguin Books.

GLOSSARY

Amma: Mother in spoken Malayalam

Achan: Father in spoken Malayalam

Ammamma: It is a Malayali word used by either grandchildren or younger children to addresses one's mother's mother or a female elder in the family.

Ammavan: Mother's brother

Ammayi: Mother's brother's wife

Balawadi: Baby nursery or child playhouse.

Chakkarachorru: Jaggery rice made with rice, jaggery and coconut of thick consistency

Champaka: A type of Luau flower

Chechi: It is a Malayali word used to address an elder sister.

Ellemma: Derived from Elle-little, Amma-Mother or mother's little sister.

Ettan: Brother

Kallam: A traditional decorative folk art from India usually using rice flour. These are decorative designs made on floors of living rooms and courtyards during Hindu festivals and are meant as sacred welcoming areas for the Hindu deities. In North Malabar these rice flour designs are absent among the Nayars. They only use flowers and fresh leaves of plants to make elaborate and intricate designs for festivals.

Kamadevan or *Kama*: God of love, and erotic sexuality

Karnavar: The senior most maternal uncle and also, the head of the Nayar matrilineal joint families of Kerala. Usually the authority of the Karnavar in a family is unquestioned but there are also matriarchal families where the women's decisions take precedence over the Karnavar. Even after the decline of matrilineal system, the word is used to denote authority, an elderly person.

Karnavarathi: The wife of the Karnavar

Kavu: Sacred Grove

Kindi: It is a type of a pitcher made of bell metal and usually found in Kerala homes. It is used to keep water at the entrance of the house, so that visitors can wash their feet with this water, and also to wash hands after meals. It is also used in rituals to pour water.

Kohl, Kajal, Kanmashi: It is a cosmetic made for the eye and widely used in India by the women.

Kullam: Man-made water pond usually present in *taravads* or Temples. It is used for swimming and bathing. Most *Kullam* have separate entrances for women and men.

Kunnikurru: Small red pepper like fruits that grow on a shrub.

Kuruthola: Fresh young leaves of the coconut tree

Kurava: Ululate or the far-hitched sound made by women on special occasions

Malayalam: The language spoken by the people of Kerala.

Malayali: Native of Kerala or one who speaks Malayalam

Marumakkathayam: A system of inheritance along the mother line.

Mattu: A freshly washed ritual cloth presented by the low cast women to the Nayar women on the fourth day of menstruation for the ritual bath.

Muringa: Drumstick Plant

Nayar: Nayar is a caste from the South Indian state of Kerala, traditionally matrilineal living in large joint family that housed descendants of one common maternal ancestress.

NelluKathir: Fresh paddy flowers

Nellavillakku: Traditional Kerala Lamp made of bell metal.

Neyyi-appams: Deep fried (in clarified butter) rice dumpling made with ground rice, jaggery, banana, and coconut

Oonjal: Long swing tied on tree branches.

Payasam: A liquid porridge made usually of rice and milk

Pativrata: Usually used to describe a traditional Hindu wife—devoted and vowed to her husband as God and his welfare, happiness, health and prosperity being her first priority and responsibility.

Puram: Festival celebrated by young girls for Kamadevan. It occurs during the *Meena* month. This year (2012) it is happening on the 29th of March.

Pullikombu: Branch of the tamarind tree

Sambandham: Visiting relationship practiced in Kerala

Set-Mundu (or *Mundum Neriyathum* or *Mundu-set*): This is the traditional clothing of women in Kerala, South India. It is the oldest remnant of the ancient form of the saree, which covered only the lower part of the body. In the Mundum Neriyathum, the most basic traditional piece is the mundu or lower garment, which is the ancient form of the saree denoted in Malayalam as 'Thuni' (meaning cloth), while the Neriyathu forms the upper garment the mundu. The Mundum Neriyathum consists of two pieces of cloth, and could be worn in either the traditional style with the Neriyathu tucked inside the blouse, or in the modern style with the Neriyathu worn over the left shoulder.

Taravad or *Taravatu*: A large ritually significant house and land unit consisting of all the matrilineally related kin, male and female, descended from a common female ancestor, living together.

Thiyyan: The community of ritual specialists who embody the deities in the theyyam ritual.

Theyyam: A ritual dance form of worship of North Malabar in Kerala state

Thirandukulli: Name of the Menarche ritual

Thiruvathira: Festival celebrated by young women for Kamadevan

Thumba: A small white medicinal flower that grows wildly in Kerala. It is used in many rituals and festivals.

Urrapu: Malayalam word meaning to strength, to lock, to secure, to firm, etc

Urulli: A special thick vessel made of bronze present in most Kerala household. Different vessels used for cooking, rituals, and in festivals.

Vallukannadi: A typical bell metal hand held mirror of Kerala

Vannan: It was the ritual right of the women of this community to wash and clean the menstrual clothes of the Nayars. In the complex caste system of Kerala they were considered *lower caste*

Vannathan: It was the ritual right of this community of people to wash and clean the clothes of everyone. In the complex caste system of Kerala they were considered *lower caste*

Vayasu-ariyikucha: another name for *Thirandukulli*

Vellichapadu: Known as the revealer of light, a mediator between the deity and the devotees. Possessed by the deity, Vellichapadu dances in frenzy at the festivals in Bhagavati temples.

Thesis Collage

Leading Yoni Mandala Workshop

Hosting a Art Show

SOME GLIMPSES FROM MY RESEARCH LIFE.

Hosting Pongala @ITP - Year 2

Vagina Monologue

Hosting Pongala @ITP - Year 1

Rediscovering Goddess @Malta

ABOUT THE AUTHOR

Photo Courtesy Robin Ruth

Rekha Govindan Kurup is a freelance writer, poet, artist, blogger, social media activist and more importantly sees herself as a modern-day feminist yogini.

Rekha is a native of Kannur, Kerala (India). She grew up across the different states of India. Following her marriage, she went to United States where she has been living for the last 14 years, At the peak of her decade long career in IT, she gave up her Silicon Valley job to engage in service activities. She served as the West Coast director for the Youth Development Initiative of the International Association for Human Values.

Life took an unexpected turn when her deep longing to understand and embody the feminine led her to the Institute of Transpersonal Psychology (ITP; now known as Sofia University) in Palo Alto, California, where she got M.A in Women's Spirituality. Over the last few years, Rekha has passionately engaged in reconnecting with her feminine purpose through various academic, spiritual and social engagements including visiting the ancient pre-historic goddess temples of Malta, driving alone across five states of United States to attend the 11th council of the thirteen indigenous grandmothers in Montana, hosting Attukal Pongala at ITP for 2 consecutive years, participating in Eve Ensler's VM initiatives, leading Women's Circles and workshops, etc. Recently she has returned to India to further her research work. She is also in the process of establishing a foundation to educate, empower and engage women and girls to embody the sacred feminine in their daily lives through the discovery and investigation of indigenous matrilineal feminine practices. Her upbringing in India in the eastern philosophy combined with her life in United States gives her the ability to bring a unique perspective to contain, assimilate and research cross-cultural differences and commonalities.

Rekha Govindan Kurup is an instructor of the Art of Living Foundation and has taught several workshops internationally to youth and adults. She is also, serving as the advisory board director for Udne Ki Asha, a non-profit trust working with underprivileged children in Bangalore city.

Website: http://www.rekhagovindankurup.com

Made in the USA
Middletown, DE
24 October 2014